LIVING DECENTLY

Material Well-being in Australia

PETER TRAVERS • SUE RICHARDSON

Melbourne

OXFORD UNIVERSITY PRESS

Oxford Auckland New York

OXFORD UNIVERSITY PRESS

Oxford   New York   Toronto
Delhi   Bombay   Calcutta   Madras   Karachi
Kuala Lumpur   Singapore   Hong Kong   Tokyo
Nairobi   Dar es Salaam   Cape Town
Melbourne   Auckland   Madrid
and associated companies in
Berlin   Ibadan

OXFORD is a trade mark of Oxford University Press
© Peter Travers and Sue Richardson 1993
First published 1993 LKP

National Library of Australia
Cataloguing-in-Publication data:

Travers, Peter (Peter Denis).

Living Decently: material well-being in Australia.
Bibliography.
Includes index.
ISBN 0 19 553360 7.

1. Cost and standard of living—Australia. 2. Poverty—Australia. 3. Poor—Australia. 4.

Wealth—Australia. I. Richardson, Sue, 1946– . II. Title.

339.470994

Printed in Hong Kong by Yau Sing
Published by Oxford University Press,
253 Normanby Road, South Melbourne, Australia

• CONTENTS •

CONTENTS

CONTENTS

• PREFACE •

Material well-being matters. In this book we argue the case for this proposition, analyse the nature and distribution of material well-being in Australia, and draw implications for public policy. We understand material well-being to be that aspect of human well-being that can be affected by a change in produced goods and services. It is clear from this definition that we are dealing with only one aspect of life—albeit a very important one. To place it in perspective, we also examine the relation between material well-being and other dimensions of human well-being—that is what lies behind our choice of title: *Living Decently*. The concept of 'living decently' has many overtones, including a reasonable standard of living, respectability, and being able to hold one's head high in the community—all of which are touched on in this study of material well-being.

There is always a gap between the collection of data and the publication of a book such as this. In our case, much of our work is based on the results of the Australian Standard of Living Study, dating from the end of 1987. You will find the Study described in detail in an appendix at the end of the book. We also draw on surveys of the Australian Bureau of Statistics (ABS), the most recent of which was conducted in 1989.

Our chief conclusion is that at the end of the 1980s most Australians were indeed 'living decently'. Material affluence was at an all-time high. Australia was not the world-leader in equality, but it still ranked around the middle of the dozen most equal countries in the world. Australia is a world-leader when it comes to social mobility; that is, both privilege and disadvantage are less likely to be inherited in Australia than in any other country. There is disadvantage, of course, but one of our more positive findings is that disadvantage in one aspect of life is often offset by advantages elsewhere. For instance, the aged in Australia do not rank high in terms of income. However, they do rank high in terms of home-ownership, and in other material comforts. Similarly, the spillover from income level to social activities such as visiting friends or having friends around for a visit, engaging in hobbies, or simply feeling happy about life, is small.

Our positive picture of high levels of affluence and of relative equality is at variance with the 'gloom and doom' that is typical of many editorial writers and political and social commentators. One reason for this is that we use rather more complex measuring-sticks of affluence and of material disadvantage than are common in Australia. By far, the most common indicator of affluence is current income; the most common indicator of poverty is a poverty line based on current income. We argue (in Chapter 1 for income, and in Chapter 5 for poverty) that these sorts of indicators are inadequate. Of course income matters when it comes to measuring both affluence and poverty, and the measures we propose always start with income. But they include much more besides.

In Chapter 1 we describe our preferred measure, 'full income', which supplements current income with the value of assets and of non-employed time. People's material well-being depends not only on their income, but on the assets they have accumulated. It also depends on the time they have available for productive work in the home, for leisure, and for social activities. With this sort of measure, a couple living in a rented home, who are employed for a combined total of 80 hours a week, for a combined income of $50 000, are judged to have a much lower standard of living than their neighbours who also earn $50 000, but who own their home outright and are employed for a total of only 40 hours a week.

We also go beyond current income when it comes to measuring poverty. In Chapter 5 we argue that there are two aspects to thinking about poverty, especially in rich countries like Australia. First, we want to know who is on the bottom of the scale of material well-being. We want to know which groups fare worst, how big the gap between the average and the bottom is, and how these things compare across time and with other countries. To be precise, these questions are to do with inequality rather than poverty. To answer them we would use full income if it is available; otherwise, current income would serve well enough. In order to move from questions about inequality to questions about poverty, we ask what life is like when one is on the bottom of the income scale. Does it mean hunger, homelessness, and social isolation? Or does it mean 'a condition of frugal comfort estimated by current human standards' (Higgins, 1907)? We would argue that the first situation clearly constitutes poverty and the second clearly does not, and that there are many situations in between where we would expect to find strong disagreement in the community. Before we get to such judgments, however, we need information about hunger, homelessness, social isolation, and 'frugal comfort'. Such information cannot be gleaned from information about income alone (unless income is unambiguously high). We need direct information about how people are actually living. Much of this book is devoted to the presentation of this sort of information—and it is this information that leads us to our generally positive conclusions.

• • •

This book is a collaboration between an economist (Richardson) and a sociologist (Travers). This gives it the potential both for the rich development of diverse perspectives, and for falling between two stools. From our own point of view, there has indeed been a great deal of cross-fertilisation, and both of us have modified our views considerably in the course of writing.

We have sought to accommodate a broad readership by writing for non-specialist audiences. The first test of this was whether each of us could understand draft chapters written by the other. The elimination of unintelligible concepts and expression was the easy part. The less tractable issues involved the broader philosophical assumptions that are ingrained in the two disciplines. These differences were most apparent to us in two areas: the place of moral values in the research enterprise, and the relationship between negative and positive freedom (freedom from and freedom to). In the end we not only agreed, but we found the debates the most fruitful part of our collaborative effort. These issues are dealt with at some length in Chapters 5 and 6, but we think it worthwhile to highlight now what is at stake.

We regard it as a truism that 'value free' study of human affairs is impossible. Rival theories are 'underdetermined' by facts—that is, though theories are constrained by facts, they cannot be derived from facts alone (Hesse, 1978). A theory that is not coherent with facts will be implausible. However, since several rival theories may be equally coherent with facts, all social sciences rely on something approaching value judgments to choose between them.

In Chapter 5 we confront the issue of how values also enter into the very definition of 'facts'. Our definition of poverty, for instance, relies on a moral judgment about what constitutes 'living decently'. We then go on to say that we are prepared, as researchers, to make some moral judgments in this context, but draw the line at making others. We do not say that the facts about poverty are so stark in some instances (malnutrition, famine) that no moral judgments are needed. What we say is that the moral consensus that famine and malnutrition indicate poverty is so strong that we do not hesitate to affirm it. When it comes to the moral judgment that in a rich country such as Australia people are poor if they lack a certain level of income, or lack the capacity to engage in common activities such as going on holiday each year, we do draw back. This is not because we refuse to make moral judgments, but because we do not believe there is any likelihood of a consensus in such judgments. We regard them as political judgments that are best left to the political process. What researchers can do is to inform that debate by describing how people live, pointing out who is on the bottom, what the relative gap between the privileged and the disadvantaged is, how things are changing over time, and whether disadvantage in one area spells disadvantage across the board. This stance is itself a value judgment on the task of researchers, and it is the judgment that underlies this entire book.

We found it somewhat easier to agree on the nature of truth than on the nature of freedom. Economists tend to regard sociologists—especially those whose field of interest is the welfare state—as at best misguided sentimentalists, at worst as interfering busybodies who think they know better than people themselves what is good for them. Sociologists in turn regard economists as quite naïve in their understanding of how people's preferences are shaped by their circumstances. Whereas economists' understanding of freedom is mainly in terms of negative liberty (freedom from interference), sociologists are much more ready to stress positive freedom (the capacity to act). These issues come to a head in questions such as whether inequality should be addressed at all, or, if addressed, whether it should be by means of raising incomes (thus allowing people to choose between, say, education, health, and a new car), or by providing some services 'free'. The 'free' services are, of course, not free, but are funded compulsorily, usually by taxes.

We had no difficulty in agreeing that some forms and degrees of inequality are a proper reason for public intervention. It was less obvious whether the focus of public intervention would be on incomes or on services. Once again, we did agree in the end, and our proposals are set out in Chapter 6. Our general bias is towards solutions that result in higher incomes, and thus permit greater choice. But we also list many important exceptions to this general rule, and see some services—education in particular—as having even greater importance in the world we are now entering.

The chief ground for the positive conclusions of this book is the snapshot we offer of Australian society at the end of the 1980s, rather than any prediction about the future. In fact, in the final chapter, we identify four factors that have been decisive in producing the present situation, all of which are under threat in the 1990s: low unemployment; a 'good enough' social security system; very high levels of home-ownership; and high quality government provision of specific goods and services. Of these, low unemployment is so important as to be in a category of its own. The policy proposals we draw from our study relate to sustaining the last three—social security, housing, social services—in such a way that they interact favourably with the first—low unemployment. Our confidence that the rosy picture we have painted in this study will be sustained in the future depends on how successfully that can be achieved.

• ACKNOWLEDGEMENTS •

Many people have assisted us in this enterprise. The Australian Standard of Living Study on which much of our work is based was supported by grants from the Australian Research Grants Council. Fieldwork for the study was conducted by AGB:McNair—we are particularly indebted to the 1695 Australians who completed our rather lengthy questionnaire. We have received extensive assistance in data analysis from Frances Robinson, Simon Molloy, and Melissa Gibbs, and have been greatly assisted by patient critics who have commented on various drafts of chapters. Among them we note, in particular, Keith Hancock, Jonathan Pincus, Hugh Stretton, Dick Blandy, and David Johnson.

• INTRODUCTION •

In this Introduction we discuss two issues that are basic to this book. The first is the importance of material well-being. By material well-being we mean that aspect of human well-being which can be affected by a change in produced goods and services. This excludes such things as self-respect, freedom, dignity and love. Needless to say, material well-being is only one aspect of life, but we argue that it is important enough to merit most of a book. And because our interest in material well-being extends beyond describing who has what, we ask how it relates to the rest of life. We also have an interest in distributive justice—that is, whether there is a fair allocation of goods. This leads on to the second issue, that of how the distribution of material well-being relates to public policy. By public policy we mean state intervention to influence the distribution of resources. We examine both the wide divergence of opinion on the role of the state in seeking to bring about the good life, and the points on which there is agreement. We conclude the Introduction with an outline of the policy implications that we take up in more detail in the final chapter.

MATERIAL WELL-BEING AND HUMAN WELL-BEING: SOME BASIC CONCEPTS

In this section we do three things. We ask why material things matter at all. We then talk about 'spheres of life', by which we mean the various domains of life, only some of which are to do with material things. And we discuss distributive justice, or the rules by which a community decides on the fair division of goods, whether they be offices, honours, money, housing or goods pertaining to other spheres of life.

• Material Things Matter •

We have chosen to focus on an aspect of life that is crucially important for human well-being. Aristotle has perhaps best summarised
why material things are important when he argued, in the context
of a debate on what was needed to lead a fully human existence,
that it is impossible or difficult to do fine things without resources.
In answering whether someone deprived of basic human goods—a
prisoner, for instance—could still live well, Aristotle conceded that
he could certainly lead an heroic life, but that being good is not the
same as living well. To live well, we need resources, and these
include material resources.

Behind this claim lies the notion that values such as wealth,
courage, beauty and generosity are goods in their own right, without reference to an overarching ultimate good. If life consisted of a
single value—courage, for instance—then a courageous prisoner
might indeed be living well. But if we refuse to measure well-being
on this single dimension, then the prisoner is clearly not living well
(Nussbaum 1986, pp. 296–333). A similar point can be made with
reference to contemporary events. We may be filled with admiration
for the heroism of those who have endured life under repressive
regimes, or who have shown generosity or fortitude in the face of
famine. But this does not deny the extent to which those same lives
have been stunted by the repressive regime or by material deprivation (Ash 1989).

• Spheres of Life •

Aristotle is not the only writer to have focused on the different
dimensions or spheres of life. Later in this book we draw on a more
recent philosopher, Michael Walzer, who has also stressed the
importance of the various spheres of life, only some of which
involve material resources.

Walzer's chief insight is to observe that there are different spheres
of life, and that the exchanges that take place within them have different *meanings*, and therefore operate under different sets of rules.
For instance, if we are operating in the sphere of life which is governed by the rules of the market, we would expect to pay for what
we want. But if we attempt to pay a jury for a favourable decision,
or a public official for an office we are seeking, we violate the very

different meanings of those spheres of life: we are attempting to apply the rules of the market where they do not apply. In these examples, we are violating rules sanctioned by law. If, on the other hand, we attempt to buy friendship, we may commit no crime, but we will probably discover we are violating something even more powerful—the very meaning of friendship. In a capitalist society, market exchanges and the rules of the market are clearly of immense importance. But so are exchanges in other spheres, those involving justice, public office, friendship, marriage and procreation rights, basic welfare services and civic duties such as jury and military service. Walzer gives a long list of 'blocked exchanges', or attempts to limit what money can buy, even in a capitalist society. These include the sale of human beings, the sale of public office, of Divine Grace, of basic rights, such a freedom of speech, and of prizes. So-called 'desperate exchanges' are also prohibited: safety regulations and minimum wages place boundaries on what can be negotiated between employers and employees (Walzer 1985, pp. 100–3). In each case, these limitations on what money can buy are a recognition of the varied meanings we attach to different dimensions of our lives.

• Distributive Justice •

We have said that in this book we will not merely describe how goods are divided among Australians, but will also ask whether this distribution is as it should be. In other words, we are asking questions about distributive justice. We will be asking whether the distribution of goods that we describe is to be applauded or lamented, and whether public effort should be made to defend the present distribution or to alter it. Our approach to distributive justice has already been foreshadowed in the discussion of spheres of life and the work of Michael Walzer.

For Walzer, injustice occurs if one of the many spheres of life comes to *dominate* the others, so that one's standing in one sphere determines one's standing in all. For instance, if the rules of the market-place come to operate outside their appropriate sphere, and one could buy and sell not only carrots and cars, but also public office, ecclesiastical office, friendship, and the right to marry or emigrate, we condemn it with words like 'bribery', 'simony', and 'corruption'. What lies behind this is our realisation that valued goods are somehow being corrupted by the intrusion of the sphere of money.

This suggests a pluralistic approach to distributive justice. Once we talk of the 'meanings' of different human goods, we are talking of something that will vary in time and place. In contrast to Rawls (1971), Walzer argues that 'the principles of justice are themselves pluralistic in form; that different social goods ought to be distributed for different reasons, in accordance with different procedures, by different agents; and that all these differences derive from different understandings of the social goods themselves—the inevitable product of historical and cultural particularism' (Walzer 1985, p. 6).

If we start from a particular culture and history, we observe different standards of distribution applying to different social goods. However, though these specific standards exist, they are 'often violated, the goods usurped, the spheres invaded, by powerful men and women' (Walzer 1985, p. 10). What we find in fact is that most societies are organised so that one good or set of goods is dominant—that is, individuals who have one good can command a wide range of other goods. The dominant good may be birth, religious truth, wealth or physical prowess. 'History reveals no single dominant good, but only different kinds of magic and competing kinds of magicians' (p. 11).

Fortunately, the magicians are never entirely successful in persuading the rest of the population that one particular good should dominate, and in the struggles that ensue, three kinds of counter-claim are commonly made: 1) that the dominant good should be redistributed more equally; 2) that it is dominance itself, rather than the unequal distribution of the dominant good, that is unjust; and 3) that the current dominant good should be replaced by another dominant good (p. 13). Walzer himself opts for the second claim: that distributive justice should focus on the reduction of dominance. He describes this goal as 'complex equality'—that is, citizens' standing in one sphere or with regard to one social good should not be undercut by their standing in some other sphere, with regard to some other good (p. 19). So this notion of equality can accept that one citizen should enjoy, say, greater fame and prestige than another, so long as this does not spill over into advantages in other areas, such a health care, education or gaining public office.

One of the more controversial implications of Walzer's approach is that redistribution is not seen as a primary goal of distributive justice. This is because the first concern of distributive justice is to ensure that the separate meaning of different goods is retained in the face of imperialistic encroachments of dominant goods. For instance, if money is the dominant good, and everything could be bought, including friendship, it is small consolation to be told that a redistribution of wealth will result in equality in the friendship market. Bought friendship would still mean the destruction of the good we know as friendship. The second objection to a focus on redistribution is the pragmatic one—that it probably would not work. Even if a powerful state periodically returned everyone to an equal starting point, the equality would not last long—inevitably, luck, skill, cunning and ruthlessness would be brought to bear on the market where everything could be traded. Moreover, state officials would, presumably, also be bought, and the redistributive regime would soon be subverted. In his later writing, Walzer concedes that the pragmatic argument can also be turned against his favoured regime of complex equality and separate spheres. Unlimited wealth, power and office make it possible for those who win such goods to close off opportunities to everyone else (Walzer 1986). There may thus be *some* point at which directly redistributive action may be called for, even for Walzer.

We will follow Walzer in two later chapters. In Chapter 4 we discuss how material well-being relates to three dimensions of 'the rest of life': happiness, health and social participation. We will show there that the distribution of these goods is only weakly related to that of material well-being and, to that extent, Australia would pass Walzer's test of a well-ordered society. In Chapter 6 we discuss issues of redistribution, and examine there, in the light of Walzer's approach, the public policy implications of our distributional findings. Our task at this stage is to place that discussion in context by outlining the kinds of debate that lie behind current political struggles concerning social policy.

MATERIAL WELL-BEING AND PUBLIC POLICY

One reason why material well-being is important is because it involves a sphere of life that is easily influenced by public policy. It is much easier for the state to raise taxes, pay pensions and to build schools and hospitals than it is to produce virtuous citizens. But why does the state pay pensions and build schools and hospitals? Why does it outlaw slavery, set minimum income and safety standards for employees, or have laws against bribing officials? Presumably because it has some notion of what would constitute a good life for its citizens, and it sees a world utterly dominated by a single good— such as money—as offending against this concept of the good life. But it is precisely at this point that many object, and ask what business the state has deciding what the nature of the good life is. Theorists inspired by Kant argue that the state is not in the business of teaching or enforcing morality, nor has it any specific conception of happiness. In a pluralist democracy, the state simply has no knowledge of what objectively constitutes human flourishing (Arneson 1989). This view of the neutral state is strongly challenged on a variety of grounds, not the least being that even the so-called 'neutral theorists' do in fact implicitly espouse quite strong positions on the good life (Galston 1982). They want a state that is strongly committed to a view that the good life is based on self-direction and autonomy.

The outcome of these debates on whether the state should have a substantive view on what constitutes the good life will obviously affect public policy choices. This will be the case with regard both to the areas covered (a Ministry for Happiness?) and to the extent of redistributive intervention.

One form in which this debate emerges is in relation to so-called 'negative' and 'positive' freedom. Negative freedom is to do with freedom *from* interference by others. Positive freedom is to do with freedom *to* do certain things, and is concerned with one's capacity to act. If we are free, say, to write a best-selling novel in the sense that no one is stopping us, then we enjoy negative freedom. However, if we lack the capacity to write well, then we lack the positive freedom to be a novelist. The weight one gives to these two sorts of freedom is all-important when it comes to one's stance on public policy and distributive justice. In brief, the more one emphasises negative freedom, the less one is likely to be in favour of state intervention. Those who place greater emphasis on positive freedom, on the other hand, are much more likely to call for public intervention. Fortunately, there is a degree of convergence between these two positions, and we will look at this before we go on to discuss where the policy implications diverge.

• Convergence: Minimum Decency •

Where the different positions converge is in their agreement that the state has *at least* a minimal concern with material well-being as we have defined it. All liberal states are concerned, for instance, with minimum decency in the sense of avoiding desperate poverty. Similarly, even those who place maximum emphasis on the freedom of all individuals to pursue their concept of the good life as they see fit will usually recognise that this implies ensuring at least that degree of affluence which is a prerequisite for the pursuit of all other purposes (Galston 1982; Goodin 1988). Much of this book will be devoted to an examination of the data that permit us to judge whether all Australians enjoy at least that degree of affluence.

The consensus that the state should ensure at least minimum levels of decency does not take us very far. As we shall see in Chapter 5, even the punitive British Poor Law Report of 1834 could say piously that all civilised communities recognise their duty to relieve the indigent (British Parliamentary Papers, Poor Law 1834, vol. 8, p. 143). It then went on to define 'indigent', 'poor', 'decency' and 'relief' in such a way as to make its recognition of the practices of civilised communities sound very hollow indeed. If the commissioners who reported in 1834 were to be transported to contemporary Australia, they would find that little had changed in the terms of the debates. They would find particularly heated debates as to the extent that the state should be in the business of ensuring its citizens could live decently, as opposed to leaving them free to shape their own lives. We now examine these conflicting views on the nature of freedom, and then the important implications they have for public policy.

• Divergence: Positive and Negative Freedom •

The issue here is the boundaries of public policy. Even if we have agreement on whether public policy has a legitimate concern with minimum standards of living of citizens, it is by no means clear where we should draw the line on what constitutes the standard of living.

You could be well off *without being* well. *You could be* well *without being able to lead the life you* wanted. *You could have got the life you* wanted, *without being* happy. *You could be* happy, *without having much* freedom. *You could have a good deal of* freedom, *without* achieving *much. We can go on' (Sen 1987, p. 1).*

Sen does in fact go on. Consider the difference between being well-off (opulent) and being well. In a famous debate on the effects of the Industrial Revolution on the standard of living of the British working class, Hartwell painted a rosy picture of rising standards, while Hobsbawm claimed the opposite (Hobsbawm 1957; Hartwell 1961; Hobsbawm and Hartwell 1963). Who was right? Hartwell was right in that he showed a rise in opulence. But Hobsbawm was right in that he showed this was accompanied by great misery, including rising death rates between 1820 and 1840 (Sen 1987, p. 15). Those who define the standard of living in terms of being well-off will find Hartwell convincing. But those who place importance on the proportion who stay alive to enjoy the opulence will be more impressed by Hobsbawm.

What if one is alive and well, but unhappy? Many would say that happiness or utility is the final criterion by which living standards are judged. The focus is on achieved results, not freedom to achieve. Valuation is according to inner states (pleasure, happiness, pain) of the person affected. If all people were alike, and all shared similar backgrounds, this might make sense. But critics like Sen note the deeply conservative bias of this calculus. People adapt to their circumstances. For instance, many in the most appalling circumstances take some joy from small mercies. Some slaves were indeed happy. Rural Indian women are not obviously dissatisfied despite alarmingly high gender-biased death-rates. Illiterate Indians are not acutely unhappy about being illiterate (Sen 1990).

This criticism suggests that notions such as freedom in the sense of the positive freedom to achieve should be at centre stage. The broader a person's real freedom to achieve, the higher their standard of living. This may or may not bring with it greater happiness. Literacy may well result in greater discontent, as people come to see the gap between what is and what might be.

The distinction between negative freedom (freedom from interference by others) and positive freedom (freedom to achieve) is itself hotly contested. When each is taken to the point of caricature, the issues are easy to see. Negative freedom understood only as the absence of external physical or legal obstacles takes us back to Hobbes and Bentham, and the hollow sham of 'freedom' when there are gross disparities in the power of contracting parties. ('God for us all, and the devil take the hindmost!' as the elephant said as it danced among the chickens.) On the other hand, positive freedom has repeatedly been the ideological façade of the totalitarian leader who rejects citizens' demands on the ground that they merely reflect the internalisation of repressive conditions of the *ancien régime*. The first caricature ignores the effect on freedom of dire material want, while according to the second, affluence and bourgeois freedom are mere façades, masking the absence of 'true freedom'—the kind that would come only with collective self-government (Taylor 1979). According to both caricatures, the study of material well-being would be, at best, of secondary interest.

Berlin noted that 'the rise and fall of the two concepts [of negative and positive freedom] can largely be traced to the specific dangers which, at a given moment, threatened a group or society most: on the one hand excessive control and interference, or, on the other, an uncontrolled "market" economy. Each concept seems liable to perversion into the very vice which it was created to resist' (Berlin 1979, p. xlvi). He went on to observe that ultra-individualism was scarcely a rising force at the time he was writing (1969). He may have had in mind the events in France of May and June 1968 and their turbulent aftermath, when there was a sustained assault on the very concept of liberal scholarship and liberal society. It was a period when Marcuse was denouncing the evils of a consumer society where rising living standards were based on the satisfaction of 'false needs':

> The so-called consumer economy and the politics of corporate capitalism have created a second nature of man which ties him libidinally and aggressively to the commodity form. The need for possessing, consuming, handling, and constantly renewing the gadgets, devices, instruments, engines, offered to and imposed upon the people, for using these wares even at the danger of one's own destruction, has become a 'biological' need in the sense just defined. The second nature of man thus militates against any change that would disrupt

and perhaps even abolish this dependence of man on a market ever more densely filled with merchandise—abolish his existence as a consumer consuming himself in buying and selling. The needs generated by this system are thus eminently stabilizing, conservative needs: the counterrevolution anchored in the instinctual structure' (Marcuse 1969, p. 11).

It is easy to see both the appeal of Marcuse's argument and its perils. His argument is that the formal liberty offered by capitalist societies is hollow, even when it is accompanied by affluence, since this affluence merely feeds 'needs' which do not reflect true human values. Every liberation movement has to contend with variants on this argument as it confronts the way in which people's aspirations can be narrowed and shaped by an oppressive situation.

But the exposing of 'false needs' carries with it ominous implications of an enlightened élite who understand people's 'true needs'. A representative sample of such reasoning can be found in a contemporary textbook on social planning during the period of transition to socialism in an advanced capitalist country:

The purpose of the planning system is to create a society organized along socialist lines. ... This means that the role of social planners would be not simply to reflect locally expressed needs, but to confront experience under capitalism with a socialist critique, and to encourage a dialogue about socialist policies. Put another way, the social planners are intended to be not researchers or reporters, but catalysts and facilitators. This means, of course, that local planners would often have to counter expressed needs and expectations with alternative explanations, needs and priorities. This would particularly be the case in the first stage of socialist reconstruction, lasting at least 15 or 20 years, when needs created under capitalist organization would continue to be articulated during the transition to socialism (Walker 1984, p. 237).

It might well be argued that Walker is one of the last people ever to have written in this vein, and that, especially since the fall of the Berlin Wall in 1989, Hayek is a far more widely read author than Marcuse. Once again the proponents of negative freedom are in the ascendancy, and the chief threat to freedom comes from the ideology of the unrestrained market.

One set of risks stemming from the concept of negative freedom has been described particularly well by Taylor (1979; 1989). The cruder forms of negative freedom as espoused by Hobbes reject all qualitative distinctions between different kinds of freedom, and focus on a purely quantitative assessment. Taylor's reductio *ad absurdum* is to note that whereas all practice of religion in Albania was banned, there were virtually no traffic lights. On the other hand, there are countless traffic lights in London, affecting the freedom of movement of the entire population, and though the practice of religion is free, few, in fact, take advantage of it: there was, therefore, more freedom in Tirana than in London. That is, of course, unless we think freedom is important because we are purposive beings, and some purposes are more significant than others (Taylor 1979). This line of reasoning has important consequences for social policy, where judgments are made about the qualitative importance of some goods (for example, education) compared to others (for example, gambling), with the consequent restriction of some freedoms and enhancement of others.

• Policy Implications •

The policy implications of the importance given to freedom, and specifically to positive freedom, will become apparent in our final chapter. It is one thing to examine one aspect of life (material well-being) for analytic purposes, as we do in this book. It is quite another to go on to draw out public policy implications based only on this facet of life. For example, suppose we show that among a certain group there is perfect equality in cash incomes, but one quarter get their money from employment, one quarter get theirs from interest on capital, the next quarter are welfare recipients, and the rest are supported by relatives. Does this difference in the source of income matter? It would not matter if our only interest is material well-being—$100 is $100, and its source is irrelevant. The fact that the recipient of the welfare dollar may have to comply with a humiliating process to ensure 'genuine need' (Besley 1990; van Parijs 1990), or that the recipient of the intra-family transfer may experience it as a reinforcement of dependency (Atkinson 1989, pp. 12, 86) are

11

relevant considerations only if one introduces such concepts as positive freedom and rights.

If our interest is in material well-being only, it makes sense to have a social security system that ensures that all attain a certain minimum material standard of living, measured as accurately as possible, with payments targeted as accurately as possible. But, if our interest is more on rights and on freedom the emphasis would be on ensuring that all have an entitlement to a sufficient income, the disposal of which would be a matter for them. Note that the argument here is not that income is a good proxy for standard of living. It is the quite separate one that an important aspect of human well-being is the autonomy that comes with income, or, more precisely, with income to which one has certain rights.

If an assured income is important to human well-being, so is the public provision of certain goods and services. We discussed earlier Walzer's observation that a society in which literally everything could be bought and sold would be one that is radically different from any we know, and one few of us would wish to see. That seems clear enough if we have in mind the buying and selling of people, friendship, or a judge's decision. Here we are dealing with what cannot be bought and sold because it cannot be owned in the first place (people), or things whose very meaning would be corrupted by sale (friendship or judicial rulings) (Andre 1992). But what of access to health care, education, recreational facilities and housing? In practice, market-based societies, including Australia, have given mixed answers to this question. To some extent these goods and services can be bought and sold, but there is also vast public provision. We explain in Chapter 6 why we agree with this mixed strategy, and we also argue there why we think that in Australia today, the balance is moving too far in the direction of the market.

We will argue in Chapter 6 that, until recently, the public provision in Australia of both income support and of community services has had some very strong features. In the early 1990s the form of this public provision is changing rapidly. We do not like the direction of much of this change, and we are dismayed when the rationale for it is to increase people's 'independence and autonomy'. We argue that words like independence and autonomy ring hollow, not only when people lack basic necessities, but also when they lack the kinds of opportunities that have been a feature of the Australia we describe in this book. It has been a society typified by relatively easy access to employment, and to good housing, health care and education. We cannot envisage Australians 'living decently' in the future if they are denied access to those goods.

1

INDICES OF MATERIAL WELL-BEING

INTRODUCTION

Is it possible to obtain a reliable picture of how the standard of living differs among individuals? This is an important question. Views about individuals' standard of living underlie all welfare and other redistributive government policies. They also underlie views about the performance of the economic system of one country as compared with others. The traditional index of standard of living has been money income (or, for countries, Gross Domestic Product per capita). However, there is increasing dissatisfaction with a sole reliance on money income for this purpose. In this chapter we explore some of the sources of this dissatisfaction and pay particular attention to the ways in which information about other aspects of the standard of living may be incorporated into an overall measure.

Our purpose is to provide readers with an awareness of the main strategies and their strengths and limitations. We do not provide sufficient detail to enable newcomers to implement these strategies for themselves. Rather, we want to provide an intelligible account of the ideas that underlie the techniques for measuring standard of living and some capacity to assess their results.

Material well-being (or standard of living) is an intangible concept and numerous strategies have been devised to represent it empirically. Although our interest is the relative standing of individuals, much of the literature on techniques for measuring the standard of living refers to countries, with a particular focus on less developed countries.[1] The dissatisfaction with GDP per capita has caused a search for superior alternatives. The dissatisfaction arises from the facts that 1) it cannot always be reliably measured, and 2) it excludes important dimensions of the standard of living. The most notable sources of error in measurement arise from activities which are not transacted through the market (such as the production of food and other commodities at home), barter and the activities of the black market. Dimensions such as levels of literacy and life expectancy have an importance that is separate from the availability of produced commodities and there is thus a desire to incorporate these into a measure of the standard of living in their own right. There are analogous problems in the quantification of the standard of living of individuals.

A complete survey of the techniques which have been used for the construction of representations of material well-being would be too lengthy to provide. Instead we give a sample that illustrates the types of strategies which are available and some of the strengths and weaknesses that the careful reader should be alert to. In order to understand better the practical techniques for quantifying the material standard of living of individuals we commence at an abstract level to identify what we would ideally like to know, and then move to concrete approximations of this.

Before constructing or assessing an index of material well-being it is important to have a clear idea of the intention that lies behind the construct. In the standard economic approach the satisfactions that people derive from economic activity and material resources are termed 'utility'. The extent of utility that is experienced by an individual is judged entirely by that individual and is purely subjective: it cannot be assessed by an outside observer. Furthermore, only the economic sphere of life is relevant—namely, activities associated with the production and consumption of goods and services.

This characterisation of the standard of living has been challenged in two ways. One is to contemplate human well-being in a broader sense, which may be associated with high levels of positive freedom, of which the freedom made possible by access to material resources is a part. This may be assessed by an outside observer and judged in terms of 'functioning well', to use Sen's phrase (Sen 1982; 1985). The second is to reject as unreliable the economists' emphasis on self-assessed levels of well-being—the chief reason being that people adapt to constrained circumstances. As Sen puts it (1985, p. 29), 'A poor, undernourished person, brought up in penury, may have learned to come to terms with a half-empty stomach, seizing joy in small comforts and desiring no more than what seems "realistic". But this mental attitude does not wipe out the fact of the person's deprivation'.[2] We shall now examine each of these approaches to see how they relate to indices of material well-being.

• Utility •

Economists use the term 'utility' to represent the satisfactions which people receive from economic activities such as consumption, saving and work. Welfare economics focuses on the impact of particular events on the level and distribution of utility. Early in the history of this idea, utility was treated as something which could be observed and measured in such a way that the amount of one person's utility could be added to or subtracted from another's (that is, it was taken to be a cardinal measure). The maximisation of economic well-being then meant maximising the sum of individual utilities. However, the idea that this abstract concept could be quantified and made commensurable across persons came under increasing attack and was abandoned in the 1930s (partly because it was found to be unnecessary for much of the predictive and analytic agenda of economics).

Economists use the term 'utility' in a way that may confuse philosophers. To the economist it has the modest interpretation of representing the extent to which a particular commodity satisfies the wants of the individual (as this is judged by the individual him or her self). It implies no views as to how those wants are formed nor whether they are somehow life-enhancing. The purpose of the construct is chiefly as a basis for determining the price that people will pay for a commodity, which is the foundation of the theory of demand. It is a separate step to say that the purpose of an economic system *should* be the maximisation of the extent to which these individual wants are satisfied. We noted in the Introduction, for example, the argument that the wants satisfied by the economic system are largely created by the system in the first place.

The amount of utility experienced by an individual is determined by a number of factors. One is the quantity of goods and services consumed in a period (including those provided publicly and by the natural and built environment). Another is the skill that the person has in converting these goods and services into valued consumption. For example, a person may be better or worse at converting a bundle of food items into a tasty and nutritious meal. To obtain valued consumption from purchased commodities one also needs time. The importance of time has been heightened by the surge in two-earner families, especially those with children.[3]

Time is also an essential input into leisure, which is both a direct source of utility and frequently enhanced by combining time with purchased goods and services, such as a yacht or ticket to a football game. Hence the amount of adult time that is not spent in earning an income (non-employed time) is both a direct and an indirect source of utility.[4] Tastes will also affect the amount of utility a person obtains from any bundle of goods and services consumed. This is true regardless of how the tastes have arisen—whether they are autonomous, imposed by advertisers or culture or by peers or parents. Finally, of major importance is the quality and character of the work experience. People spend a high proportion of their adult lives at work and they derive much more from this than just income.

A focus on the concept of utility rather than on commodities thus has the virtue that it encourages paying attention to these other sources of material well-being. And it keeps commodities in their place: they are a means to an end, not an end in themselves.

It is now widely accepted that utility cannot be either observed directly or quantified on a numeric (as distinct from rank order) scale. Thus, in order to make use of the idea of utility it is necessary to make an assumption and develop some proxies. The assumption is that, in terms of material well-being, people are insatiable—that is, more total consumption and non-employed time and a better work and natural environment is always preferred to less. This assumption need not apply to any specific item of consumption, such as cars or sweet biscuits; for single items it clearly is possible to have enough—an additional car is just a nuisance once one has run out of people to drive it and parking space. The assumption of insatiability means that people would always prefer more *general* purchasing power to less—when they have had enough biscuits they buy something else. For this assumption to be satisfactory it need not be true for all individuals, it need simply be a predominant tendency.

Since utility cannot be observed, the first approximation is to use material resources in its stead. We draw on the assumption that more is always preferred to less to posit a positive and monotonic relationship between utility and material resources. That is, every increase in material resources is assumed to translate into an increase in utility, and for the individual there is only one corresponding utility level for each level of material resources. This is not an innocuous assumption: there are whole branches of thought which argue that material possessions and the never-ending pursuit of more are essentially barren. Plato was an early exponent of the view that an elevated human existence involved separation from and rejection of the pursuit of material goods.[5] The assumption of insatiability is justified on the grounds that it is consistent with observed behaviour: most of the time most people behave as if they want more material resources (note that leisure is included in this term).

• Functioning •

To represent the school that is an alternative to utility we draw on Amartya Sen's concepts of functioning and capability to function (1982, 1983, 1985). Sen argues that utility is not a good measure of *overall human well-being*, because it a) focuses only on the material, and b) ignores the fact that people's tastes and aspirations may become severely restricted by their life experience. He also argues that utility is not a good measure of the more limited idea of *standard of living*, which is not the good ' ... but the ability to do various things by using that good ... and it is that ability rather than the

18

mental reaction to that ability in the form of happiness that ... reflects the standard of living' (Sen 1982, p. 334).

Instead of focusing on either utility or goods, he advocates that we think of a three-stage process in which we start with material and human inputs. These are combined according to the needs and abilities of the individual to produce 'capacities' or 'capabilities to function'. Capacities, in turn, are used more or less effectively to deliver the ultimate result, which is human functioning. To illustrate the idea of capabilities, Sen gives an example of a bicycle. A bicycle is a *commodity* (or good) which, when combined with other inputs such as a path, the skill of the rider etc., produces the *capability* to move in a certain way, which may in turn produce happiness or *utility*. Which of these comes closest to the notion of standard of living? It cannot be commodities, since of themselves they do not tell us what one can do (I may have a disability which prevents me from riding my bike; I may lack the skills to do so; there may be no roads; there may be a prohibitive tax on cycling). He argues that it is the *capability* to do certain things (in this example, to have transport) that we are trying to capture with the idea of the material standard of living.

At times we may wish to go further and enquire into quality of life in the sense of functioning well as a human. This idea is imprecise but powerful, and may be seen as the endpoint of purposeful human action. The chief reason for concentrating on 'capability to function' rather than on the endpoint of functioning well is to give full weight to *choice* in human well-being. Sen is very much in the Aristotelian tradition here in distinguishing between citizens having 'the capacity to do fine things' (which is the aim of good government) and what citizens then choose to do with their capacities (Nussbaum1990).

In this context, the idea of functioning is valuable in that it reminds us that material well-being is not all that matters in life. Several of the techniques discussed in this chapter draw explicitly or implicitly on this approach, in particular the Human Development Index, the Scandinavian levels-of-living studies and an index constructed by means of distance functions.

The achievement of both utility and functioning requires the application of human skills to the material resources which are available. Material resources themselves are not the endpoint against which a satisfactory life should be judged. One reason for drawing attention to this is that there are two ways in which a specific level of individual functioning or utility may be enhanced: one is by increasing the levels of resources available to that individual; the other is by enhancing the person's skills and the environment in which those skills may be exercised. Figure 1.1 illustrates the relationships between the concepts which have been discussed in this section.

Figure 1.1

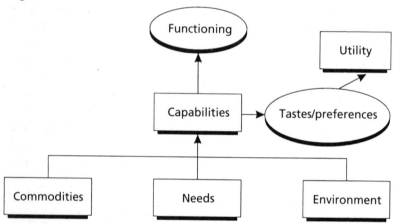

The remainder of this chapter is devoted to the development and exposition of practical proxies for utility and functioning at the individual level—proxies that may be quantified and which enable people to be ranked.

• Constructing Indices •

There are two different paths which may be taken in the construction of indices of material well-being. One is to convert all items into a common numeraire such that they may be added together to produce a single score for each person. People can then be ranked unequivocally on the basis of this score. The capacity to produce a clear ranking makes this strategy an attractive one. However, its drawback is that many relevant items are very different in character and it may be straining credulity or concealing important distinctions to represent them in terms of a common numeraire. If items are reduced to a common scale it implies that more of one can compensate for less of another.

There are situations where this does not make sense. Vickery (1977), for example, argues that time and money are not perfect substitutes in household production. By this she means that there are some things produced in households which cannot be replaced by a purchased substitute: parenting is the prime example. She concludes that one needs a two-dimensional index of a family's resources: time and money. Similarly, it may not be possible to compensate for poor health by providing more money: to be bedridden and rich is scarcely the same as to have fine health and little wealth. The second strategy is a response to this point. It defines separate spheres that contribute to material well-being, such as consumption, time, the work experience, health and natural environment, and ranks people separately on each of them. No attempt is made to produce an overall ranking or aggregation. It is the first of these two strategies—the single index—that is the more complex, and for this reason we pay most attention to it.

A SINGLE INDEX

The conceptual task of constructing an index boils down to two decisions. One is what to include in the index. The other is what weight to give each item. Once these decisions have been made, the remaining task is to find reliable empirical estimates of the items to be included, or acceptable approximations of them. We shall keep these steps in mind as we proceed to discuss specific strategies for the construction of a quantifiable index of material resources.

• What to Include? •

The first decision to be made when constructing an index is what to include. Ideally we would include every item that has a non-trivial impact on the material well-being of individuals. The list of such items is very long, and would include:

- all goods and services which were purchased and consumed in the period (a value for total expenditure on non-capital items would suffice—it is not necessary to identify every item separately)

- services received from assets which are owned, such as a car, house and consumer durable goods
- adult non-employed time
- all goods and services received (by each individual) from government, such as education, policing, the judicial system, health services, foreign policy, wilderness protection, local council regulations and so on
- goods and services received in kind from an employer, including the quality of the working environment
- all goods and services received in kind from other sources, such as friends and family, less any such which are given
- the natural and built environment to the extent that this can be influenced by produced goods and services: this includes congestion, quality of public and private buildings, air and water, public spaces and gardens and conservation areas.

It should be remembered that even if we were able to quantify all these things satisfactorily for each individual we would still have only a proxy for the concept of ultimate interest—namely, utility or capabilities. People who possessed equal amounts of these things may none the less obtain different levels of satisfaction or different capacities from them.

In practice, of course, it is scarcely possible to quantify each of the items listed above and to allocate an appropriate value to each individual. Some items, such as the value of the environment and of council regulations, are extremely difficult to quantify. Others, such as the value of policing and elegant public buildings, are extremely difficult to allocate to individuals. Thus, only a subset of the full list of influences on material well-being is likely to be included in any particular quantitative index. Within this subset many items will not be quantified with great accuracy, for reasons of sample error, inherent difficulty and the need to make estimates where the real value cannot be observed directly. We should note that any item that is excluded is implicitly given a value of zero. Thus, any estimated value will improve the overall index if it is on average a closer approximation to the real value than is zero.

A comparison between what we would *like* to measure and what we *can* measure shows there to be a large gap between the two. In practice, what we have is a proxy (some subset, more or less accurately estimated, of the full set of items which contribute to material well-being) of a proxy (material resources as a proxy for utility or capability). And this is not the end of the slide from what we want to what can be attained: it is also necessary for us to aggregate the different things in the list somehow. We concentrate first on the strategy which involves converting the measure of each item to a common numeraire.

• A Single Unit of Measurement: Money •

Economists have a long tradition of seeking a common denominator for the measurement of things, starting with the idea of wealth. J. B. Clark wrote, at around the turn of the century, 'the entire study of wealth is, indeed, meaningless unless there be a unit for measuring it; for the questions to be answered are quantitative'. (Clark 1908, p. 136). Many of today's issues of distribution and inequality are also quantitative, although not exclusively so. The measurement of wealth in earlier times took on many of the features of today's interest in the broader idea of material well-being (of which wealth is a part). In particular, wealth has been held in many and diverse forms and the issue of how to aggregate them has been a major one. One metric commonly proposed was the price at which it could be sold. Another, which became contentious, was the amount of labour embodied in a stock of wealth. Contesting this measurement of a stock of physical assets was the view that things are valuable, and valued, for the satisfactions they provide: thus it is the flow of satisfactions rather than the existence of the stock which should be valued. Adam Smith, writing in the eighteenth century, put it thus:

> *Every man is rich or poor according to the degree in which he can afford the necessaries, conveniences, and amusements of human life. (Smith 1976, p. 47)*

This is an important distinction, because the flow of satisfactions is a function of the state of mind of the individual and not just of the objective characteristics of the items themselves. But how to value and sum this flow of satisfactions? Is it not like trying to sum individual feelings or experiences?

There are several ways in which weights may be given to the different (and initially non-commensurable) sources of material well-being. We begin by examining the use of money as the numeraire.[6]

• Full Income •

The scope of income is a trade-off between two objectives, to include all benefits to consumers as part of income, even benefits arising from non-market activity, and to construct statistics that are reasonably precise and beyond dispute. (Usher 1987, p. 748)

The difficulties of producing measures of the material standard of living which are 'reasonably precise and beyond dispute' apply both to nations and to individuals. The convenient index of 'cash income received' is unreliable because both countries and families differ widely in the extent to which economic activity occurs outside the market. This problem arises even for the relatively homogeneous group of OECD countries, principally in the form of variation in labour market participation rates and the extent of home ownership.

When measuring the resources available to an individual it is preferable to quantify expenditure rather than income. Expenditure generates the flow of services from which material well-being is derived. Income, in contrast, provides the *capacity* to purchase things. There will be occasions when the level of income is a direct source of utility, as when people feel that their social standing, self-worth and security are affected by their level of income. But generally income is valued not for its own sake but for the ability it provides to buy goods and services. It is thus more satisfactory to measure directly the level of goods and services bought. The distinction is important when there is a significant divergence between a person's income and his or her levels of expenditure, as occurs, for example, when either borrowing or saving are at substantial levels.

The drawback of using expenditure as a measure is that it is difficult to collect the data. One procedure, used by the Australian Bureau of Statistics (ABS), is to ask households to keep a diary of all expenditures over a short period, such as two weeks. This is a costly exercise and it should be noted that in ABS surveys a very high proportion of households report spending more than their income (net of income tax). For example, in the 1988–89 Household

Expenditure survey about *60 per cent* of households reported, on average, expenditure which exceeded their net income (ABS 1990b, p. 8). It is implausible to suppose that 60 per cent of households are persistently dissaving, and this result invites the conclusion that either expenditure is being over-estimated by respondents or income is being under-recorded.

Over a lifetime, expenditure and income are likely to be very similar for a family (if a family can be imagined to have a lifetime). But data are usually collected for much shorter periods, such as a week or a year. Although in principle expenditure is to be preferred over income, in practice it is frequently (money) income that is used because this is the information which is at hand. There are additional reasons why money income alone is likely to be a poor proxy for the material standard of living of an individual.

One reason is that, generally, people do not live alone. When they live in families or even as unrelated members of a household, many of the important sources of material well-being, such as the house and its contents, are shared. The clearest example of where it can be most misleading to look only at the individual's own cash income is the married couple with one partner earning an income and the other partner providing home-produced goods (or enjoying leisure). The person at home has no recorded income, but shares in the goods and services purchased out of the partner's income. To attribute the income only to the partner who receives it overstates the resources available to the earner and understates the resources available to the non-earner. An assumption needs to be made about how such income is shared. One assumption, which we prefer, is that it is shared according to need. We acknowledge that this is a controversial assumption that will be resisted by some. In its defence we make three points: 1) there is little empirical information on actual sharing arrangements and simple guesses are preferable to complex ones;[7] 2) it is hard *not* to share a good deal of the standard of living of a household, such as the quality and location of the house and its contents and food; 3) the assumption does *not* imply that each member of the family has equal levels of autonomy, self-esteem, power etc.—it refers solely to material standard of living.

The assumption of allocation according to need begs the question of how 'need' is defined. The most common approach is to use an equivalence scale. This scale provides a weight to each type of family depending on the number of adults and children it contains. The weights may also vary with the age, gender and work-force status of family members. The idea is to find a weight which will give a family of, say, six children and two adults the same *equivalent income* as the numeraire single adult. The weights given to an extra child typically are within the range 0.25 to 0.50. That is, the needs of an extra child are taken to be between 25 and 50 per cent of the needs of a single adult. The use of per capita measures is one form of equivalence scale, that is, one in which each person is given equal weight. The construction of the weights contained in any equivalence scale is more an art than a science and a variety of equally plausible scales are available.[8] Unfortunately the results of various inequality and poverty measures are quite sensitive to the choice of equivalence scale. For example, reporting on international comparisons of poverty, Gruen (1989, pp. 17–18) notes that on one measure about 5 per cent of the aged in Australia are recorded as being in poverty while on another measure this figure is 22 per cent. He attributes the difference chiefly to the use of different equivalence scales.

A second qualification to the use of recorded money income as a measure of material well-being is the need to deduct personal income tax: it is purchasing power rather than gross income which is relevant.

We conclude that where income is used as the proxy for material standard of living it should be income net of tax and after adjustment by some equivalence scale. But even then, as noted above, it is not sufficient to count only money income. Equivalent after-tax money income should be supplemented by the addition of other major sources of material well-being, to produce a measure known as 'full income'. Full income is a measure, expressed in dollars, of all the major sources of material well-being, including money income.

The selection of money as the numeraire with which to aggregate diverse components of material well-being resolves the question of what weight to give each component: the weight is its (after-tax) money value. The difficult part is to put sensible money values on things which are a source of material well-being but which are not traded in the market place: that is, are not purchased in the conventional way. The most important of these are: the time that adults in the household have for things other than earning an income (such as parenting, household chores, leisure, gardening, volunteer services and education); the services provided by the owner-occupied house and its contents; and indirect benefits provided by governments. Data from the authors' Australian Standard of Living survey suggest that owner-occupied housing provides the equivalent of about 10 per cent of average full income and the contribution of adult non-employed time is about 26 per cent.[9] The ABS (1992) estimates the value of government-provided housing, education, health care and non-cash social welfare benefits to be 22 per cent of the value of household disposable income. It is clear from these figures that these non-cash sources of material well-being are not trivial. It is therefore necessary to take care in their estimation and incorporation into an index of full income, a value of which will be attributed to each person. Before we proceed to discuss how this may be done, however, we consider whether the effort is worthwhile.

There are usually two reasons for computing an index of standard of living. One is to examine inequality and the related idea of poverty. The other is to compare average values of the standard of living either across countries or across time. Money income will be a good proxy for full income if a) the rank order of households is the same on the two measures; and b) the ratio of the non-money components to the money components is stable over time and between comparison countries. Do these conditions hold? The brief answer is 'no' to the first question and 'probably not' to the second. We shall show later that the inclusion of the major non-money items into full income changes the rank order of individuals to a non-trivial degree. It also alters the picture of who is on the bottom of the distribution. In our judgment the differences in the pictures produced when using full as compared with money income are sufficient to justify the extra effort of constructing full income, except perhaps where fairly crude rankings are satisfactory. We have not seen any examples of full income measures compared across countries or across time. However, in order for the relation between full and money income to be stable in such comparisons, there must be comparable labour force participation behaviour, patterns of home ownership and distribution and level of government indirect taxes and benefits. These are stringent conditions.

• *Imputation techniques* •

There are two basic strategies for imputing a money value to sources of material well-being which are not purchased directly from the market. One is to find the opportunity cost (in money terms) of the resource—that is, the amount which could have been received if the resource had been used to earn income. The other is to find some equivalent which is bought and sold in the market and to use its price to indicate the value of the item which is not. In principle the two approaches give the same answer: in practice they may not. We give examples of each of these approaches below.

The opportunity cost method can be used to impute the values of non-employed time and household durable goods. With regard to non-employed time, the basic assumption is that the labour market is in equilibrium and people can choose between working or not working a few extra hours per week. In this case, if they choose not to work extra hours then it may reasonably be inferred that the value to them of the other things they will do with their time—their non-employed hours—is at least equal to the extra income (after tax) they could have received by working.

This precise notion can only be imprecisely applied in practice. People often do not have a free choice about the number of hours they work. A decision to work full-time does not imply that every hour worked is valued more highly than an hour of non-employed time. All it implies is that the total amount earned is preferred to the total number of hours spent doing something else. Where part-time work is reasonably available we can go further and say that the choice of full-time rather than part-time work means that the pay for the extra hours exceeds the alternative value of those extra hours. The average hourly (after-tax) pay of a person in either full- or part-time work thus gives an approximation of the value placed on an hour spent not employed, but it is not an exact valuation.

Clearly there are times when the labour market is not in equilibrium; that is, there is unemployment and people spend more time not employed than they would choose. It is difficult to value the time of people who are recorded as unemployed as they are likely to embrace a wide spectrum of valuations of non-market time. For some, non-market time may be so highly valued that they would rather not be employed. They would rather hone their surfing skills or build their own house or look after their young children. For this group, the imputed value of non-employed time is equal to or more than the difference, after-tax, between their likely wage and the value of unemployment benefits received. For others, unemployment is a thoroughly miserable experience, and the marginal value of non-employed time may even be negative. A negative marginal value does not, of course, imply a negative average value, and it is probable that the unemployed person is able to make *some* substitution of time for purchased goods and services in home production. How much can only be guessed at.

An imaginary experiment is to ask the unemployed people what is the minimum amount they would have to be paid in order to work a full week. Some people may say they would do this for nothing, because of the boost it would give to their skill levels, self-esteem and subsequent employability. This answer does not imply a zero value for non-employed hours: rather, the benefit from employment is expected to be in the form of future rather than current income. Generally, the answer to the question gives an estimate in money terms of the value of their non-employed time. Because of the absence of a firm basis for imputing a value to the non-employed time of the unemployed, we believe a conservative position should be taken and a low value such as zero imputed. The same views apply to people who cannot work for reasons of disability or ill-health.

Unemployment can also appear in the form of working fewer hours than desired or complete withdrawal from the labour force. Especially for older men, the problems of finding work appear to be a substantial cause of retirement before the age of 65. Clearly, if non-employed hours are not voluntarily chosen, it is misleading to value them at the market wage rate.

For people who are not in the work-force but who are of working age, the value of non-employed time must be approached differently, because there is no direct observation of their average hourly wage. Instead, it is possible to *estimate* the wage that the person would have received had he or she been employed. This can be done by use of what economists term an 'earnings function'. An earnings function shows how the wages of people are related to attributes such as the amount of their education, the amount of experience they have had in employment, the amount of time they have been in their current job and perhaps additional factors such as city or country location, whether they are migrants, their marital status, the industry in which they are employed and so on. The relationship between such attributes and a person's earnings can be established through the application of regression analysis to data from people who are in employment. The results can then be used to predict what people *could be expected to earn* were they in employment, given their education, experience, migrant status etc. It is usual to estimate these relationships separately for men and women since experience shows that they can be different. The earnings function should be calculated using after-tax earnings as the dependent variable, since the purpose is to identify the value of purchased goods and services which a person is giving up by having an hour non-employed.

Most adult males of working age are in employment. This is not true, however, for women. It is mainly women, therefore, to whom this technique of imputing a wage is applied. In estimating an earnings function for women, careful studies take into account the fact that the women who *are* in employment are not a random sample. It is possible to make some adjustment (known as a Heckman correction) for this sample selection bias.

The use of an observed or predicted wage to put a value on non-employed time is an example of the 'opportunity cost' approach to valuation. An alternative is to work out what people would have to pay to buy the services with which they provide themselves in their non-employed time. For example, time-use studies have been conducted for households which identify the time spent in activities such as housework, child-care and home maintenance, as well as recreation and rest. The first group of activities can be 'bought in' by employing someone else to do the housework and maintenance and look after the children. The cost of buying such services then provides as estimate of the value to the family of having them produced by a family member who works at home rather than in a paid job. The three major objections to this approach are: a) that it requires detailed information for each household on patterns of time use; b) it cannot be comprehensive because, for example, it is not possible to employ someone else to experience leisure for you; and c) purchased services may not be very close substitutes for home-produced ones, especially in the case of parenting.

The 'cost of equivalent services' approach is a useful way to measure the value to the household of the services it receives from its stock of durable assets. This can be illustrated for the case of people who own their own homes. The ownership of a home provides the household with a flow of 'housing services' that is does not have to use current income to acquire, unlike a household which is renting. (For a household which is still paying off a mortgage, the equity in the house is the source of the 'non-purchased' services). What is this worth? One answer is that it is worth the rental that the house could command. In an equilibrium world of no taxes or agents, this would be the same amount regardless of whether the household receives or pays the rent. This sum would also equate to the (risk-adjusted) returns which the household could obtain on equivalent funds invested in some other asset. In fact there are taxes, agents and asymmetries between borrowing and lending which mean that, in practice, alternative valuation approaches can give different results. For a more detailed discussion of these issues with respect to housing see Yates (1991). We note that the Australian Statistician, in constructing the national accounts, imputes an annual value of 5 per cent (real) to the equity that home owners have in their houses.

To summarise, money values may be imputed by:
- estimating the opportunity cost of the resource that is used within the household (such as adult time and equity in the home); *or*
- estimating the price which would have to be paid to obtain the goods or services were they to be purchased rather than produced at home.

The practical application of these general principles can be difficult and imprecise. The existence of taxation, inflation, expected capital gains, asymmetries between buyers and sellers, quality differences between home-produced and purchased services and disequilibrium in the market all present hazards to the accurate imputation of money values.

• *An illustration* •

The principles discussed above have been applied by the authors in the construction of an index of full income using data from the

Australian Standard of Living survey. Here we briefly outline the steps taken in the construction of that index.[10]

First, individuals were located in their households. Total annual money income was recorded after subtraction of personal income tax and then adjusted by application of an equivalence scale.[11] Each adult member of the household was then deemed to receive this amount of equivalent after-tax income.

The (after-tax) value of adult time not spent in employment was then estimated for each family member. This was quite a complex task. Each person was assumed to have 50 hours per week available for employment. For those currently in employment, their non-employed time was valued as the product of their average hourly wage and (50 minus the number of hours in employment). For people of working age who were not in the work-force (these were chiefly women employed in home duties and men who had voluntarily retired early) the above procedure was replicated but with the actual wage being replaced with their predicted wage. A zero value was attributed to the non-employed time of people who were unemployed or invalids or who were judged to have retired early because they had been unable to find a job. Full-time students were assumed to be available for employment for one third of the year and thus had their estimated wage imputed to them only for this period. People over the age of retirement had their non-employed time valued as 25 per cent of average after-tax earnings.

The estimations were deliberately conservative. We wished to reduce the force of any charge that our results were being driven by unreasonably high estimates of the value of non-employed time. Table 1.1 provides a summary of the numbers of people who were in each category and the basis on which their non-employed time was valued. It is quite clear that the imputations made for the value of non-employed time are inaccurate. They are justified on the grounds that to remain silent with respect to non-employed time is the same as imputing a value of zero to this vital household resource. In our judgment, the use of an implicit value of zero involves an error which is much larger than that involved in the above imputations.

To compute the full income of the family, the value of non-employed time of both spouses has been included, together with

Table 1.1: *The valuation of non-employed time: numbers and basis for estimation of value of non-employed time for different groups*

PERCENTAGE IN CATEGORY		BASIS OF ESTIMATION
Employed	68	own after-tax wage
Unemployed	4	0
Invalid/disabled	<1	0
Home duties	18	predicted wage
'Voluntary' early retirement	5	predicted wage
'Involuntary' early retirement	1	0
Retired	4	25% of average after-tax wage
Students	<1	33% of predicted wage

their cash income. The average value of own non-employed time is $4910 and the average value of partners' non-employed time is $3701. Of course, not all individuals had partners. Together, own plus partner's value of non-employed time provided 26 per cent of total full income, on average.

For owner-occupiers, the services they receive from their house are a major form of income in kind. As with non-employed time, this income has the additional value of being tax-free. In our sample, 33 per cent owned their houses outright and 37 per cent were paying off a mortgage. To impute a value to this service, we drew on estimates of the value of their house made by our respondents. The imputed value of the house was calculated as 5 per cent of the family's estimated equity.

Part of the full income received by a household is the services of consumer durables and other possessions. Our list of these assets is not comprehensive, and in particular excludes items which are most likely to be found among very well-off households. Thus the imputed value of services from possessions which we recorded is likely to be more compressed than a full enumeration of asset position would reveal. The possessions we do value are: car, second car, boat, holiday house, caravan, shares (for each of which we have a broad indication of value from respondents), life assurance, refrigerator, washing machine, telephone, colour television, video recorder, microwave oven, stand-alone deep-freeze, dish-washer and stereo equipment. Each of these has had an income value imputed which equals the annual interest (after tax) that could have been received by the household on its purchase price, less an allowance for depreciation. (This is an example of the opportunity cost method of valuation).

Some households receive benefits in cash or kind from family members who live outside the household. We have information on such family help as it relates to child-care, housing, transport, meals, occasional gifts of furniture and gifts of cash. Such services provide a benefit to the household which receives them and a cost (though not necessarily of the same amount) to the household which provides them. The value of flows in both directions are imputed. Both the numbers of households involved and the value of the flows are quite small. For example, six per cent of people received regular help with child-care, five per cent received regular help with housing costs, six per cent received regular meals and seven per cent received regular or occasional financial help. Slightly higher percentages said that they helped other family members in these ways than said that they received help.

The other benefit in kind for which allowance has been made is that accruing to people on government pensions or benefits. An amount of $1200 per annum has been imputed as the value of these benefits, based on an update of estimates made of their value by the Department of Social Security in 1984.

The full income of the household is reduced by medical expenses (over and above that refundable from health insurance) and the amount of repayment of debts other than a house mortgage.

Finally, the components of full income are in two groups, the first of which is adjusted by the use of an equivalence scale to account for differences in the size and composition of the household and the second of which is not. The first group comprises cash income, the value of adult non-employed time, the value of benefits in kind, both given and received, health expenses, debt repayments, and the estimated annual value of life assurance and shares. The second group comprises the annual value of consumer durables together with a boat, holiday house, caravan, house (for owner-occupiers) and assistance from family with housing and furniture. All values are calculated after income tax. We thus have an estimate of the value per adult of after-tax equivalent full income.

• Is full income different? •

What do we learn from this measure? We refer to it frequently in the rest of this book but here simply summarise a few interesting conclusions.

First, as is to be expected, the absolute values of full income exceed those of equivalent after-tax money income: the mean values, respectively, are $33 169 and $19 535 (a 70 per cent difference), while the median values are $30 742 and $17 345 (a 77 per cent difference).

Second, people's ranking in the distribution of income is sensitive to how income is measured. Table 1.2 reports a number of different income measures and the rank correlations between individuals' standing on each of them. The income measures are: a) own pre-tax earnings (OE); b) after-tax family income (FI); c) equivalent after-tax family income (EI); and d) equivalent after-tax full income (FULL).

The correlations suggest that each of the measures of income is capturing something distinctive. Full income includes equivalent income as its major component. Despite this, the correlation between people ranked on the two indices is only 0.80. We may conclude that the other items, such as the value of non-employed time and of owner-occupied housing, are not closely correlated with equivalent income and that the inclusion of such sources of material well-being does change our views of how relatively well-off individuals are. The following correlations support this view: equivalent income and imputed rent from owner-occupied housing, 0.34; equivalent income and equivalent value of *own* non-employed time, -0.02; equivalent income and equivalent value of *household* non-

Table 1.2: *Rank correlations between people ranked according to their values on pre-tax earned income (OE), after-tax family income (FI), equivalent income (EFI) and full income (FULL)*

	OE	FI	EI	FULL
OE	1.0	.61	.57	.45
FI		1.0	.87	.74
EI			1.0	.80
FULL				1.0

employed time, 0.07; equivalent income and services of other assets, 0.22. Support is also found in the fact that 66 per cent of people are in a different quintile when ranked by each measure and 21 per cent of people who are below the median on one measure are above the median on the other measure. Seven per cent of people move from the top quintile to the bottom quintile, depending on the measure used.

Third, for the full sample, inequality in the distribution of full income is very similar to inequality in the distribution of equivalent income, with Gini coefficients of 0.26 and 0.28 respectively. This similarity disappears when we consider only the bottom half of the distribution (ranked by equivalent income). Then, with a Gini coefficient of 0.16, equivalent income is much more equally distributed than is full income (Gini: 0.25).

Fourth, Table 1.3 displays an important finding: inequality in the distribution of the *components* of full income (imputed rent, own non-employed time, partner's non-employed time and 'other') is considerably higher than for either full income or for equivalent income. However, these components are not highly correlated, so that when the several unequal distributions are added together the

Table 1.3: *The degree of inequality (as measured by the Gini coefficient) and correlation between full income and its components (as measured by the Pearson correlation coefficients)*

				CORRELATION COEFFICIENT			
	Gini	*FULL*	*EI*	*IR*	*ONET*	*PNET*	*Other*
Full income (FULL)	*0.26*	1.0	.80	.60	.35	.41	.25
Equivalent income (EI)	*0.28*		1.0	.34	.02	.16	.10
Imputed rent (IR)	*0.56*			1.0	.05	.15	.15
Own non-employed time (ONET)	*0.52*				1.0	-0.1	.09
Partner's non-employed time (PNET)	*0.62*					1.0	.06
Other	*0.75*						1.0
Full inc. (lower 50%)	*0.23*						
Equiv. inc. (lower 50%)	*0.16*						

Source: Australian Standard of Living survey

resulting aggregate is more equally distributed than is any of its components (apart from equivalent income). For example, the correlations between the value of own non-employed time and both imputed rent and value of one's partner's non-employed time is negative (and very small). These low correlations tell an important story. *Inequalities in the different spheres of material well-being tend to offset each other.* Instead of those people with the highest incomes also having the greatest imputed rent, other net assets and time, we find that they may rank quite low on these other dimensions. This is especially, but not uniquely, true of the aged, who tend to have low incomes but relatively high imputed rent, other net assets and value of time.

Table 1.3 shows, for example, that the degree of inequality in the distribution of imputed rent, as measured by the Gini coefficient, is 0.56, and that people's levels of imputed rent and levels of equivalent income have a correlation coefficient of 0.34.

Another way of examining this point is to see what contribution each of the components of full income makes to inequality in its distribution. Table 1.4 reports the results of decomposing the sources of inequality, based on a technique developed by Robert Lerman and Shlomo Yitzhaki (1985). (Note that 'Full income' incorporates the net impact of government indirect taxes and benefits in kind from health, education and housing services).

Table 1.4: *Sources of inequality in the distribution of full income*

	GINI COEFFICIENT FOR FULL INCOME	SHARE OF FULL INCOME	PERCENTAGE CONTRIBUTION TO INEQUALITY
Full income	0.23	1.0	100
Equivalent income	0.28	.55	52
Imputed rent	0.56	.09	14
Own non-employed time	0.52	.13	13
Partner's non-employed time	0.62	.09	11
Netgov*	0.43	.07	-4
Other	0.75	.08	14

* **Netgov** *stands for the net effect of government indirect taxes and expenditures on education, housing, health and non-cash social welfare, as reported in ABS (1992)*

Table 1.4 can be interpreted as follows. The Gini coefficient measures the degree of inequality in the distribution of full income and its component items. The figure of 0.56 for imputed rent, for instance, is derived by first ranking people according to their level of imputed rent and then calculating the inequality in this distribution. An analogous interpretation applies to each of the other components of full income. It is thus perfectly possible for an item to have a high degree of inequality in its distribution but also to *reduce* the degree of inequality in the distribution of full income, as is the case with own non-employed time. This arises if the ranking of people on the item in question is not closely correlated with their ranking on other items (in particular, equivalent income). We see, for example, from Table 1.3 that own non-employed time has a trivial (and negative) correlation with equivalent income: the summation of the two of them produces a distribution which is more equal than either is alone.

The column headed 'Share of full income' shows the proportion of total full income which is contributed, on average, from each source. The column headed 'Percentage contribution to inequality' shows the contribution made by the inclusion of the item in question to the Gini coefficient for full income. To judge whether the inclusion of imputed rent, for example, increases or decreases total inequality, it is necessary to compare its share in the value of full income (9 per cent) with its share in contributing to inequality (14 per cent). If the latter is greater than the former, as is the case with imputed rent, then inclusion of the item increases aggregate inequality. Of the items listed, equivalent income, own non-employed time and net government indirect taxes and expenditures are the ones which contribute less than their share to total inequality. The last of these is the only one to make a negative contribution to inequality, and note that it does this despite the fact that it is quite unequally distributed, with a Gini coefficient of 0.43.

Table 1.4 illustrates well the important role played by the degree of correlation between people's ranking on different sources of material well-being. The distributions of each of the items we added to equivalent income to construct full income are highly unequal. And yet when they are aggregated the resulting total is more equally distributed than is equivalent income.

Fifth, when people are ranked by full as distinct from equivalent income we obtain a different picture of who is at the bottom of the distribution. In particular, people of retirement age are much better off while blue collar families are worse off than their equivalent income would suggest. To illustrate, when the population is ranked by *equivalent* income, 60 per cent of single people aged 60 to 74 are in the bottom quintile. In contrast, when the population is ranked by *full* income, only 16 per cent of this group are in the bottom quintile. The single aged are either not a disadvantaged group, or are profoundly disadvantaged, depending on which measure is used. The same relative differences are found for aged couples, but the absolute numbers are much smaller. *There are almost no aged couples in the bottom quintile of full income.*

While less dramatic than the story for the aged, the use of full income shows people from unskilled backgrounds, single parents, and non-aged single people to be substantially more disadvantaged than their equivalent income would suggest. Conversely, migrants from non-English speaking countries and people on pensions or social welfare benefits (which includes but is not confined to those on the old-age pension) are better off than their equivalent income would suggest. Whereas social welfare recipients comprise 52 per cent of the bottom quintile of people ranked by equivalent income, they comprise only 39 per cent of the bottom quintile of full income.

Who are worse off—widows or the divorced? The answer depends entirely upon which of the two income measures is being used. On the basis of *equivalent* income, widows rank with single parents as the most disadvantaged group, with 65 per cent of them being in the bottom quintile. The divorced, while clearly disadvantaged, are not as severely so, with 47 per cent in the bottom quintile. If *full income* is used as the indicator, widows are scarcely more disadvantaged than the population at large (24 per cent are in the bottom quintile) whereas the divorced are severely disadvantaged and more than twice as likely as widows to be in the bottom quintile.

Sixth, we find, as expected, that the distribution of full income over the life cycle is flatter than is the·distribution of money income. We show this in Figure 1.2 (over the page), which reports the profile by age of two measures of money income—family income and equivalent income—and contrasts this with the profile for full income.[12] The income plotted for each age group is expressed as a fraction of the median for the relevant income type, in order that the scale on the vertical axis be common for each.

Figure 1.2: *Three measures of the life cycle*

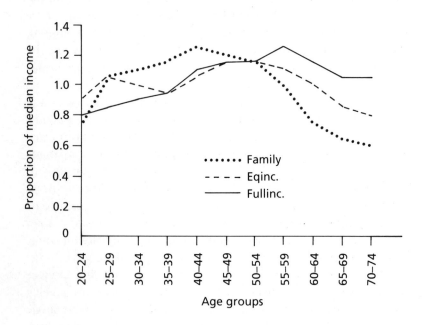

• *Strengths and weaknesses of full income* •

The advantages of full income as a measure of the standard of living that people attain from material resources are:
- it is a single index on which everyone can be ranked unambiguously
- there is a clear theoretical rationale for
  a) the items which are to be incorporated into the measure
  b) the values which are imputed to each item
- it is more comprehensive, in important ways, than is money income.

The *disadvantages* of full income are:
- it measures resources only and is still some distance from giving a picture of utility or functioning
- it makes heavy demands on data
- the many imputations which are required may reduce the credibility of the index
- it cannot plausibly be comprehensive.

• Alternatives to Income •

In the discussion of full income we saw that one way to obtain weights for the components of material well-being was to impute a money value based on their market opportunity cost or the cost of purchasing an equivalent service. But not all things can sensibly be reduced to money values. For example, it strains credulity to express degree of health or level of optimism in terms of money equivalents. Scandinavian studies have shown that a question which is very effective in identifying degrees of material hardship is 'In an emergency, could you raise $1500 in a week?'. The answers to this useful question cannot be reduced to a money numeraire. Similarly, there are aspects to people's ability to function satisfactorily which go beyond the material, such as freedom from stress and degree of autonomy. These concepts lose their power if they are squeezed into a money metric. Is there, then, some way in which such aspects of life can be quantified and aggregated to produce an index which has a single value for each individual? We here describe three ways in which this may be done. We remind readers that it is not our intention to provide sufficient detail to enable a person who is not familiar with these techniques to themselves apply them in practice. Rather, we intend to provide a feel for the underlying strategies and for the strengths and weaknesses inherent in the techniques so that their results may be interpreted in a knowledgeable way.

• Factor Analysis •

Factor analysis does not require components to be expressed in a common metric (such as dollars). Nor is it necessary to have a cardinal measure for each component. It is sufficient to be able to rank each person in order on each component, which is expressed in whatever unit is most convenient. These are most useful features of the technique and enable it to be applied to a disparate array of information. For example, in calculating standard of living it is possible to include indicators such as 'went away on a holiday last year' and 'obtained help from a welfare agency'. These are qualitative variables which cannot sensibly be reduced to some common numeraire.

To use factor analysis to compute a measure of standard of living, it is necessary to assume that there exists a uni-dimensional measure of standard of living, along which everyone has an ordered ranking. This measure is not directly observable, but is correlated with a number of attributes that are observable. Factor analysis is a multivariate technique for extracting this underlying variable, and for deriving weights that give the strongest correlation between the underlying variable and the observable attributes. If the assumption is valid, the first principle factor which is extracted from the application of factor analysis to the data represents this hypothesised 'standard of living'.[13] Of all the variables in the data set, factor analysis may identify only a subset as being related to each other and to the first principle component. The remaining variables will then be grouped into a second and possibly third or more component. The extraction of more than one component implies the existence of more than one underlying commonality. If this is inconsistent with the hypothesis of the researcher, the subsequent components can simply be ignored and the index constructed only out of the items in the first principle component. In this sense, factor analysis can help in the selection of the items in the index as well as with the weights to be given them.

Among the more accessible presentations of factor analysis are the ABS information paper *Socio-Economic Indexes for Areas* (ABS 1990), and Gould's excellent critique of the uses and abuses of this, and other, measurement techniques in *The Mismeasure of Man* (Gould 1988).

One of the main uses of factor analysis is to simplify a large array of complex data, and it has been applied with particular success in the study of fossils. For instance, Gould found that in his study of pelycosaurian reptiles, the fourteen dimensions he was measuring were so highly correlated that they could be summarised in a single dimension, the first principal component, with practically no loss of information. The reason for this was simple: large animals have large bones, and small animals have small bones. His single size dimension told him all he needed to know (Gould 1988, pp. 248–50).

A major caveat about the use of factor analysis is that just because a mathematical summary of an array of data can be made, it would be the error of reification to assume that this somehow conferred a physical meaning on the principal component. This *may* be justified, as in the case of Gould's interpretation of the fossil analysis as a size dimension, but it would be perilous to deduce it from the mathematics alone. 'A factor analysis for a five-by-five correlation matrix of my age, the population of Mexico, the price of swiss cheese, my pet turtle's weight, and the average distance between the galaxies during the past ten years will yield a strong first principal component' (Gould 1988, p. 250). In other words, neither factor analysis nor any other statistical technique can absolve us from the need to think about what we are doing, and whether it makes sense.

When the ABS used factor analysis to construct indices of socio-economic advantaged and disadvantaged *areas* (as distinct from our focus on individuals), it heeded Gould's warnings in the sense that the initial variables chosen for each index were selected on the basis of their known performance in earlier indices, and in the light of comment from academics and research institutions. For instance, the indices of relative advantage, relative disadvantage, and of economic resources all contain variables relating to income and to housing. The rationale for this is that these are clearly variables one would expect to be important in this context . When the indices were constructed with the aid of factor analysis they were not immediately accepted, but were 'validated' in the sense that their performance in practice was examined to see if they 'made sense'. For instance, if high income were not given a high weight in an index of socio-economic advantage, we would suspect that something was wrong. Similarly, local knowledge was used to check whether rankings of districts intuitively made sense. A further useful check is to examine the extreme rankings to see if there was a plausible rationale for their ranking—the most obvious one being a homogeneous district, with uniformly high or low incomes, levels of education, and rates of home-ownership (ABS 1990).

Gould's warning about the danger of reification in factor analysis applies to the construction of all indices. Provided this warning is heeded, indices can be useful devices for summarising and simplifying complex data. The more sophisticated and complex the technical process of constructing the index, the more likely it will be that it will be reified (if for no other reason than that few people can understand the process well enough to criticise it). The ABS practice of using experts with local knowledge to check whether the results 'make sense' is a useful antidote to reification. It could well be objected that this is reminiscent of Rowntree's practice at the turn of the century of supplementing his poverty line with opinions of local residents as to who was living in secondary poverty (Rowntree 1902), and implies an appeal to an independent source of 'true' knowledge. At the very least, it highlights the fact that statistical techniques for aggregating data produce results which are no better than the information they have to work with, and need to be interpreted with care and insight.

• *Strengths and weaknesses of factor analysis* •

The *advantages* of factor analysis are:
- it provides a means of selecting which components to include that is not simply arbitrary or idiosyncratic to the researcher
- it is capable of dealing with items which are not measured in a common metric
- there is a statistical rationale behind the process by which weights are determined for each item: thus the weights are not arbitrary.

The *disadvantages* of factor analysis are:
- the initial selection of items must be appropriate to the assumption that each of them contributes to some common, higher level, function (the first principle component)
- there is no intuitive appeal to the weights which are determined for each item
- there is no theoretical rationale for the weights which are determined for each item, apart from their statistical properties.

• Distance Functions •

Whereas factor analysis assists in the selection of what to count as well as determining the weights to be given to each item, distance functions are a technique only for determining weights.

Distance functions, which have uses in the measurement of the quantity and quality of output in areas such as education,[14] have only been lightly used in the field of income distribution and poverty measurement. The example to be discussed here is taken from a paper by Lovell, Richardson, Travers and Wood (LRTW) (1993), which draws on the same data as are used in the construction of full income (described above).

Distance functions have the attraction that they can aggregate sets of data (in our case, different sources of material well-being) which are measured in different units and for which we have no a priori weights. It is necessary simply for the observations in each set of data to be ranked in order, with the observations which make the least contribution to the output ranked lowest. For example, in the construction of an index of material standard of living (referred to as a resources index), LRTW use information for each individual on the following items:

- whether an owner-occupier
- equivalent after-tax income
- value of residence
- whether own a second dwelling
- value of car
- value of consumer durables
- ratio of non-housing debt to income
- combined value of holiday house, caravan and boat
- whether have a telephone
- annual value of shareholdings
- whether got behind in payment of utility bills
- whether received material help from a welfare agency
- whether could raise $5000 in a week in an emergency.

On each of these, each person was assigned a rank order number: in the case of housing, for example, this number lay between 1 and 16, with 1 being the lowest value of house recorded in the data and 16 being the highest.

To illustrate the idea of a distance function, we consider only two variables—say value of dwelling (House) and ratio of non-housing debt to income (Debts). In Figure 1.3 (over page) the observed values of each of these are measured on the axes. The curve LL traces out the combinations of *minimum* values of each variable which are found in the data. For example, the person marked x^1 has a score of 1 (the minimum value) on house value and 4 on debts. This implies that, among the people who scored 1 on house value, the lowest

Figure 1.3

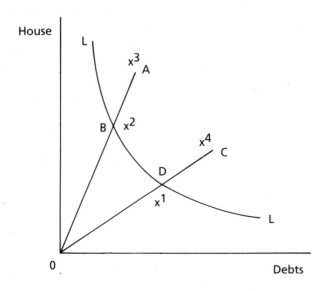

observed score on debts was 4. Person x^2 scores higher on house value (3) but lower on debts (2). This says that, among the people who scored 3 on house value, the lowest observed score on debts was 2. Conversely, of those who scored 2 on debts, the lowest observed value on house was 3.

Thus LL defines a lower bound: nobody has a combination of house value and debts which is worse (that is, closer to the origin) than that traced out by the curve. The definition of this boundary is a key step and its distinctive feature is that it is derived from the data: no externally derived values need be assumed. All people on the boundary are taken to have the same minimum value of standard of living while all people beyond the boundary (further from the origin) have a standard of living which is higher than this. But how much higher?

Consider person x^3. How much must this person's resources be shrunk in order to put him or her on the boundary—that is, at the minimum observed level? The answer may be found by drawing a line from x^3 to the origin and measuring the ratio of distance AB to A0. This ratio provides a measure of how far above the observed minimum x^3 is. Consider now whether x^4 has a higher or lower

46

standard of living (as captured by the two measures used in this example) than x^3. The answer can be found by comparing the ratio CD/C0 with AB/A0. These ratios are the values for the distance function, which we here interpret as an index of the material standard of living. The actual computation used 11 variables and cannot therefore be illustrated on a two-dimensional diagram. But the principle of identifying the lower bound as the envelope of the minimum observed combinations of values remains. So too does the strategy of radial shrinking of an observed value to this boundary to obtain its score on the index.

LRTW use the same technique to compute a 'quality of life' or 'functionings' index, again drawing on data from the Australian Standard of Living survey. The nine variables used were:

- self-assessed level of health
- how well get along on family income
- can obtain support in case of illness
- can have company if desired
- can have someone to discuss personal problems if desired
- self-assessed level of happiness
- how well one is doing in life
- expectations of the future
- have social contacts with friends
- comparison of past with present
- have activities outside the home.

The distance function technique is especially valuable for variables such as these since they clearly cannot be reduced to some common numeraire.

Finally, LRTW examine the relation between people's standing on the two indices: do more resources translate consistently into a higher quality of life? In brief, they find:

- the distribution of resources is highly compressed (with a coefficient of variation of 2.12 and a Gini coefficient of 0.009)—much more so than is the distribution of equivalent income, for example
- the distribution of quality of life scores is compressed but not as much so as are resources (with a coefficient of variation of 9.20 and a Gini coefficient of 0.048)
- the 'efficiency' with which people convert resources into quality of life is about a dispersed as is quality of life

- this variation in levels of 'efficiency' provides an opportunity for people with relatively low levels of resources to lead a relatively high quality of life, and vice-versa: 22 per cent of all individuals rank among the top third in one of the 'resources' or 'quality of life' indices and among the bottom third in the other.

They conclude that Australia looks to be highly egalitarian in two dimensions. One is that the distribution of resources and of quality of life is very equal. The other is that these two distributions are largely independent of each other, so that having a high level of material resources is neither necessary nor sufficient in order to have a high quality of life.

• *Strengths and weaknesses of distance functions* •

The *advantages* of distance functions are:
- they can deal with items which are not measured in a common metric and where it is possible to rank responses only in terms of more or less (hence qualitative variables may be used)
- there is intuitive and theoretical sense in the processes by which lower bounds and relative scores are determined.

The *disadvantages* of distances functions are:
- the technique is computationally complex which reduces the power of the reader to judge whether the results are plausible
- continuous variables need to be converted into a smallish number of (necessarily arbitrary) intervals
- computation becomes very onerous if large numbers of variables are used
- it is necessary to determine a priori which variables are to be used.

• Arbitrary Weightings •

Dissatisfaction with GDP per capita as an indicator of the performance of countries in their levels of human well-being has led to the construction of a number of alternatives. These involve adding other information in addition to GDP. For practical reasons the additions are small in number and ad hoc in selection. They typically include some measure of health outcome, such as infant mortality and life expectancy, and perhaps an educational outcome, such as literacy rate or average years of schooling.

These indices face several problems. The selection, largely arbitrary, of what to include is one of them. A second is that it is recognised that the achievement of basic levels of literacy, health, GDP per capita and so on is likely to contribute more to well-being than similar increments achieved at higher levels. That is, there is not a linear relation between the level of the selected indicator and its contribution to standard of living. Kakwani (1991) makes a related (but inverse) point. The achievement of a given absolute improvement in any element, such as GDP per capita or infant mortality rate, becomes harder as a country gets closer to international best practice. Thus, if one is measuring a country's *achievement*, or improvement over time, rather than its absolute level of standard of living, then a given improvement implies a smaller achievement if the country starts from a low base.

There are three contentious points in the construction of such indices:
- the selection of which factors to take into account
- how to aggregate these
- the assumed relation between the *level* of each factor and the contribution made by an *increment* in it.

• Human Development Index •

We next examine how one important example, the multivariate Human Development Index (HDI) by the United Nations Development Programme, has been dealing with these problems in its annual publications, beginning in 1990 (UNDP 1990).

In brief, the HDI starts from the assumption that it is desirable to have an index that measures not only income (a means of human development), but also an indication of outcomes. With this in mind, the 1990 version of the index supplements the commonly used ranking of countries in terms of per capita Gross Domestic Product (an indication of available means) with two indicators of outcomes: life expectancy and adult literacy. Furthermore, to take account of differences in costs of living, GDP is adjusted for purchasing-power. The idea is that a dollar adjusted in this way can buy roughly the same amount in Japan, Australia and China.

The construction of the 1990 index proceeds as follows:

Step 1: Define a maximum and a minimum value for each of the three indicators in the deprivation index: life expectancy, literacy, and real GDP per capita. Each country is given a score on each indicator, ranging from 0 (not deprived in relation to the whole range of countries) to 1 (the greatest degree of deprivation among the countries).

Step 2: Take a simple average of the three indicators to form the deprivation score.

Step 3: The human development score is 1 minus the deprivation score.

The *Human Development Report 1990* illustrates this by applying the formula to Kenya:

Maximum life expectancy	78.40
Minimum life expectancy	41.80
Maximum adult literacy rate	100.00ß
Minimum adult literacy rate	12.30
Maximum real GDP per capita (log)	3.68
Minimum real GDP per capita (log)	2.34
Kenya life expectancy	59.40
Kenya adult literacy rate	60.00
Kenya real GDP per capita (log)	2.90

Kenya's life expectancy deprivation (1)
$= (78.4 - 59.4) / (78.4 - 41.8)$ 0.519
Kenya's literacy deprivation
$= (100.0 - 60.0) / 100.0 - 12.3)$ 0.456
Kenya's GDP deprivation
$= (3.68 - 2.90) / (3.68 - 2.34)$ 0.582
Kenya's average deprivation (2)
$= (0.519 + 0.456 + 0.582) / 3$ 0.519
Kenya's Human Development Index (HDI) (3)
$= 1 - 0.519$ 0.481
(UNDP 1990, p. 109).

The 1991 and 1992 versions of the HDI retain its three components, longevity, adult literacy, and income, but refine two of them so that they would better distinguish between the various rich countries. The original version measured human knowledge by adult literacy rates only, and resulted in 19 rich countries all scoring 99 on a scale where the maximum value was 100. The later versions include also years of schooling, giving it a weighting of .33 to a weighting of .66 for literacy. One effect of this is a substantial improvement in the ranking of the US. In the case of income, the original version set the maximum value at the log of the average poverty line value of 9 rich countries adjusted by purchasing power parities, namely, $4861. In other words, income above this value was given a weighting of zero. The result was an index that did not differentiate among the 34 richest countries. In the revised version, income above the poverty line is regarded as having sharply diminishing returns, but it is given some weighting, sufficient to differentiate among rich countries.

Examples of the change in rankings between the 1990 and the 1992 versions are: Australia, stable at 7; UK stable at 10; US, from 19 to 6; Costa Rica from 28 to 42. The HDI rankings and values for industrial countries only are given in Table 1.5. Note that the 'missing' rankings indicate that some industrial countries have lower rankings than developing countries.

The 1991 and 1992 editions of the HDI show that it has considerable flexibility, and can be modified to include further refinements such as for male/female disparities in the HDI and for inequality in

Table 1.5: HDI ranking for industrial countries 1992

Country	HDI rank	HDI value	Country	HDI rank	HDI value
Canada	1	0.982	Israel	18	0.939
Japan	2	0.981	Luxembourg	19	0.929
Norway	3	0.978	Italy	21[a]	0.922
Switzerland	4	0.977	Ireland	22	0.921
Sweden	5	0.976	Spain	23	0.916
USA	6	0.976	Greece	26	0.901
Australia	7	0.971	Czech.	27	0.897
France	8	0.969	Hungary	28	0.893
Netherlands	9	0.968	Poland	32	0.874
UK	10	0.962	USSR	33	0.873
Iceland	11	0.958	Bulgaria	35	0.865
Germany	12	0.955	Yugoslavia	37	0.857
Denmark	13	0.953	Malta	38	0.854
Finland	14	0.953	Portugal	39	0.850
Austria	15	0.950	Albania	49	0.791
Belgium	16	0.950	Romania	60	0.733
New Zealand	17	0.947			

Source: UNDP, 1992, Table 1.1

[a] 'Missing' ranks belong to developing countries with a high HDI score.

the income distribution. Moving into more uncharted waters, the HDI methodology can be applied to an index of human freedoms.

One of the major consequences of using the HDI rather than GDP is to change substantially the rankings of some countries. The most extreme examples are given in Table 1.6. The first column shows countries whose GDP gives little indication of their relatively high achievements in the areas of life expectancy and education, while the fourth column shows countries whose income is not matched by achievements in the other domains. Though the components chosen to construct both the 1990 and 1991 versions of the HDI are plausible, there is always an arbitrary element, and one that can substantially change the ranking of countries. For instance, the United States has the highest ranking of all countries in terms of years of schooling (an input indicator). When this is combined with adult literacy (even with a weight of only .33 relative to literacy rates) to measure educational attainment, the US substantially improves its relative position. The decision to include years of schooling (or any other component) is a value-laden, or political judgment, rather than a technical one.

The decision to include a particular component in the index leads to the second contentious decision, the weighting to give it. The HDI solution to this problem is to give each component an equal weighting. Thus, if a country improves its score by five on the literacy scale, remains constant on the income scale, and drops five units on the life expectancy scale, it would show no change in overall ranking. This has the advantage of simplicity—it is easy to understand what is going on. The objection is that there is no rationale for the equal

Table 1.6: *HDI and GDP rankings*

	GDP rank	HDI rank		GDP rank	HDI rank
China	130	79	UAE	12	57
Sri Lanka	120	76	Oman	37	82
Viet Nam	146	102	Iran	45	90
Myanmar	148	111	Gabon	48	91
Poland	66	32	Iraq	46	85
Chile	68	36	Libya	36	74
Tanzania	158	126	Saudi Arabia	33	72
Albania	80	49	Algeria	58	95

Source: UNDP, 1992, 127–9

weighting, beyond the assertion that all three components are essential to human well being. It also implies that welfare losses in one area (such as infant mortality rates) can be offset in a one-to-one manner by gains in another (such as average GDP).

The 1991 edition supplements this argument by experimenting with some alternative weightings—for example, leaving the three components separate; then ranking each country on each component; then averaging the three rankings. Changes in final ranking are, in fact, minimal, and the Spearman rank-correlation between the two is 0.996 (UNDP 1991, p. 88). All in all, a strong case is made that the HDI is not sensitive *overall* to the more obvious alternative weightings of the components. However, for individual countries this will be the case only to the degree that the components are correlated. For instance, in 1991 Japan had the highest rank on all three components. A change in weighting would therefore make no difference to Japan's top overall ranking on the HDI. Similarly, Niger's extremely low ranking on all three components would mean a change in weighting would have little effect on its HDI. But when we come to Oman (very low literacy, low life-expectancy, very high GDP), or Cuba (low GDP, but very high literacy and life expectancy), the weighting is all-important in determining the final score.

There is no obvious solution to the problem of appropriate weights. One response is, in fact, to reject the very concept of a single index of this kind. For instance, the 1990 version showed Saudi Arabia equal 1st on income; 88th on literacy; and 66th on life expectancy. Its overall ranking was 64th, just ahead of the Dominican Republic, but behind the Philippines. A strong case could be made that this final aggregation involves such a loss of information as to be highly misleading. One would be better served by retaining the rankings on the individual components.

An alternative approach to the same problem is presented by Kakwani (1992). He explicitly incorporates the belief, which is shared by authors such as Sen and Dasgupta, that 'as the standard of living reaches progressively higher limits, incremental improvement would represent much higher levels of achievement than similar incremental improvement from a lower base.' (p. 1) He incorporates this into an achievement index, which measures the difference in levels of standard of living in two different time periods. The variables used are GDP per capita, adjusted for purchasing-power parity, aggregate life expectancy at birth, female life expectancy at birth and the infant mortality rate. Like the HDI, these are chosen on an ad hoc basis. Kakwani does not aggregate them into a single index, but reports country performance and achievement for each item separately; these achievements are then compared with GDP. The novel aspect of Kakwani's index (for the purposes of this discussion) is the incorporation of the idea that a given absolute increase in a score on an index is a greater achievement the higher the initial level of that index is.

It should be noted that the ranking of nations according to standards of living and changes therein is an ambitious task. It requires believable, comparable data across up to 160 nations. The choice of which factors to include to supplement GDP per capita is inevitably dictated largely by what is available.

MULTIPLE INDICATORS

To this point we have explored ways by which diverse information may be collapsed into a single index on which each person/country may be given a numerical score. Some of the hazards of doing this were mentioned in the discussion of the Human Development Index. It is a matter of judgment whether in any particular case the drawbacks of aggregation exceed the advantages of having a neat summary of diverse information and an unequivocal ranking.

The Scandinavian levels-of-living measures provide an example where the judgment has gone strongly against a single index. Our illustration draws on the Swedish case (Erikson & Uusitalo 1987).

Detailed surveys of nine different dimensions of individual standard of living have been conducted in Sweden on a number of occasions, starting in 1968. The surveys cover:

- health, access to care, and longevity
- employment and working conditions
- economic resources
- knowledge and educational opportunities
- security of person and property
- family and social environment
- recreation and culture

- political resources
- housing and local resources.

Each person is ranked separately on each of these nine different dimensions of standard of living. One important reason for keeping the dimensions separate is that it has been found that the ranking of individuals varies considerably from one dimension to another. This information would be lost if the dimensions were to be compressed into a single index.

Use of a single index also implies that standing on any one dimension can be substituted for standing on any other dimension. For example, a person who scored 8 out of 10 on each of health and personal safety and 2 on economic resources and knowledge and education, would be deemed to be in the same situation as an otherwise similar person who scored 8 on economic resources and knowledge and 2 on health and personal safety.

While the low correlations between the standing of individuals on the different dimensions provides one reason for not aggregating them, the opposite conclusion may also be drawn. It is important to know whether individuals or groups suffer an accumulation of disadvantage. A single index will show this in an aggregated way: if no one suffers multiple disadvantage then there will be no absolutely low scores. Another way to obtain this information is to see how many people (and who) have a low score on each of a specified number of dimensions. For example, in Norway 10 per cent of the population, and in Sweden 6 per cent, fared badly on three or more of the nine dimensions (Ringen, in Erikson & Uusitalo 1987). Once this group has been identified it is then possible to examine who they are and why they might be particularly disadvantaged. Note that the selection of 'three or more' as the criterion of multiple disadvantage is itself arbitrary and subject to the same criticism that disadvantage on any one dimension is viewed as the same as disadvantage on any other.

CONCLUSION

While it is not possible to produce an index on which individuals are ranked according to their levels of capability or utility, we have shown a number of ways in which rankings may be obtained on dimensions which should correlate positively with these. We have also shown one example of the measurement and ranking of individuals by something which approximates functionings. There are occasions when it is not utility, capabilities or functionings but material resources which are the dimension of interest. Then we are on more secure ground in the construction of an index, although controversies will remain.

A major question is whether the well-being which we wish to capture is best represented by a single-valued index or whether it is preferable to rank people separately on different scales. Where the dimension of interest is personal material resources there is a strong case for using a single-valued index, represented in money terms. Money provides a convenient and theoretically appropriate numeraire and there are sound procedures for expressing most of the important resources in money terms.

Pressure to construct a single index is strong even when to do so requires some straining of the data. It stems chiefly from the desire of users of the results to be able to rank people in an unequivocal way and to summarise the relevant information. If these two attributes are not attained formally they will frequently be imposed informally. Though this pressure to compress different types of information is understandable, it can be hazardous. The hazards arise from the difficulty in placing a clear interpretation on what the resulting index measures and the sensitivity of the ranking to variation in the weights given to the components of the index. When there is no natural common dimension to the components, then to aggregate them into a single index forces an unreal homogeneity. The price paid for ease of digestion is credibility: a person who does not like the results need only question the basis on which the components were added, unless it can be shown that the rankings produced by the index are not sensitive to the weights used. The irony is that if it is not sensitive then it is doubtful whether the inclusion of extra dimensions adds much extra information.

NOTES

[1] See, for example, Kakwani (1991) and the references therein; Sen (1973).
[2] As an illustration we cite the example of a poor Bangladeshi woman. Married at age 12 by her family to a young man who, it turned out, beat her regularly, she was deserted with a small child by the age of 16. Today, at the age of 20,

she operates a sewing machine in a garment factory and sends half her monthly pay of about $30 home to her mother, who takes care of her 5-year-old son. 'I feel I'm the happiest woman on earth', she said. 'No one beats me anymore almost every night. I'm independent and I earn my own money.' Quote from McConnell and Brue (1992), p. 3.

3   It is not surprising to see, in response to this, substitution of purchased goods, such as meals out, for time-intensive home-produced goods, such as meals prepared at home.

4   A useful work on the consequences of *not* putting a value on time is Waring (1988). For a popular account of the uses of time cf. Bittman (1991).

5   A contemporary example is provided by Paul Wachtel in his book *The Poverty of Affluence*. He argues, among other things, that it is not the absolute level of material well-being that provides utility but its rate of change: people feel good only if they have more—relative to their own past and to other people with whom they compare themselves. In this view, utility is a function of the first derivative (or rate of change) of material well-being, rather than of its level. See also the arguments of Marcuse (1969) presented in the Introduction of this book.

6   In the discussion we focus on money as the single dimension index of material well-being. There have been other suggestions, however, for abbreviated proxies to summarise relative material well-being. For countries, examples include average life-expectancy, infant mortality rates and energy consumption per capita. For individual households one suggestion is number of pairs of shoes possessed by each person—perhaps to be dubbed the Imelda Marcos index of relative prosperity.

7   Among the few empirical attempts to study sharing arrangements are Edwards (1981) for Australia, and Pahl (1989) for Britain.

8   For a discussion of different equivalence scales, see Buhman, Rainwater, Schmaus and Smeeding (1988).

9   The way in which these figures were calculated will be discussed later in this chapter.

10   For details see Richardson and Travers (1992).

11   The equivalence scale used was that known as the 'Henderson scale', after Professor Ronald Henderson, who first used this scale in his pioneering work on poverty in Australia. In the broad it weights an additional adult at 0.7 and an additional child as 0.2.

12   Family income is the sum of cash received by all family members from all sources. While it is computed as after-income tax, it is not adjusted by an equivalence scale to take account of variations in the composition of the household.

13   'If the variables have been sampled appropriately to hypothesise that the underlying dimension of interest is the factor determined by the weighted composite of the variables which accounts for the most possible variance, then the first principal factor is the solution' (Gorsuch 1974, p. 86).

14   See, for example, Eric Hanushek (1986). For a different illustration of the use of distance functions, see Angus Deaton (1979).

THE LEVEL AND DISTRIBUTION OF
MATERIAL WELL-BEING IN AUSTRALIA

Is Australia an egalitarian society, not just in terms of political and other citizenship rights, but also in the distribution of material resources? This is a contested issue. On the one hand, Raskall (1992) can say 'Let's get a few facts straight. Australia is one of the most unequal societies in the world'. On the other hand, Australia had been judged to be one of the most egalitarian in the distribution of both earnings (Lydall 1968) and income (for example, Sawyer 1976). Who is right? Do we know enough to say who is right? Where does the information on which such judgements are based come from? How does the distribution in Australia compare not just with other countries but also with itself in earlier times? These are some of the questions to which this chapter is directed.

SOURCES OF INCOME DATA

In this section we concentrate on providing a description and evaluation of the sources from which conclusions about the distribution of income and wealth in Australia are drawn. Later sections describe and discuss these conclusions.

• Australian Bureau of Statistics •

One reason for the uncertainty about the degree to which Australia is an egalitarian country in its income distribution is that pertinent reliable information only became available in the late 1960s. At that time the Australian Bureau of Statistics began to collect survey information on individual and household incomes on a regular basis. Prior to that, the last official word on the distribution of income was to be found in the census of 1933, and before that in the census of 1915. The absence of good information had two effects. One was that issues of the distribution of income went unexamined. The other was that researchers turned to inferior sources. These included information on the structure of award wages and statistics on the broad distribution of taxable income which were published by the Commissioner for Taxation. In 1967–68 a private study known as the Australian Survey of Consumer Finances and Expenditure (or the Macquarie Survey) was conducted.[1] It provided information on both income and wealth and was the main source of data until the ABS published its data from the survey of 1968–69. The former survey was a bold enterprise, but it suffered from a large non-response rate and consequent suspicions that it was not adequately representative. The picture of Australia as highly egalitarian was derived from these data, together with those on the structure of award rates of pay.

Today the situation is very different. There are regular, frequent and exhaustive enquiries by the ABS into levels of income, both in the form of surveys designed explicitly for this purpose (the Income Distribution Surveys, now called Survey of Income and Housing Costs and Amenities) and in the form of questions about income attached to other surveys, such as those on expenditure, health, labour force participation and the census. The data from the ABS are now detailed and high quality. They do, however, possess two major drawbacks.

One is that there is no information on the level and distribution of private wealth, apart from the single item of housing status. In consequence the distribution of wealth, and even more so its relation to the distribution of income, remains shrouded in ignorance, despite the imaginative efforts of a number of researchers to construct such a distribution from ad hoc sources (see, for example: Williams 1983; Podder and Kakwani 1976; Raskall 1977; Piggott 1984, 1988; Dilnot 1990; McCallum and Beggs 1991; and Shanahan 1991). One of the more complete sets of information on this topic is provided by the data from the Australian Standard of Living survey (ASL), of which more later. These data are especially useful for their capacity to link income and wealth. They do not, however, enable a fully reliable rank order of household or individual wealth to be computed.

The other major shortcoming of the ABS data is their silence on sources of standard of living other than current money income. The ABS has gone to great lengths to obtain accurate measures of money income, which is especially difficult for the self-employed. For example, in the 1986 Income Distribution survey it asked about 180 different questions about income. But this zeal has not been matched in the pursuit of other major sources of material standard of living. For instance, there is no direct information on the amount of non-employed time, although the labour force status of the reference person can be obtained. Nor, as noted above, is there any information on assets (apart from the house) which provide a flow of current services to the household. With one notable exception, the difficult territory of assessing differential access to public services, such as transport, recreation, medical services, libraries, education and differential environmental quality has been left vacant by the ABS. The notable exception is to be found in the 1984–85 and 1988–89 Household Expenditure surveys. These enabled the ABS to compute an estimate for each household of its direct and indirect tax payments and its receipts of benefits from government expenditure on education, health, housing and non-cash social welfare benefits. This provides a most useful advance in the measurement of the standard of living.

We note that the Institute of Family Studies is, during 1992, conducting a large survey of families with children in a (non-random) selection of lower socio-economic areas. One important focus of this survey is the range of public services available and the ease of access to them.

• Luxembourg Income Study •

It is difficult to imagine what a perfectly equal distribution of income or of the standard of living would look like. Need income be the same for every individual at every moment of time? Or is it sufficient if it is equal over a lifetime? Is it the income of the individual or the income of the household which is the central interest? What is the lifetime of a household? These questions are especially pertinent when standard of living is measured by money income, for then equal money incomes may be associated with quite unequal amounts of leisure, home production, assets and so on. We raise these points in order to explain why the absolute value of measures of inequality, on their own, are not very informative. Is a Gini co-efficient of 0.30 a lot or a little? For the most part, we cannot assess it against a norm of perfect equality, because it is hard even to con-ceive of such a thing. It has certainly never been observed in practice in modern societies. Paglin (1975) makes the point that there is some level of inequality in annual incomes that we would expect to observe simply because of the typical lifecycle pattern of income, even if lifetime incomes were identical. It is for this reason that inequality is judged in terms of comparisons. Rather than ask whether, say, the distribution of household equivalent income in Australia is equal or unequal, it is more informative to ask whether it is more or less equal than the comparable distribution in Australia at some earlier date or in other countries.

The main danger in making such comparisons is that like is not being compared with like. Technical details, such as exactly how the household is defined (for example, whether it includes adult sib-lings/children/parents), the equivalence scale used, the period over which income is measured and what is included in the definition of income, must all be comparable before it is possible to say that one distribution is more or less equal than another. Computed levels of inequality can be quite sensitive to differences in these details. For example, the ABS defines an income unit to be couples with and without dependent children, single parents with dependent children and single people. Dependent children are any living at home who are aged 15 or less or are full-time students aged 16–20. If there are any other family members living in the same house, such as an elderly parent, a sibling of one of the adults, or an adult child, then these are counted as separate income units. It is thus possible, and indeed it happens, for an income unit to record a very low or even zero income and yet have quite a high standard of living in the form of a comfortable house, access to transport, plenty of food and so on. Other comparable countries tend to define the income unit, or family, in a more inclusive way—for example, to include all occupants of a dwelling who are related by blood or marriage. The more inclusive is the definition of the income unit the lower will be the recorded levels of inequality, because redistribution is going on within the income unit. This redistribution is not recorded in the ABS data when it occurs among any family members who are not a spouse or dependent child. Thus, other things being equal, we expect that the distribution of income among families or income units will appear more unequal in Australia than elsewhere.

In recognition of the sensitivity of inequality measures to the specification of income, income unit and equivalence scale, a major project known as the Luxembourg Income Study (LIS) was established in 1983 (see Mitchell 1991 and Green *et al.* 1992). Australia is now one of the fourteen or so countries in this study (the numbers participating continue to rise). One of its main objectives is to place the income distribution data from participating countries on a comparable basis. It is not possible to do this completely, but great progress has been made. It is thus now possible, for the first time, to make quite accurate comparisons between the distribution of income in Australia and in other participating countries. The other countries are mainly northern European, together with the United Kingdom, Canada, Israel and the United States. The countries in the LIS project are among the most equal in the world. The Australian data used in the LIS programme come from the ABS Income Distribution surveys.

• Australian Standard of Living Study •

The ASL is a private survey conducted by ourselves in 1987. The survey sampled randomly the Australian population aged between

20 and 74 who lived in private dwellings (that is, were not homeless or in caravan parks or institutions). People who lived in remote country areas were also excluded. The sample frame covered 96 per cent of the relevant age group. The questionnaire was personally delivered and collected and completed by the respondent, with assistance when requested. The response rate was high: 76 per cent of eligible people with whom contact was made and 65 per cent of the estimated total eligible sample. In all, 1578 dwellings were approached and 1659 usable responses were received. The respondents matched well with ABS census data on age, education, housing status and income.[2]

A major purpose of the ASL survey was to learn more about the standard of living than was revealed by just money income. Thus, information was sought on: the stock of household assets from which a flow of services was received (such as hi-fi system, video recorder, dishwasher, telephone, car, boat, caravan, holiday house); items of wealth (rental property, superannuation, liquid funds, life assurance, whether shares were owned etc.); the amount of adult time that was not committed to employment; assistance given and received between family members outside the household; welfare receipts in kind from the government; major health expenses; debt repayments; and so on. In addition there is information on family background, education, workforce experience, and attitudes such as optimism and happiness.

At present the ASL data provide probably the most complete set of information on the standard of living that is available for Australia. They are especially useful for their capacity to link income and items of wealth. But the inventory of private wealth is not complete: in particular, items which distinguish large wealth holdings are under-represented. Further, in most cases there is little detail on the value of each item, so that not even a fully reliable rank order of people according to their wealth may be established. It is only possible to compute standard inequality measures for the distribution of wealth if dollar values are imputed to the list of possessions. The data are also limited by the size of the sample. This becomes a problem if the analysis requires a very detailed breakdown of the population. It is then possible to find only small numbers of people in some cells.

SOURCES OF WEALTH DATA

It is difficult to obtain good information on the distribution of wealth. Because wealth is a stock (unlike income, which is an amount received annually) it is likely that many people do not have an accurate knowledge of their own wealth. Further, the distribution of wealth is much less equal than the distribution of income. It is necessary, therefore, to have good information on the wealth of the top tail—the truly rich. The two main sources of data on the distribution of wealth are surveys and taxation statistics. The latter are only available if there is some form of direct taxation of wealth, either in the form of some regular tax on the stock of wealth of the living, or as a tax on inheritance, for which a value of the estate must be assessed. Neither source will be entirely accurate. The numbers of people in the top tail are small and thus easily missed in sample surveys. People are often reluctant to reveal their wealth and, even if not, may not know its value with any accuracy. Tax-based data have the advantage over surveys of being comprehensive and involving severe penalties for misstating true values. However, they suffer from the problem of tax avoidance. The rich, in particular, have both the resources and the incentive to avoid taxes on wealth. On balance, tax-based data are believed to be the more accurate, especially at the top end (Piggott 1988).

Australia has no data on wealth from either source. Not since 1915 has there been an official survey of wealth. The only direct taxes on wealth were the death and estate duties levied by the state and Commonwealth governments. The last of these was abolished in 1976. In the absence of good survey or direct tax data on wealth holdings, a number of researchers have created wealth distributions by imputation. These imputed distributions describe only the main components of wealth, such as housing equity and financial assets, and are mostly unable to link levels of wealth with other attributes of the household or individual, such as occupation, education and income.

The two main ways to impute a distribution of wealth are, first, the estate duty multiplier method (Raskall 1977, Gunton 1971, Shanahan 1991) and a contemporary equivalent-records from division of property on divorce (McCallum and Beggs 1991); and, second, inferences from investment income recorded in income distribution surveys (Dilnot 1990). The only survey of wealth holding in Australia since 1915 is the Macquarie Survey referred to above. This is considered to be somewhat unreliable, especially at the top end.

The estate duty method combines information on the value of estates left at death with the probability of death at given ages to infer a distribution of wealth among the living. This is supplemented with data on aggregate wealth to impute the top tail. It embraces only estates that are subject to duty, and relies upon the assumption that the pattern of wealth-holding at death mirrors that among people who are the same age but still living. (This implies no connection between mortality rates and levels of wealth.) Contemporary application of the estate duty method has been seriously hampered by the abolition of death duties in Australia, since it was the compliance with these duties which provided the source of data. Of course, the existence of the duties encouraged the dispersal of wealth prior to death, and its holding in non-taxable forms, and thus undermined the reliability of the data. Probably because of the abolition of death duties, the studies using the estate multiplier method are now quite old: they draw on data from the 1960s and early 1970s (Gunton 1971, 1975; Raskall 1977). The thesis by Shanahan (1991) is of interest for historical reasons: it is based on data for South Australia in the early part of this century.

The most recent estimates of the distribution of wealth are provided by McCallum and Beggs (1991). They use the data from a private survey by the Institute of Family Studies titled 'The Economic Consequences of Marital Breakdown'. This survey was conducted in 1984 and is described in McDonald (1986). The 825 respondents represented only 25 per cent of the initial sample, which was drawn from divorcing couples in Victoria. It thus excludes single people. Nonetheless, the respondents were claimed by McCallum and Beggs to be reasonably representative of married couples in Australia. The assets included in the data were house and furniture, motor vehicles, superannuation and insurance, farm or business, liquid cash, real estate, jewellery, furs and tools (p. 59). McCallum and Beggs combined this information with other survey data on the frequency of receipt of bequests and some information on their value, which was obtained from the 1984 National Social Science survey. Unlike the estate multiplier method, it is not necessary with divorce-based data to infer the wealth distribution of the living from that of the dead. It is necessary instead to infer the wealth of single people from that of married people, and to assume that people who divorce and contest the division of property have wealth which is typical of all married couples. These remain strong assumptions.

THE AUSTRALIAN STANDARD OF LIVING

There has been much concern expressed in recent times that the once (relatively) very high standard of living in Australia is now slipping to the point where we no longer rank in the First Eleven. We do not propose to canvass this subject in any comprehensive way, but wish to offer a few observations on the current standard of living.

It is a theme of this book that the material standard of living is much more than just current income. This applies just at much in the assessment of the relative standard of countries as it does in the assessment of the relative circumstances of individuals. Thus we can draw directly on our earlier discussion of the nature of individual material well-being to identify the items which should be considered in assessing the standing of a country.

First, it is plain that any concern about Australia's decline arises from a comparison, not with Australia at earlier periods, but with other countries. Any historical comparison makes it clear that in absolute terms the standards of the present have never been equalled. This is true whether we look at real purchasing power per person, at average hours worked over a year (and even more so over a lifetime), at standards of housing and extent of education, at the quality of medicine, the extent of support of people who have few resources of their own and at equality of opportunity.

As one example, consider the world of work. Fifty years ago most people left school at age 13 or 14 and went directly into employment. On marriage, women had little option but to retire completely from paid employment. Men, in contrast, had little option but to continue in full-time employment until old age. For many, this meant working well past the age of 65. There was little leisure. Paid annual holidays had only recently been introduced for most people and they consisted of one week. Rare were the workers who had superannuation or long service, maternity or sick leave or redundancy payments or workers' compensation. Most people who were too old to work were dependent on their children for financial support or were poor. Today we have a new leisured class: instead of comprising the rich aristocracy whom most people could only envy, it now comprises the retired. The idea that fit and active adults should and could cease work, simply because they had reached an age around 60, and should have fun instead, is a truly modern one. And it produces a truly egalitarian leisured class.

While there was an old-age pension (most meagre by modern standards) and invalidity benefits (first introduced in 1909 and 1910 respectively) there was no systematic support for children, the unemployed, the sick, single parents, or students. Since the 1930s the distribution of income has become more equal (McLean and Richardson 1986), home ownership has gone from 55 to 73 per cent and a whole system of income support for people with low incomes has been created. In the earlier period the Commonwealth was confined by the Constitution to the provision of the old-age pension and invalidity benefits. The amendment to the Constitution passed in 1946 broadened the scope of Commonwealth social welfare activity. Today such payments comprise 50 per cent of the Commonwealth budget and cover many of the contingencies which prevent the earning of an income.

In 1947 the life expectancy at birth was 66.1 years for males and 70.6 years for females. Today these figures are 73.9 and 80.0 (ABS 1991a). 'In comparison with other countries, Australia ranks amongst those with the highest expectations of life' (ABS 1991b). Japan (75.8 years) is one of the few countries whose life expectancy exceeds the Australian average of 73.3 for all persons (ABS 1991b, p. 134).

In 1933, 55 per cent of households were owner-occupiers and 38 per cent were tenants. By 1947 these figures had changed to 59 per cent and 37 per cent. In contrast, by 1988, 73 per cent of households were owner-occupiers and only 26 per cent were renting.

In 1933, 12 per cent of people aged 15–19 were students and only 80 per cent of children aged 5–14 were at school; the figures today are 50 per cent and virtually 100 per cent.

In 1947, 8 per cent of 'houses' were made of fibro-cement, calico, canvass or hessian, lath and plaster or wattle and daub. Today the number is trivial. In 1947 the average number of total rooms per person in private dwellings was 1.35. In 1986 there was approximately one bedroom per person in private dwellings.

Since the prosperous early 1970s, real GDP per head has risen by 50 per cent.[3]

INTERNATIONAL COMPARISON

Australia is not the only country that has seen progress in its material standard of living. One reason to compare ourselves with others is to see if we could do better, and it is on this test that Australia fares not so well.

The evidence for a decline in Australia's relative standard of living comes from a comparison of levels of GDP per capita. As we have emphasised, this is an inadequate indicator of standard of living. At the least it should be supplemented with information on hours worked. For a more accurate picture we need information also on the stock of assets, both public and private, which provide a flow of services to households, such as housing, hospitals, education facilities (both quantity and quality), roads, urban amenities, national parks, personal security and the quality of the environment and of the workplace. Each of these may cause a divergence between changes in standard of living and changes in measured GDP per capita. We comment on a few relevant aspects below.

Because of the way in which GDP is measured, only productive activity which occurs in the market-place is counted. Thus, all the work which goes on in the home and in the voluntary sector is omitted. If the proportion of the average adult lifetime spent in paid employment rises substantially it is possible to have a substantial rise in GDP yet no rise in the standard of living—people now spending more time in employment would be giving up education, voluntary work in schools, hospitals, for charities and so on, domestic work, care for elderly parents, child-rearing and leisure. It is quite possible that the total amount of work done would not rise at all: the only change is that more of it would be going through the market-place.[4] It is necessary, therefore, for accurate assessments of relative standards of living, and how these have changed, to take account of differences in the proportions of lifetimes that are spent in employment. Ian Castles provides a good illustration of this in an illuminating study in which the standard of living in Sydney is carefully compared with that in four large Japanese cities (Castles 1992). In order to attain his income, the average Japanese male employee works for 50 hours per week, while the average for all adults is 30 hours per week. The comparable Sydney figures are 38 and 21. At the age of 60 to 64, Japanese men worked on average about 33 hours per week, while the figure for Sydney was half that. Males over the age of 64 worked on average about 16 hours per week in Japan and virtually not at all in Sydney.

More generally, the total supply of time to the paid workforce has been subject to some major changes in recent decades. These include the large rise in the average number of years of education, the large rise in the supply of female labour to paid employment and the emergence of quite large-scale early retirement among men. To these movements must be added a (small) decline in average weekly hours worked and a rise in the amount of paid leave of various sorts. Similar movements have occurred in other comparable countries, but to differing degrees. In consequence it is necessary to take account, where possible, of total hours worked when comparing levels and changes in the standard of living. As an example of the potential significance of such adjustment we cite the results of McLean and Pincus (1983). They augment the annual rate of growth of real GDP for Australia between 1891 and 1938–39 by adjustments for reductions in the length of the average working week (0.3), earlier retirement (0.2) and increase in life expectancy (0.4 at a zero discount rate) (p. 201). The figures in brackets show their calculations of the amount by which the real rate of growth of GDP per capita rises as a result of the inclusion of each item. Together, they more than double the annual growth rate. That is, when account is taken of changes in hours worked and life expectancy, the rate of growth of the Australian economy between 1891 and 1939 doubles compared with the growth rate of GDP as conventionally measured.

The environment is largely an unpriced input into the production of GDP. A given level of GDP may be produced in a way which leaves the air, water and land largely unscathed. Alternatively, it may be produced at the expense of great pollution, reductions in soil fertility, wilderness, biodiversity, fish stocks, natural timber and so on. This use of the environment, while contributing to the value of *outputs*, is not counted as an *input* into production, or a cost of production. It thus leads to the net value of output being over-estimated. A clear example of where GDP figures were misleading on this account is Eastern Europe, where the attained levels of output have been achieved at great, and unmeasured, cost to the environment. By European standards, the quality of the environment in Australia in general is very high, no doubt in large part attributable to the absence of population pressure.

A second measure of international standards of living that goes beyond GDP per capita is provided by the United Nations Development Programme (UNDP), which has constructed a Human Development Index on which all countries are ranked.[5] The index ranks countries according to their score on a combination of factors. In 1990 these factors were GDP per capita, adult literacy and life expectation, each of which was given equal weight. Australia ranked 9th in the world in this index, whereas on a straight GDP per capita basis Australia ranked 17. Since 1991, various supplementary indices have been constructed. One takes account of the different experience on the relevant items of men and women. The UNDP describes this as a 'gender sensitive' HDI. On this index, in 1992 Australia ranked 6th (with a score of 0.88), behind Sweden (0.94), Norway, Finland, France and Denmark (UNDP 1992, Table 1.3). In a similar vein, an income-distribution sensitive index sees Australia ranked 11th (0.93) with Japan at the top (0.98) (UNDP 1992, Table 1.4).

INEQUALITY IN THE DISTRIBUTION OF INCOME AND WEALTH IN AUSTRALIA

The previous sections have discussed the sources of data and the ideas which underlie our understanding of the level and distribution of the standard of living in Australia. In this section, we briefly summarise the results of existing studies which use these data and ideas to describe the distribution of income and wealth in Australia.

We have a rather spotty picture of inequality in Australia and how this compares with other periods and other countries. The historical picture is particularly thin because of the poor data available for earlier periods. Exploration of the distribution of income is expanding quite fast, due in part to the availability of good quality data. The same cannot be said of our knowledge of the distribution of wealth.

• The Distribution of Wealth •

Our theoretical understanding of the shape of the distribution of wealth is no more satisfactory than is its empirical estimation. Nonetheless, there is great interest in the extent, nature and causes of inequality in the distribution of personal wealth. For this reason, we report the conclusions which have been drawn from empirical studies in Australia. First, we note that wealth (as measured by home-equity, other property, shares, superannuation, life-assurance, fixed interest deposits and cash) is much less equally dis-tributed than is income. This is partly explicable by the fact that wealth is a stock which is accumulated over time. Some people have little wealth because they have not yet had the time to acquire more. The inequality in the distribution of wealth does not *necessarily* aggravate inequality in the distribution of income; and whether or not it does is a most important question for assessment of inequality in the distribution of the standard of living, for each are central com-ponents of that distribution. Only the ASL data are capable of throwing light on this link. This evidence suggests that people with higher incomes also tend to have greater wealth, but the link is a weak one—many people who have quite high wealth have low incomes and vice versa. This is particularly true of retired people.

Most of the studies of the distribution of wealth in Australia have concentrated on the task of providing a satisfactory *description* of that distribution. Such a description is a preliminary to any analysis of cause and has presented a considerable challenge to researchers because of the poor database which is available. What have these descriptions found?

- The richest 1 per cent of the adult population owns about 20 per cent of private wealth; the richest 10 per cent own about half the wealth; and the poorest 30 per cent have no net wealth (although they may own consumer durables and a car).
- Compared with other countries, such as the UK, the US, Canada, Sweden and Denmark, this is not a particularly unequal distribution.

- The patient saving out of income does not explain much of the wealth of the *top* wealth-holders: factors such as inheritance, luck and entrepreneurial flair are more important.
- By far the most important form of wealth is the family home: 75–80 per cent of Australians eventually own their own home free of debt and the house represents 55–60 per cent of total household wealth.
- The other major forms of household wealth are superannuation, rental properties, equities and interest-bearing deposits.
- Wealth-holding peaks at around age 58–65 and then falls somewhat.
- Wealth rises with education (about 10 per cent for each additional year) and age (about 2.5 per cent for each additional year up to age 58).
- Twenty-two per cent of adults report having received some inheritance: this figure rises to nearly 40 per cent for those aged 70 to 79. (Inheritance tends to come in two waves, one on the death of parents and the second on the death of the spouse.)
- People hold their wealth first in interest bearing deposits, up to an amount of about $4000, then in housing and superannuation; it is only among the top 5 per cent of wealth-holders that equities start becoming important, with the top percentile holding about 60 per cent of their wealth in this form. (For further details see: Dilnot 1990; Piggott 1988; McCallum and Beggs 1991.)

• The Distribution of Income •

Empirical studies of the distribution of income in Australia have mostly focused on annual money income, expressed as equivalent money income where possible. It is notable that the quality of both the concepts used and the data have improved markedly over time. Early studies of the distribution of income had to rest content with, at best, individual average annual incomes presented in grouped form. The use of grouped data means that any inequality within the group is suppressed: all individuals with incomes falling within the boundaries of a particular group are usually assumed to receive the same income, frequently set as the mid-point of the income range. The income intervals used to group the data were large and the boundaries of the highest income group were undefined, so that the top incomes had to be guessed at. Contemporary data are free of many of these problems: it is now possible to group people into the households in which they live in order to identify household income and adjust it for the size and composition of the household to produce equivalent income. Frequently it is also possible to deduct imputed or reported income tax in order to identify disposable income. A most important advance has been the provision of unit record data in which the researcher has access to information on the exact income of the individual or household and not just the income interval into which they fall. These unit record data also enable the personal characteristics of the individual/household to be linked with their income. It is thus possible to move beyond description to examine the causes of high and low incomes.

• *Comparisons of income inequality* •

As noted earlier, one of the informative ways in which to present conclusions about income inequality is to make comparisons with earlier periods and with other countries. A number of studies have done this for Australia and we summarise their findings below.

The distribution of income became more equal in Australia between 1915 and 1981, particularly because of a fall in the share of the top 10 per cent but also because of a rise in the share of the bottom ten per cent. The Gini coefficient for males fell from 0.46 to 0.37 and for females from 0.65 to 0.54. This decrease in inequality occurred after the Great Depression of the 1930s and much of it had occurred by 1968 (Lancaster-Jones 1975; McLean and Richardson 1986).

Inequality in after-tax equivalent family income per person rose slightly between 1981 and 1986: the share of the bottom quintile fell from 7.7 to 7.6 and the share of the top quintile rose from 38.2 to 39.3; the Gini coefficient rose from 0.31 to 0.32. These inequality figures place Australia, out of a total of eight countries, ahead of only the United States in the equality league (Saunders, Hobbes and Stott 1989).[6] They have been used to conclude that the distribution of income in Australia is relatively unequal. Before endorsing this conclusion, we note two points. One is that these comparisons, though they are based on the best international data available (those from the Luxembourg Income Study), are still not without problems. Saunders et al. note two problems in particular. One is that the distributions in most of the countries became somewhat more unequal during the first half of the 1980s. The timing of the data varies from 1979 (US, UK and Norway) to 1981–82 (Australia and New Zealand). Given the small differences in Gini coefficients between the four least equal countries, rankings could be affected as a result of this timing problem. Furthermore, the measured levels of inequality are quite sensitive to the choice of equivalence scale. Australia and New Zealand have relatively large family sizes compared to most of the other countries in the group. They are thus especially sensitive to this issue. The other point to note is that the countries which are included in the Luxembourg Income Study have among the most equal distributions of income in the world.

• Sources of change in the distribution of income •

The distribution of income can change as a result both of independent changes in the demographic, family formation and economic situation and as a result of government policy. We note here that, despite the large changes which have occurred within these spheres, the distribution of income has proven to be remarkably stable (Rivlin 1975; Phelps Brown 1988). Phelps Brown goes on to observe that 'One major conclusion emerges from this survey: the distributions of income and wealth are resistant to great imposed changes' (p. 475). It is a very difficult task to unravel the causes of changes in the distribution of income. None the less, several authors have undertaken this task, in an understandably partial fashion, and we here report their results.

A micro-analytic simulation of changes in the level and distribution of real household income has been conducted based on unit record data from the 1985–86 ABS Income Distribution survey (Bradbury, Doyle and Whiteford 1990). From this base year, the picture has been extended backwards to 1982–83 and forwards to 1989–90. In doing so, allowance has been made for changes in employment, demographic composition, sources of income and the differential impact of these on different family types. While not without flaws, this sort of simulation is a major development in the provision of timely information on the effects of recent large economic changes. During this period real wages fell and farm incomes recovered from the very low levels of 1982–83. The increase in median real family income was 6.5 per cent for all families and 3.3 per cent for non-farm families. The authors conclude that this increase was not equally shared. The greatest gains went to sole parents (12.8 per cent), non-aged couples without children, and farm families. The period was one of rapidly rising home interest rates and house prices. Together, these virtually wiped out the gains in real income of non-aged couples without children and *reduced* the incomes of couples with children. In contrast, the rise in house prices increased the income gains of people over the age of 65, on average, because of their high rate of home equity. The groups who did least well were young single people and couples with children. *Within* each family type, the distribution of income has generally become more equal and this is probably also true for families overall.

The payment of income tax and the receipt of government social welfare payments reduce inequality in the distribution of household income. In 1975–76 the Gini coefficient was reduced from 0.40 to 0.35 as a result of the receipt of pensions and benefits and fell further to 0.33 as a result of the payment of personal income tax (Kakwani 1986). Note that both these conclusions rest upon the assumption that the distribution of *private* income is not affected by the existence and level of government welfare payments and taxes. While this assumption is almost certainly wrong, we know little about the level of any interdependence between private and public income and service provision.

Inequality in full income, as calculated from the data in the Australian Standard of Living survey, is only slightly less than inequality in after-tax equivalent income. If we add to the full income of individuals an estimate made by the ABS (1992) of the effects of indirect taxes and receipt of government-provided education, health services, housing and non-cash social welfare benefits, then the Gini coefficient falls from 0.26 to 0.23. (See Chapter 1 for a discussion of the estimation of full income.) That is, the net effect of indirect taxes and the listed government services is substantially equalising.

• *Expenditure compared with income* •

Economists have long argued that it is expenditure rather than income which determines the material standard of living of the household. It is expenditure, not income, which measures the level of consumption of goods and services in a period. The two will differ as a result of saving, borrowing and repayment of debt. Most measures of inequality focus on income, usually for the pragmatic reason that it is easier to collect data on income than it is to collect data on expenditure. Is there any difference in the picture of inequality if expenditure is used instead?

When households are ranked by levels of household income, their expenditure is more equally distributed than their income. Furthermore, each is more equally distributed when it is expressed per capita than when it is expressed on a household basis. The reason for this is that average household size rises with each higher quintile of household income. The differences are substantial. In the next chapter we show this in graphic form (Figure 3.5).

The ASL data have been used to estimate a distribution of material resources and of human functionings, using distance functions to aggregate non-comensurable components. This study concludes that the distribution of both material resources and functioning scores is highly compressed. Most importantly, it also concludes that the two distributions are not correlated, so that it is quite likely that a person with relatively low levels of resources will be functioning well and vice versa. This separation of the two distributions is itself an egalitarian feature. It is not only, or even, the rich who are living satisfactory lives. (Lovell et al. 1993).

• *The distribution of earnings* •

The degree of equality of the distribution of earnings in Australia is a matter of considerable interest because of the unusual institutions which this country has for the setting of wages (the system of industrial tribunals for conciliation and compulsory arbitration). Note that we cannot automatically attribute any relative equality in the earnings distribution to the existence of these tribunals. Comparisons of the pay of managers (who are outside the award system) across a number of industrial countries shows that this pay was substantially more compressed in Australia than in the comparison countries (Richardson 1981).

One area in which the industrial tribunals have had a distinctly equalising effect is in the relative pay of men and women. For twenty years prior to the equal-pay decisions of 1969 and 1972 the index of women's award rates of pay was steady at around 72 per cent of the male index. It rose to around 90 per cent following the equal-pay decisions and has remained at that level since. This increase in relative award rates of pay has been matched by increases in actual earnings (Gregory and Daly 1990). A move to more equal pay for women is generally equalising (for earnings) because women's employment is disproportionately in the lower paying jobs. It may *not*, however, equalise household incomes, because two-earner families already tend to be placed relatively high in that distribution.

In a study which compares the distribution of male adult full-time employees in the United States, the United Kingdom and Australia, McNabb and Richardson conclude that the rate of return to education is lower (at about 7 per cent) in Australia than in the other two countries, where it is about 10 per cent. That is, the increase in earnings which is associated with an extra year of formal education is lower in Australia than in the other two countries. Furthermore, the Australian labour market seems to be rather different in that experience on the job has been quite a good substitute for formal education as a means to higher pay. Both of these conclusions imply a relatively egalitarian pay structure; first because the more highly educated are relatively modestly rewarded, and second because there are several paths to the attainment of good jobs, namely formal education and learning on the job.

The most recent and complete comparison of the distribution of earnings in Australia with that in other countries is that of Green et al. (1992). These authors use the LIS data to compare the earnings distribution of adult male employees who are heads of households and employed full-time and full year. The countries in the comparison are Australia, Canada, the United States, West Germany and Sweden. Two periods are examined, the first in the early 1980s and the second in the mid 1980s.

For all countries there has been some increase in inequality over the early 1980s, although this is least apparent in Australia. In fact, in Australia, as in West Germany, the Lorenz curves for the two periods intersect. While the share of the top quintile increased, so too did the share of the bottom quintile. In the other three countries the movement was unambiguously in the direction of greater inequality. For example, in the United States the top quintile increased its share of total earnings from 35.0 per cent to 38.1 per cent. The comparable figures for Australia are 31.6 and 32.4. Green et al. compute six different inequality indices for both periods. In the

United States, Sweden and Canada inequality rose for all six measures. In Australia and West Germany, inequality rose when measured by the Gini and Theil indices and by the Atkinson index when relatively low weight is given to the bottom end (that is, e = 0.5 or 0.8). The two measures which are sensitive to the bottom of the distribution (the Atkinson index with an e value of 1.5 and the variance in the logarithm) show a fall in inequality in the two countries (p. 12).

A comparison of the absolute level of inequality in male earnings in the mid 1980s shows Australia to be in the middle of the rankings on all six indices. Its distribution was more equal (for example, its Gini = 0.21) than that in the United States (0.30) and Canada (0.25) and less equal than that in West Germany (0.20) and Sweden (0.19). On all the measures the United States in particular but also Canada stand out as having distributions which are substantially less equal than those found in Australia and the two European countries.

CONCLUSION

We are now in a position to answer the questions asked at the beginning of this chapter. Australia clearly is *not* one of the most unequal countries in the world. Developed countries tend to have more equally distributed incomes, especially when the services of government are included. Among the developed countries, those included in the LIS survey with which Australia has been compared probably rank in the 15–20 most egalitarian countries in the world. Australia is located in the middle of this group. Thus, it is safe to conclude that Australia ranks in the top dozen or so countries in the world in terms of equality in the distribution of income. The evidence we have on the distribution of earnings is consistent with this assessment.

Not only is Australia relatively egalitarian in the distribution of income, it is more so now than in the past. This move toward a more equal distribution applies not only to income but probably also to wealth. In both cases it seems to have been a modification in the shares of both the top and bottom tails which has been the equalising force. Were a more comprehensive measure of income to be used which embraced government-provided services such as health and education, the decrease in inequality over time would be even more pronounced.

Our ability to draw reasonably firm conclusions about the relative distribution of income and earnings in Australia owes a great deal to the decision by the ABS to collect income data from regular surveys. The inclusion of Australia in the LIS project has also been of great value in preventing erroneous conclusions about Australia's relative equality. International comparisons are irresistible, and if the information is not there to enable them to be made reliably then they will be made unreliably. This was apparent in the period before the LIS project commenced. Statistics were asked to carry a burden they could not bear. As a result, the conclusion was drawn that Australia was more egalitarian than it actually is in its distribution (although the evidence still supports Australia as being very egalitarian in the opportunities it offers each new generation, in the form of inter-generational class mobility; for more on this see Chapter 3).

The satisfactory levels of information now available for money income do not carry through to two other important areas. One is the key constituents of full income, namely non-employed time and housing equity plus consumer durables. The other is wealth. Analysis of the ASL data has shown that the supplementation of money income with a few extra pieces of information can have an important impact on our understanding of who is at the bottom of the income distribution and why. We believe that the inclusion of these extra pieces of information (for example, questions about the use of adult time, especially but not exclusively concerned with the division between employed and non-employed time) would greatly enrich the results of the income distribution surveys. If the length of the questionnaire is a constraint then perhaps some of the great detail sought about money income could be sacrificed.

It is unlikely that there will ever be satisfactory data on the distribution of wealth unless the ABS decides to get into the field. Inferences from data collected for other purposes will continue to be used until something better is available. But it is unlikely that these can be very accurate or that they will have the crucial feature of being able to link levels of wealth with levels of income and other resources (such as time and access to public services). It is vital to know whether or not the correlation between individuals ranked according to wealth and individuals ranked according to income is high. If it is, then the disadvantages of low income are compounded. If it is not (and the bits of evidence from the ASL suggest it may not be very highly correlated) then the overall levels of inequality are thereby reduced. This has implications both for our understanding of the society and for public policy.

Even official surveys have difficulty in obtaining a high response rate and good quality answers to questions on wealth. Private surveys have little chance of being satisfactory. Yet the limitations of the survey method must be accepted because of the absence of any direct taxation of wealth from which data may be generated. The ideal is to have both a tax-based source of data, because there are costs to lying about tax liability, and a survey-based source of data, because this can seek complementary information about socio-demographic characteristics. In Australia there is neither.

NOTES

[1] This survey is described in Edwards, Gates and Layton, 1966.

[2] Full details of the design and conduct of the survey are available from the authors.

[3] Data are from the 1933 and 1947 censuses of the Commonwealth of Australia and contemporary ABS sources, including the 1988–89 Household Expenditure survey.

[4] We note that this point seems to be overlooked by 'supply side' enthusiasts, who see a rise in the supply of effort to the labour market as an unqualified improvement in productive effort.

[5] The details of how this index is constructed were discussed in Chapter 1.

[6] The countries are in ascending order of Gini coefficient values, calculated on equivalent net family income among quintiles of individuals: Sweden (0.20), Norway (0.24), West Germany (0.25), United Kingdom (0.27), New Zealand (0.29), Canada (0.30), Australia (0.31) and the United States (0.32) (Saunders et al. 1989, p. 67).

3

WHY SOME PEOPLE ARE RICH AND
SOME POOR

In this chapter we shift our focus from *who* is rich and poor to *why* they are rich and poor. One possible explanation is that riches and poverty are inherited. We have already examined inheritance in the strict sense in the previous section. Here we focus on 'inheritance' in the looser sense of social mobility.

• Equality of Condition and Equality of Opportunity •

By social mobility we mean the degree of stratification or 'openness' of a society. Societies range from the highly stratified, where people's class origins and destinations are tightly linked, to the very open, where knowing a person's family of origin would tell us little about where they end up in life. Social mobility is not the same as equality of condition. There is no logical contradiction in a high rate of social mobility going hand in hand with great inequality in terms of riches and poverty. However, in practice, a high rate of mobility is usually a good indicator that a society also enjoys relative equality of condition.[1]

Many writers have seen Australia, together with the United States, as exceptional in their high rates of social mobility when compared to the 'old' societies of Europe. Erikson and Goldthorpe point out that for Marx and Engels, the exceptional features of the US (the open frontier, wide range of opportunities, independent entrepreneurship) would be a passing phase, at the end of which it would follow the European model of mature capitalism. However, for de Tocqueville, the US was the forerunner of democratic societies, and would be followed by the older European nations. A third school saw the US as being permanently exceptional in its degree of openness and mobility (Erikson and Goldthorpe 1992, p. 310).

Though many early writers had commented on Australia's exceptional degree of both equality of condition and equality of opportunity, it was Hancock (1930) who stated the case in terms that became the received wisdom (Clark 1955, p. 660). Hancock saw Australia as notably different from the US in that equality of condition was prized above equality of opportunity. Australians had never tolerated the degrees of inequality that had been accepted in the US, but rather, somewhat to Hancock's chagrin, had put more emphasis on need than on merit. Thus, for Hancock, Australians were something of a paradox in that their tendency to cut down tall poppies both favoured and hindered equality of opportunity.

Encel, drawing heavily on Hancock, has described the distinctive feature of Australian egalitarianism as consisting of high minimum standards of material well-being accompanied by restricted scope for the unusual, the eccentric, the individual. It is the philosophy of 'equal treatment', with all its procrustean overtones, as it requires bureaucracy to enforce rules of equal treatment; bureaucracy breeds authority; and authority undermines the equality which bred it. It is typical of this attitude that prophets of rags-to-riches like Samuel Smiles and Horatio Alger were never popular authors in Australia (Encel 1970, pp. 52, 56; Berlin 1955–6).

More recently, O'Farrell has given a distinctive twist to both horns of the equal opportunity/uniformity dilemma in his analysis of the Irish contribution to the Australian ethos. The Irish contributed first through the effective protest against religious and political monopolies, and their refusal to accept discriminatory laws (O'Farrell 1986, p. 11). They had no particularly strong philosophical commitment to liberty—the opposite could be argued. 'Yet an open society in Australia was the effect of their determination to prise apart a society which threatened to become closed'(p. 11).

O'Farrell sees the Irish as also contributing to the uniformity ethos. He presents in effect the obverse of the Protestant ethic thesis. The Irish really did have 'a mind-frame inimical to capitalist aggregation' (p. 20). They were so long denied the opportunity to pursue wealth that they developed a philosophy that held it in contempt. In Australia, they adjusted their level of well-being upwards, but retained their rejection of the ethos of acquisition at all cost. 'They concluded that small and equal achievement was more fitting than great.' (p. 21)

Though Hancock and O'Farrell focus on the Australian ethos, the effect of structural factors should not be overlooked. Clark, for instance, notes how the shortage of unskilled workers had a powerful levelling effect on Australia in the nineteenth century (1966, p. 660).

Fortunately, we can now test empirically the claims that Australia may or may not have exceptionally high rates of social mobility. We now have the results of an important series of cross-national comparative studies of social mobility in Australia, the US, Japan and nine European countries (Erikson and Goldthorpe 1992). The project is based on a re-analysis of studies carried out between 1970 and 1978. The original studies examined male inter-generational mobility patterns—that is, the extent to which men's own class position differed from that of their fathers. As with all secondary analysis of existing studies, Erikson and Goldthorpe were limited by the scope of the original studies—for instance, the lack of data in some of the national studies on mobility among women, other than as wives of male respondents. In addition, they faced the usual difficulty of cross-national studies, that of comparability of data. They tackled this by recoding of the original data into common categories.

Following the European tradition, the categorical divisions are based on class rather than on a hierarchy of prestige or income. Three sets of considerations are relevant in allocating people to class positions: 1) the relative desirability of different class positions, considered as destinations; 2) the relative advantages afforded to individuals by different class origins—for example, economic, cultural and social resources; 3) the relative barriers that emerge—that is, the requirements that correspond to the resources listed under 2 (Erikson and Goldthorpe 1987a). For instance, the self-employed (Class IV) may or may not have higher incomes or enjoy higher prestige than skilled manual workers (Class VI). They are assumed to have a distinctive way of life because of their employment status, to enjoy a high degree of autonomy, to own some capital, and to experience both the risks and potential gains of their market position.

On this basis, a ten-category version and a seven-category version of the class schema are commonly used.

Table 3.1: *Class Schema*

	Ten-category version	Seven-category version
Class I	Higher-grade professionals and administrators of large enterprises	
Class II	Lower-grade professionals and higher-grade technicians; supervisors of non-manual employees	I and II: 'service class'
Class III	Routine clerical and service workers	III: 'routine non-manual'
Class IVa	Small proprietors with employees	IVa and IVb 'petty bourgeoisie'
Class IVb	Small proprietors without employees	
Class IVc	Farmers	IVc: 'farmers'
Class V	Foremen and supervisors of manual workers; lower-grade technicians	
Class VI	Skilled manual workers	V and VI: 'skilled workers'
Class VIIa	Semi-skilled and unskilled manual workers	VIIa: 'non-skilled workers'
Class VIIb	Agricultural workers	VIIb: 'farm workers'

Source: Goldthorpe, 1980

The core thesis that was tested and confirmed by Erikson and Goldthorpe was that patterns of social fluidity in industrial societies display a large commonality, variations on which tend to be nationally specific rather than open to more systematic macro-sociological explanation. In other words, the similarity in patterns of social fluidity or mobility is more striking than the national variations, where factors such as ethos might have a bearing.

Australia has few distinctive features. The model that summarises the European pattern fits the Australian data quite well when these few distinctive features are taken into account—namely, a *lower* propensity for class V/VI to recruit from white collar classes, and *higher* propensity to recruit from farm origins. Both these Australian features are explained in part by the experience of migrants (Erikson and Goldthorpe 1992, p. 322). A further feature of Australian mobility lies in the strength of common patterns. For instance, the common tendency for the children of the 'privileged service class' and of the 'petty bourgeoisie' to inherit their parents' position is found in Australia, but it is weaker than in any European nation except Hungary (p. 323).

As a general comment, Australia has a relatively high degree of fluidity, but one not outside European experience. 'If some overall characterisation of the Australian mobility regime is required, one could perhaps suggest that Australia has arrived at a version of what we have previously thought of as the Swedish pattern, although, it would need to be added, without the same degree of social-democratic political dominance' (Erikson and Goldthorpe 1992, p. 324).

One possibility is that Australia may have been distinctive, but that this has changed over time. A way of testing this possibility is to break a survey population into different age-cohorts, in order to uncover any evidence of changing patterns. When this was done with the Australian data there was no evidence of change over time (p. 324).

There is comfort in these results both for the commentators who claimed to observe very high rates of mobility in Australia, and those who noted countervailing tendencies. Australia is indeed at the high end of the mobility scale, but not to the extent that one could say a distinctively new mobility pattern has emerged. There is no support for the claim that the supposed ethos of working class solidarity and of equality of condition rather than of opportunity have had a *negative* effect on mobility (Erikson and Goldthorpe 1992, p. 324). In fact, the final conclusion of the Erikson and Goldthorpe cross-national study is a sobering one for those who see either Australia or the US as exceptional societies. 'No matter how distinctive the US and Australia may be in the economic and social histories of their industrialisation or in the ideas, beliefs and values concerning mobility that are prevalent in their national cultures, it could not, on our evidence, be said that they differ more widely from European nations in their actual rates and patterns of mobility than do European nations among themselves' (p. 337).

RELATIVE ADVANTAGES AND RELATIVE BARRIERS

We concluded above that though Australia is at the upper end of the mobility range among industrialised nations, it is not outside that range. That leaves us with the question of what is the range of the relative advantages and barriers to movement between different class positions in industrial nations?

There are many ways of presenting this information. It will be recalled that the class schema in Table 3.1 is not constructed primarily on hierarchical lines. There is no implication that Class III (routine non-manual), for instance, is in some sense 'higher' than Class IV (petty bourgeoisie). However, there clearly is a hierarchical element at the extremes of the class table, especially between Class I–II (service class) and Class VIIa (unskilled manual). (Class VIIb, farm workers, is not considered because of its small size in Australia.) Since our interest in this context is the transmission from one generation to the next of privilege and of disadvantage, we will focus on these two classes. In addition, we examine Class V–VI (skilled workers) since they represent the most distinctive feature of Australian social mobility.

Figure 3.1 shows in graphic form the European range of 'inflow' into the three classes we are considering, and where Australia lies in relation to this range. The 'inflow' rates answer the question 'Given someone's present class position, what was the class of their family of origin?'. For instance, in 3.1a we see that of the men who end up in Class I–II, 31 per cent of the Australians were from Class I–II

Figure 3.1: *Inflow rates*

a) Inflow to Class I-II

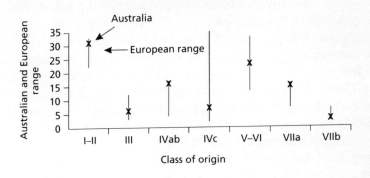

b) Inflow to Class V-VI

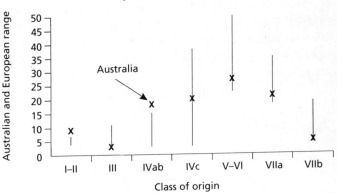

c) Inflow to Class VIIa

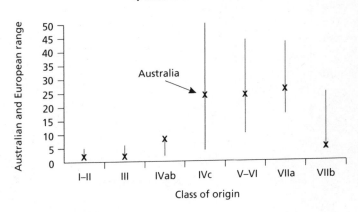

Source: Erikson and Goldthorpe (1992), figure 9.1

origins. This is just inside the top of the European range of 22 to 33 per cent and suggests relative immobility. On the other hand, 23 per cent of the Class I–II are of Class V–VI (skilled worker) origin, about the centre of the European range of 13 to 33 per cent.

In similar fashion, Figure 3.2 examines 'outflow' rates. This time the question is, 'Given a certain class or origin, where do people end up later in life?'. Thus, 3.2a shows 53 per cent of Australians born into Class I–II remaining in that class in later life. This is at the bottom of the European range of 52 to 66 per cent and suggests relative mobility.

It may seem paradoxical that Figure 3.1 seems to show that privileged Australians are rather more likely than most Europeans to retain their privileged position, while Figure 3.2 suggests a wider recruitment into the most privileged class in Australia than in most other countries. The two propositions are not, in fact, contradictory. Part of the explanation is that we are dealing with two moments in time. Class of origin is calculated at age 14, while class of destination is calculated during mature adulthood. During this interval, the size

Figure 3.2: *Outflow rates*

a) Outflow from Class I-II

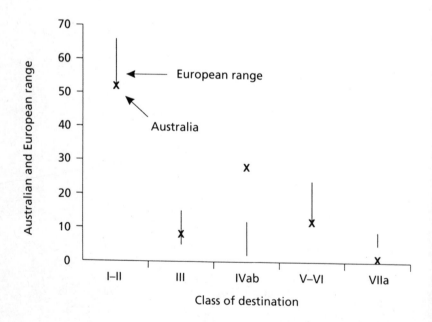

b) Outflow from Class V-VI

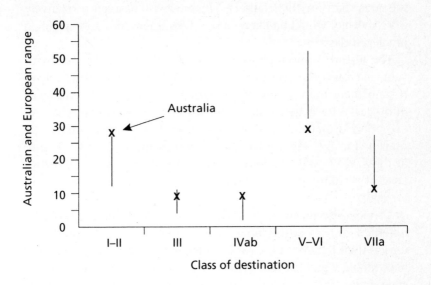

c) Outflow from Class VIIa

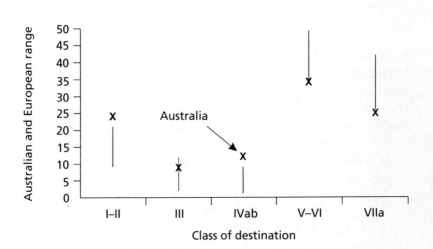

Source: Erikson and Goldthorpe (1992), figure 9.2

of Class I–II increased from 14 to 27 per cent of the population in Australia. In other words, there was much more room at the top for the sons than for their fathers. This means that even a relatively closed society would be likely to see recruitment into an expanding privileged class.

The picture is more clear-cut when it comes to the most disadvantaged class: VIIa. Australians born into Class VIIa are less likely to remain there than in any of the European countries. Recruitment into Class VIIa is generally within the European range. The one exception is that rather more come from IVab (petty bourgeoisie) than in Europe. Figure 3.1 also illustrates the distinctive feature of Class V–VI (skilled) workers, with Australia showing a higher level of recruitment from Class IVab (small entrepreneurs) than in Europe.

To what extent, then, are privileged and disadvantaged positions inherited, at least in the loose sense that sons follow the same pattern as their fathers? It is clear from Figures 3.1 and 3.2 that there is both mobility and barriers to mobility. One way of putting into perspective the different chances of moving to particular destinations is to express them in terms of odds. Odds ratios answer questions such as 'What are the relative chances of someone born into Class VII rather than Class I–II ending up in Class VII rather than Class I–II?'. In other words, what is the relative advantage of the Class I–II person in this particular competition? The answer from the ASL data is 9:1 for men and 3:1 in the case of women. Both men and women of Class VII origin have roughly an even chance of ending up in Class I–II rather than Class VII. But a male born into Class I–II has only one chance in nine of ending up in Class VII. For women, the chances are one in three. In other words, privilege has protective barriers around it for all, but they are much stronger for men.

We can conclude that the possibility of rags-to-riches is very real in Australia, both for men and for women. The possibility of riches-to-rags is remote for men, but less so for women.

• Women and Social Mobility •

We noted that the Erikson and Goldthorpe study has the limitations of the original surveys, and that one of these is that, in some cases, data on women's mobility were available only for the wives of male respondents. It has long been customary in mobility studies for married women to be classified according to their husband's occupation. In defence of this it is pointed out that, given the notion of class, it does not make sense to classify individual partners separately. It is the family that is typically the unit of consumption when it comes to sharing a dwelling, having access to health-care, or in the education of children. However, it does not follow that the family classification should be based upon the husband's occupation. In our own class schema in the ASL study, we have used a gender-blind classification method. If only one partner is employed, that partner's classification is followed. Where both are employed, a hierarchy of 'dominance' is applied (Erikson 1984). For instance, if a self-employed person (Class IV) is married to a skilled worker (Class VI), the family is classified as Class IV. There are, of course, many instances were both partners will be classified similarly, since there are strong patterns of homogamy (that is, partners are chosen from similar social backgrounds), though exceptions remain numerous (McRae 1986). Erikson and Goldthorpe followed a similar procedure when they analysed women's mobility for those European countries for which data were available (Erikson and Goldthorpe 1992, p. 264).

Would it have made much difference to the conclusions of the cross-national studies if women's mobility via their own occupation had been included? It would to the extent that women's mobility via their own occupation differs from their mobility via marriage. In an earlier study, Portocarero found that the differences were, in fact, statistically significant, but small in strength (Portocarero 1987, p. 117). In their more recent study, Erikson and Goldthorpe concluded that their most striking finding was how *little* women's experience of class mobility differs from that of men (Erikson and Goldthorpe 1992, p. 275).

The issue here is in some ways similar to one noted in the final chapter, where we discuss whether standards of living should be seen only in terms of material well-being, or whether one should also include the *source* of income. It is the difference between sharing an income, and earning it in one's own name. In the context of the present chapter, the issue is whether one focuses on the standard of living that goes with a certain class position, or on the fact that the class position is a derived one. 'If studies of living conditions support the thesis that married women's class position is more adequately described by the husband's occupation, this derived class position in itself reflects a fundamental inequality within the family unit, which becomes manifest if the unit is dissolved' (Portocarero 1987, p. 117).

• Vicious Circles, Cultures of Poverty, and the Underclass •

In discussing social mobility, we looked at the relative chances of mobility of broad social groupings or classes. We saw that though barriers to mobility certainly exist, they are weaker in Australia than in most other countries. Yet it might be argued that a discussion in terms of class misses the point. The class-based categories assume people are employed, or at least live in families where employment is decisive in determining social and market relations. But what if employment is sporadic or non-existent, and what if this has been the case over generations? Might not a way of life, or culture, have developed that places families or groups outside the mainstream to such an extent that they could be said to live in a culture of poverty, or that they are not so much a class as an underclass?

The idea that poverty might result in a self-propagating way of life has been 'discovered' about once every ten years during the past century. To its proponents, it seems a self-evident proposition. To its detractors, it is a half-truth that inflicts further injury on the poor by distracting attention from far more important causes of poverty.

• *Vicious circles* •

The issues in question are well illustrated in the writings of Charles Booth at the turn of the century. Booth uses a metaphor from logic, the 'vicious circle', to describe the situation of the London dock-workers.

> *The character of the men matched well with the character of the work and that of its remuneration. All alike were low and irregular. The vicious circle was complete. How should it be broken? (Booth 1903, p. 399)*

Booth himself shows implicitly the perils of this kind of metaphor. His perception of the 'low and irregular' character of the dockwork-ers was based on his survey of 1887. Yet within a year, the dock-workers had organised in unions, and by 1892 Booth himself had noted how their situation had changed radically. In other words, the metaphor that made sense as a retrospective description of what had happened, proved singularly weak as a prediction of the future.

• *Cultures of poverty* •

A variant on the theme of vicious circles is that of 'culture of poverty', a concept associated with the anthropologist, Oscar Lewis. Lewis is so frequently misquoted that it is important to make clear just what he did claim. Lewis saw poverty as a culture that is both an adaptation and a reaction of the poor to their marginal position in society. He did not reject 'structural' explanations. On the contrary, he saw the adaptation of the poor as perfectly reasonable, given the circumstances in which they find themselves. However, he maintained that this adaptation then develops a life of its own, and its key elements of fatalism and low level of aspiration are passed on to children. The argument is that at a certain point, the culture becomes self-sustaining, even if the original circumstances change. Lewis estimated that some 20 per cent of Americans who were poor in terms of the poverty line could justly be said to live in such a self-sustaining culture of poverty (Lewis 1969).

When put in this form, Lewis's thesis becomes rather modest: *some* poverty can be explained in terms of values and a way of life that are passed from generation to generation, and that stop people taking advantage of changed circumstances. In this modest form, the claim would be difficult to refute.

Lewis's ideas had a rebirth in Britain in the 1970s under the inspiration of the then Secretary of State for Social Security, Sir Keith Joseph. The subsequent research produced case studies showing *some* families living in something approaching a culture of poverty (Coffield et al. 1980). The questions are what weight to give to this kind of process, and whether such a focus distracts attention from other, far more important processes.

In one of the most effective examples of the debunking of theories of inheritance of poverty, Duncan (1969) pointed out that, in the context of the United States in the 1960s, when the notion of culture of poverty was at its height, a far more plausible story could be told in terms of the inheritance of race rather than the inheritance of poverty. During the War on Poverty of the 1960s, the notion of poverty begetting poverty in a near-inevitable cycle was pervasive. A series of personal characteristics were identified that were supposed to explain how poverty was inherited. These were, in fact, code-words for talking about the poverty of blacks. Duncan agrees that many blacks begin life with a series of characteristics that would be a handicap to anyone, black or white. But over and above this, they had the specific handicap of race. Duncan's empirical work makes a convincing case that race was by far the strongest influence on income differences between blacks and whites. In other words, when black and white men in the same line of work, with the same amount of formal schooling, with equal ability, from families of the same size and same socio-economic level draw widely differing salaries, the most plausible explanation is racial discrimination (Duncan 1969).

There have been several attempts to measure the extent of trans-mission of deprivation over generations. When Atkinson followed up in 1975–78 Rowntree's 1950 study of deprivation in York, he found *some* evidence of transmitted deprivation, in the sense that those who were deprived in 1950 were somewhat more likely to be deprived in the 1970s. For instance, their risk of having poor hous-ing amenities was one-and-a-half times greater than that faced by those who were not deprived in 1950, and they were nearly twice as likely to have low earnings. On the other hand, they were no more likely to be on benefit, or to be off-work (Atkinson 1989, p. 85). This finding, that deprivation at one point in time may result in a modest increase in the risk of subsequent deprivation, is a far cry from what is generally understood by 'inheritance of poverty'.

When it comes to upheavals such as the Depression of the 1930s, the evidence of transmitted deprivation is even harder to find. These studies point, rather, to the importance of the interaction of a series of events over a person's lifetime. The best known study of the life-time effects of the Depression of the 1930s is Glen Elder's follow-up study of two groups of Californian children originally studied in the 1930s. Those whose parents suffered a decline of 34 per cent in fam-ily income between 1929–33 were classified as 'deprived'. The fam-ilies were further classified into working class and middle class (Elder 1974). He found that the subsequent history of the children could not be simply read-off from their 'common experience' of the 1930s. For instance, the age of the children affected both their experience of the Depression, and their chances of benefiting from later 'facilitating' events. The middle class 'deprived' children fared particularly well in later life, especially those who were the right age to ride on the crest of the post-war boom.

Survivors of unemployment in the 1930s in Adelaide followed patterns similar to those of the children described by Elder. In a study of the employment history of men born around 1910, Travers found that those who had been unemployed in the 1930s had very different mobility patterns from those who escaped unemployment. Those who avoided unemployment followed the usual pattern of rather close links between origins and destinations. For the formerly unemployed, however, there was no relationship at all between where they started in life and where they ended up. But since the formerly unemployed were heavily concentrated in working class families, that is another way of saying that this group showed an unusual degree of mobility into the more privileged class positions. The very industries where unemployment was concentrated in the 1930s (for example, the motor vehicle industry) were boom industries during and after the war. Men whose lives appeared blighted for most of the 1930s subsequently enjoyed almost continuous prosperity until they retired around 1970 (Travers 1986).

Neither Elder nor Travers is saying that 'depressions are good for you'. What they are saying is that the life-paths of people who experience a disaster, even one as great as the Depression of the 1930s, are unlikely to be determined by that single event. Their lives were affected not only by the Depression, but by the war, the post-war boom, and the post-war migrant influx. Moreover, the effect of these events depended on what 'baggage' (Elder 1981) they brought with them in the form of their age, gender, and family background. It will also depend on the size of the generation they are born into. The small generation born in the 1930s enjoyed advantages in education and in the labour market relative to the much larger generation born in the high birth-rate 1950s (Easterlin 1980). Culture of poverty theories try to explain too much.

• *The underclass* •

The most recent version of the concept of inherited poverty is that of the underclass. Though this is a far more sophisticated and plausible variant on the theme of inherited poverty, it is still the subject of vehement controversy, and even of claims that the term is so dangerous it should be abandoned (Jencks 1989; Van Haitsma 1989; Hochschild 1991; Wilson 1991; Boxill 1991; Prosser 1991).

When William Julius Wilson uses the concept of underclass, he is attempting to describe a type of economic disadvantage that cannot be explained purely in structural terms. For Wilson, members of the underclass differ from other economically disadvantaged groups in that 'their marginal economic position or weak attachment to the labour force is uniquely reinforced by the neighbourhood or social milieu' (Wilson 1991, p. 601). Take an unemployed person living in an area of low unemployment, and another living in a neighbourhood with very high unemployment. The second faces the same overall impediments to getting a job as the first, but over and above that there is the cultural influence of other jobless families in the neighbourhood. Wilson would restrict the term underclass to those who are both disadvantaged *and* are living in an area of high concentration of disadvantage.

Despite some superficial similarities with the culture of poverty thesis, Wilson does not accept its pessimistic implication that minority groups will not respond to an improved economy. Nor does he accept Duncan's too-easy explanation in terms of racism. Wilson predicts that disadvantaged minorities will respond differently, depending on the local labour market. He illustrates this with the data in Table 3.2, drawn from Freeman's study of employment and unemployment rates among a disadvantaged group (black youths with twelve or less years of schooling) during the upturn in the US economy between 1983 and 1987.

Table 3.2: Local unemployment rate and change in local employment rate, black youths, 1983–1987

Local unemployment rate (per cent)	Change in local employment rate, 1983–1987 (per cent)
< 4	31 to 71
4 to 5	46 to 65
5 to 6	47 to 56
6 to 7	39 to 52
7 or more	41 to 48

Source: Wilson 1991, p. 605.

The data in Table 3.2 illustrate well Wilson's argument. Both structural and cultural factors operate. When there is an upturn in the economy, poorly educated minority youths across the country benefit. But the extent to which they are able to take advantage of improved circumstances varies dramatically according to cultural factors, such as the effect of living in a neighbourhood where most people are unemployed. However, the cultural factors are not free-floating, but linked to the state of the economy. Even though disproportionate numbers of minority youths remain unemployed in *all* cities, the change in employment rates from 31 to 71 per cent over a five-year period is dramatic enough to put a severe dent in theories that attribute to minority groups values that are supposed to keep them permanently outside the mainstream.

Table 3.2 is important also as an illustration of the kind of information that is needed to offset what might be termed the clinicians' bias. The clinicians in question are any workers in an agency that is in daily contact with disadvantaged groups. One reason theories of inheritance of poverty are so enduring is that they appeal to the particular experience of clinicians who frequently see case histories of disadvantage enduring over more than one generation. Of their very nature, case histories are retrospective accounts where the starting point is present disadvantage. It is scarcely surprising to find that present disadvantage is often linked to prior disadvantage. There are, of course, instances of extremely high association between disadvantage over two generations. For instance, Prosser reports a study showing white young women from welfare families having a 24 per cent chance of ever being on welfare themselves, compared to 2 per cent for non-welfare families (Prosser 1991). This is indeed a very elevated risk, yet it is no more than that. Even in this case, the disadvantage in question does *not* endure across generations for a large majority. Clinicians therefore see a statistically biased group, rather than the full cross-section of people who start with a disadvantage.

Table 3.2 points in much the same direction as the discussion of social mobility; namely, that barriers to mobility certainly exist, but they are neither as pervasive as, nor of the type that the clinician's bias suggests. Moreover, just as cultural factors are closely related to the state of the labour market, so, too, the success of affirmative action and anti-discrimination programmes is linked to the economy (Wilson 1991, p. 608).

• Life Cycle Variations •

In one of the earliest poverty studies, Rowntree suggested in 1901 that poverty among workers in York varied over the life cycle. He was referring to 'primary' poverty, that is, poverty in the strictest sense of the term. A family was in primary poverty when its total earnings were 'insufficient to obtain the minimum necessaries for the maintenance of merely physical efficiency' (Rowntree 1902, p. 86). Even with expert housekeeping and no expenditure whatsoever on anything but necessities, a family on such an income was, quite simply, underfed. As shown in Figure 3.3, there were three periods in life when poverty was more likely: early childhood, the childbearing years, and old age. To say that poverty was 'more likely' during these three phases is something of an understatement. Every labourer with three or more children spent about ten years in this phase when 'he and his family will be *underfed*' (Rowntree 1902, p. 135). A single income was not sufficient to prevent poverty during childbearing years, while the poverty of old-age came from the lack of any income-earner.

Figure 3.3: *Rowntree's life cycle of poverty*

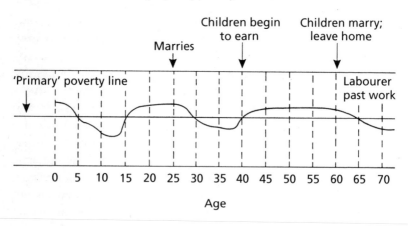

Source: Rowntree 1901, p. 137

Strictly speaking, Rowntree's diagram shows the distribution of income by age-group at the time of his survey in 1899, rather than a true picture of the development of income in the course of the life of an individual (Kaelble and Thomas 1991, p. 51). Thus, Rowntree's diagram shows families with 13-year-old children having a very

high incidence of poverty. The data from a single point in time—
1899—can correctly be interpreted as showing that both the children born in 1885 and their parents born around 1860 were in dire
poverty by 1899. A true life cycle account would tell us whether the
13-year-olds of 1899 again experienced dire poverty around the
year 1923 when their own children reached 13 years. Not surprisingly, true life cycle research is very rare, since it involves following
individuals over very long periods of time.

Among the few examples of true life cycle research is Elder's
work referred to above. It will be recalled that the age of the children he studied had a marked effect on the degree to which they
suffered from negative events, such as the Depression of the 1930s,
or benefited from later 'facilitating' events, such as the post-war
boom (Elder 1974; p. 1981). Similarly, Göbel used data from a
German worker's insurance company to track several birth cohorts,
and found that those born in 1900 fared much worse in later life
than those born in 1916. The younger group were the right age to
profit from the rising level of income in the post-war period (Kaelble
and Thomas 1991, p. 54).

If we take the term 'life cycle' in the broader sense used by
Rowntree, the question arises as to whether the same pattern
applies today. In other words, at a given point in time, does the incidence of poverty follow roughly the pattern it did in York in 1899?
The most obvious change is that poverty of the kind studied by
Rowntree in 1899 had already become rare by the time of his later
studies of York in 1936 and in 1950. In 1899, 15 per cent of 'the
wage-earning class' and 10 per cent of the total population were living in primary poverty (Rowntree 1902, p. 111). Using a similar definition, the numbers had fallen to 7 per cent of the working class
population and 4 per cent of the total population in 1936 (Rowntree
1941, p. 108). However, except for comparative purposes with the
1899 study, Rowntree used a substantially upgraded poverty line
(by some 42 per cent in real terms) in the second study, on the
ground that the early line was too stringent, and this revised measure became the basis for comparisons in the final study of York in
1950 (Rowntree 1942, p. 451; Rowntree and Lavers 1951, p. 1). By
1950, and using the higher poverty line, only 2.8 per cent of the
working class and 1.7 per cent of the total population had incomes
below the line. Moreover, one of the principal causes of poverty in

1899—low wages—had practically ceased to be a source of poverty by 1950 (Rowntree and Lavers 1951, pp. 31, 35).

Given the wholly relative nature of poverty measures in Australia today (see Chapters 3 and 6), it could well be asked whether the term 'poverty' used by Rowntree in 1899 and the poverty discussed in this book refer to the same phenomenon. It would be quite misleading to ignore the absolute rise in living standards over the period and conclude that 'nothing has changed' if Rowntree's life cycle pattern of 'poverty' is found to persist today. However, we can make a sensible comparison between Rowntree's 1899 poverty line and the Henderson poverty line applied to Australian data of 90 years later if we use them in a restricted sense, namely, to identify the periods in life when income in relation to need is at its lowest. With this question in mind, we now ask whether the life cycle fluctuations in income observed by Rowntree apply today.

One would expect that if there are changes, it would be because income from current employment is no longer the only source of income. Studies in Sweden have shown a marked decline in life cycle variations between 1967 and 1980. The biggest differences were in the fall in poverty among single parents and among the elderly (Erikson and Fritzell 1988). The story is not so clear-cut in Australia. We get quite large variations in what is going on, depending on how income is measured.

As we shall see in Chapter 5, poverty lines are usually based on so-called 'equivalent income'—current after-tax income, adjusted for certain family needs. Unfortunately for the reliability of poverty lines, equivalent income can be highly sensitive to what assumptions about family need are built into it. The wildest fluctuations of all are to do with the relative standing of the aged. For instance, single Australians aged 60 or over have either one of the highest or one of the lowest rates of poverty among the ten countries in the LIS study, depending on how equivalent income is constructed (Buhmann et al. 1988, Table 12). Unfortunately, there is no way of saying which is the 'true' figure.

If we switch from using income only to using full income, which also includes the value of assets and of time (see Chapter 2), we see another kind of variation. In Figure 3.4 the poverty line is set in the normal way using equivalent income, and results in 17 per cent of the population being below the line. We used this same 17 per cent level for a poverty line based on full income. According to both measures of income, there is an average probability of 0.83 (1 – 0.17) of avoiding poverty. Thus we hold constant the poverty *level* to enable us to contrast the difference in poverty *patterns* over the life cycle, depending on which indicator is used.

Figure 3.4: *Rowntree poverty cycle: full and equivalent income*

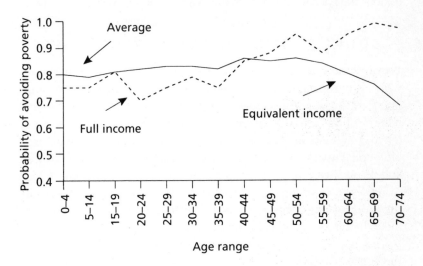

We can see in Figure 3.4 the income-only based measure (equivalent income) following something approaching the Rowntree pattern. In other words, childhood represents a period of increased probability of poverty, and retirement another, with age 40 to 50 having the lowest probability of poverty. However, when we switch to full income the story is very different indeed. On the income-only measure, young people are *less* likely to be in poverty as they leave home, whereas after age 60, chances of poverty rise sharply. The story is just the opposite for full income, with young people leaving home having an elevated risk of poverty that continues until about age 35. From then on, chances of being in poverty decline continuously with age, to the point that they are negligible around age 65. This difference arises from the fact that people accumulate assets over their working lives—including a house. Young people start out with few such assets, whereas asset ownership is likely to be at a peak around retirement age.

Our response, therefore, even to a modified version of the question of whether the Rowntree life cycle of poverty applies today is not a simple one. Childhood remains a period of greater risk of low-income in relation to need, though the 'need' of Australia in the 1980s is not that of York in the 1890s. When, in addition to income, assets and the value of time are taken into account, it is even clearer that childhood and the child-bearing years of adulthood are difficult periods today. The situation of the aged today is far less clear-cut.

SOURCES OF HIGH AND LOW INCOMES

We turn now to consider in more detail the personal attributes which are associated with having a high or a low income. We have previously *described* the types of individuals who are at the top and bottom of the distribution: whether they are young or old, male or female, migrants or local born, relatively uneducated, single parents, blue-collar workers, social welfare recipients, divorced, widowed and so on. Here we seek to *explain* the differences in income which we observe. In order to do so satisfactorily, it is necessary to isolate the independent effects of particular attributes on the position of an individual in the income distribution.

This requires moderately complex methods of analysis, some of the details of which are to be found in an appendix at the end of this book (Appendix 2). We present the analysis in terms of two sets of personal attributes. One set consists of attributes which we expect to influence a person's income but not, except perhaps in minor ways, to be influenced by that income. These attributes are, in economists' terminology, exogenous to a person's income. The other set consists of attributes which are expected both to affect and to be affected by a person's income. These are termed endogenous attributes. The attributes have been chosen to reflect the view that the systematic influences on the incomes of individuals are mostly those which affect their level of earnings, rather than other sources of material well-being. This implies that it is earnings, and savings from past earnings, which predominate in determining a person's standard of living, even when that standard of living is measured as the more comprehensive full income. In addition, a person's standard of living will be affected by sharing with a partner. We know that patient saving out of past earnings does *not* explain the wealth of the top wealth holders (Kotlokoff and Summers 1981). High levels of wealth mostly result from inheritance and successful speculation and innovation. The data on which we draw do not enable us to identify these sources of a high income/standard of living and are incomplete in this respect. But for the great majority of people, the earnings of household members over a period of time are the over-whelming source of their material well-being. McCallum and Beggs (1991) cite the finding that 22 per cent of people have inherited something and that inheritance comes in two waves: the first is when parents die and the second when a spouse dies. The amounts inherited are mostly not large. Thus it is reasonable to conclude that the standard of living which is experienced by most households is a product of their own earnings and savings behaviour.

We are able, in addition, to take some account of loss of wealth which arises from divorce.

In this section we also examine whether the effect of individual attributes on a person's level of income differs as income is defined differently. In all cases we consider the family income of individuals. But we vary the definition of income, from being simply after-tax money income to an enhanced version of income: full income. The purpose behind this exploration is to see whether the explanation of inequality in the annual money income of the household remains unchanged when a more comprehensive definition of income is used. This question fits into one of the themes of this book—namely, is it ever sufficient to use money income as a measure of standard of living, and if so, when?

• An Initial Description •

To begin, we present a simple description of the types of households which are at the top and bottom of the distribution of household income, based on recent ABS data (1992). These show several char-acteristics which stand out as typifying households that are in the bottom quintile of the distribution of gross weekly household income.[2] These are:

- They are predominantly (55 per cent) single people; only 16 per cent contain children and these are mainly single-parent households; one quarter are married couples without children.
- The *probability* of being in the lowest quintile is much higher for people over age 65 (the average age of the reference person is

59 compared with an average of 47 for all households); however, the *absolute numbers* of people aged 18 to 64 exceed those of people aged 65 or over.

• Overwhelmingly, they are dependent on government pensions and benefits for their income: these represent 84 per cent of average weekly income for the bottom quintile while wages and salaries contribute 6 per cent.

• More than any other quintile, they own their own houses outright (58 per cent compared with an overall average of 43 per cent).

In total, 12 per cent of *people* are to be found in the bottom 20 per cent of *households*.

The households in the top quintile make an interesting contrast.

• They *spend* only 1.7 times more per capita than do households in the lowest quintile, whereas their gross incomes per capita are 7 times and their gross income per household is 9.6 times that of the lowest quintile.

• Two-thirds are couples with children living in the household and another 20 per cent are couples on their own: only 2 per cent are single people.

• Ninety per cent of their income is from earnings (including self-employment income).

• Very few are over age 64.

• While only 38 per cent own their houses outright, another 42 per cent are buying their houses.

In total, 25 per cent of *people* are to be found in the top 20 per cent of *households*.

We may summarise the above information by saying that the households on the bottom of the distribution of household income predominantly contain people who are single and reliant upon government social welfare benefits. Many are also aged. In contrast, the households at the top of the distribution contain many more people: one of the reasons why they are at the top is because they have multiple income-earners. They are overwhelmingly reliant upon personal exertion income and most are married couples, many with children present.

The above observations refer to the distribution of gross household income. As we have discussed in earlier chapters, this measure does not provide a particularly good index of material well-being.

Economists argue that a better measure is expenditure, preferably measured on a household basis and adjusted by an equivalence scale. Expenditure measures the value of the goods and services which are acquired by the household in a period: it is this which is the source of material well-being. Income, by comparison, measures the capacity to buy goods and service, but does so imprecisely. Households can increase that capacity by drawing on borrowings and past savings in a way which is not picked up in a measure of income. Conversely, income can be used to increase savings or to pay off debt. Income used in this way does not contribute to the

Figure 3.5: *Lorenz curve for income per household and psuedo-Lorenz curve for expenditure and income per capital (by quintiles of household income)**

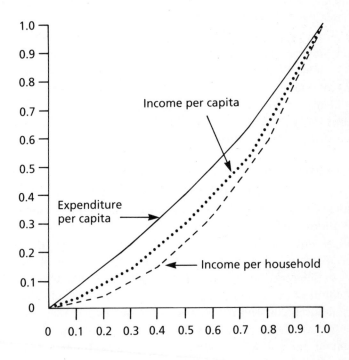

Source: ABS 1988-89 Household expenditure Survey, Australia Household Characteristics Cat. No. 6531.0 (p. 8)
*Income average weekly household income; expenditure is average total commodity and service expenditure

current standard of living (except, perhaps, in terms of peace of mind). It is therefore interesting to examine how the distribution of household income compares with the distribution of expenditure.

Figure 3.5 illustrates the Lorenz curves which result when households are compared on three different bases: 1) gross income per household, 2) household income per capita and 3) per capita expenditure. In each case the horizontal axis measures the cumulative share of *gross household income*. Thus only the first of the curves is a true Lorenz curve. The other two curves, which we refer to as pseudo-Lorenz curves, plot the cumulative share of gross household income against the cumulative share of per capita household income and the cumulative share of household expenditure per capita. They tell a striking story. Inequality in income per capita is much less than is inequality in income per household; and inequality in expenditure per capita is much less than is inequality in income per capita. When households are ranked by their gross income, their differences in expenditure per capita are a great deal less than are the differences in their income. Most studies of inequality take account of differences in household size and many also, with the aid of an equivalence scale, take account of differences in the composition of the household (see, for example, the Luxembourg Income Study data set). But the distribution of expenditure per capita is rarely used, let alone equivalent expenditure.

• Isolating the Factors Associated with High and Low Incomes •

It is a curious feature of research on the distribution of income that it has produced a weak theoretical foundation on which to base empirical work. While there is comprehensive, if contested, theory of the distribution of earnings and some hypotheses about the causes of differences in wealth, there is little theory that explains the distribution of income from all sources either among individuals or among households. This distribution is the outcome of many factors. These include the quantity and skill level of labour supplied by the household and the wages (which may be zero if members of the household are unable to find employment) which those skills command at any time. These wages themselves are a subtle outcome of competitive and non-competitive forces in the labour market and are likely to change somewhat over time. In addition to returns from employee labour, household income arises from the ownership of assets and the rate of return received on those assets; from self-employment; from the productive activities within the household and from irregular sources such as gifts, bequests and winnings. For the individual household, luck, as well as systematic components in the returns to labour and assets, will often be important. For the individual person, the composition of the household is itself a major determinant of material well-being. Changes in the composition of the household, such as through death, divorce, marriage and birth, have been shown to be an important means by which people move into and out of poverty. Finally, all the above influences are mediated by government intervention in the form of taxes, cash payments and provision of services.

It is a difficult task to separate out and quantify the effects of each of the large range of influences on individual income. This task is made more difficult by the fact that, while some are exogenous and thus may be treated as truly *causing* the observed level of income, others are endogenous and represent both cause and effect. Examples of the former are age, gender, type of school attended, parents' migrant status and parents' class: while these may be expected to affect the income of the individual, the income of the individual will not in turn affect them. Examples of the latter are labour force status (whether employed full- or part-time or not at all; whether employee or self-employed) and education; each of these may be expected to affect the income of the individual and in turn to vary with the income of the individual. Factors which are not so clearly categorised are health, own migrant-status, marital status and number of children.

The fact that an individual's income is the result of many different influences which interact in complex ways means that it is difficult to isolate the independent effect of any one factor. It is complicated further by the fact that an individual's standard of living is a result not only of his or her own attributes but also those of other family members. We wish to untangle this web in order to obtain a clearer picture of the personal attributes which are associated with a high or low income and standard of living. In order to do this, it is necessary to use econometric techniques to isolate the independent effects of particular attributes. Since the techniques themselves are not of intrinsic interest we confine their discussion to the appendix.

In the empirical analysis which we report below we do not pretend to have drawn upon a complete theory of the determination of either money or full income. Rather, we have used the data at hand to show the empirical links between a set of personal characteristics, which could not themselves have been caused by the individuals' incomes, and income measured in a variety of ways. To supplement these exogenous variables, a small number of additional variables are added which most probably do have a cause and effect relation with income (i.e., are endogenous). These variables are represented by instrumental variables in a two-stage least squares procedure.

The exogenous variables and their expected signs are:
- type of school attended—Roman Catholic (?), other private school (+) or other (–)
- migrant status of parents—English speaking background (0), non-English-speaking background (–)
- own migrant-status—English speaking (0) and non-English-speaking (–)
- socio-economic class of parents—Class 1 and 2, Class 3, 4 or 5, and Class 6 and 7 (–)
- age (+)
- age squared (–)
- number of siblings (–)
- marital status (+)
- health—represented on a numeric scale (+)
- proportion of assets lost on divorce (–) (LOSSEND).

The endogenous variables are:
- hourly earnings (+)
- labour force status—whether working full-time (+), working part-time (+), unemployed (–) or not in the labour force (–)
- years of education (+).

The regression estimation has been applied to various representations of income. We start with a measure which is close to the ordinary concept of the income of a family—after-tax income of all family members (FAMILY). The second income measure is one in which family income is divided by an equivalence scale to produce equivalent after-tax family income (EQINCOME). The third measure is equivalent after-tax full income (FULL) and the final measure is FULL with the addition of estimated net indirect taxes and benefits from government expenditure on education, health, non-cash social welfare benefits and housing (FULLGOV).[3]

The purpose of exploring these different measures of income is to see how sensitive the picture of sources of advantage and disadvantage is to the way in which income is defined. The force of the argument that money income is an inadequate measure of material well-being is greatly diminished if the picture of advantage and disadvantage, and the sources thereof, is unchanged by the measure used. We saw in Chapter 2 that the groups which were on the bottom *did* alter as the measure of well-being changed from equivalent after-tax family income to full income. Is this true also for the sources of material well-being?

We reported earlier in this chapter the finding that the degree of inter-generational mobility in socio-economic status in Australia is high compared with other countries, but not extraordinarily so. A high degree of mobility implies that parents' class does not determine that of the child. Our data will provide support for the high mobility view if the coefficient on parents' class is small and/or not significant. Parents have been divided into the three groups of high, middle and low on the class variable so that a clear ranking may be inferred (recall that classes 3, 4 and 5 cannot be ranked in terms of status). Those with the highest class are given the value 1 and those with the lowest class are given the value 3. Thus we expect parents' class to enter negatively into the determination of education and material well-being (that is, we expect the coefficient on this variable to be negative in the regression results).

The type of school a person attended is included as a vehicle by which advantage may be transmitted from parents to child. Attendance at a non-Catholic private school is expected to signal relatively high parental income, perhaps a relatively high level of interest in the child's education and higher quality schooling compared with attendance at a government high school or technical school. Attendance at a Catholic school carries less clear-cut predictions. On the one hand, for much of the period when the people in our sample were obtaining their secondary schooling, many Catholic schools were crowded and poorly funded and parents were often working class. On the other hand, the schools may have benefited from a productive level of commitment and set of values from both parents and staff.

If there is discrimination in the labour market or good language skills are important to employment success then migrants from non-English speaking backgrounds will be at a disadvantage. This expectation needs to be tempered by the knowledge that migrants, by the fact of their migration, have signalled a distinctive level of commitment to material well-being and enterprise in the pursuit of it. Numerous studies in Australia have shown that migrants from English-speaking countries look just like the local born population in their employment and earnings patterns. For these reasons we expect no effect from being the child of an English-speaking migrant, or being such a migrant oneself. If there is any effect from having a non-English-speaking background, we expect this effect to be negative (as shown by a negative sign on the coefficient for this variable).

The link between income and age is likely to vary with the income measure which is used. It was shown in the previous section how the age profile of the risk of 'poverty' varied with the distinction between equivalent and full income. Similarly, we expect the age/income profile to have a more strongly pronounced inverted U shape when FAMILY is used than when EQINCOME and FULL are used. In other words, the level of EQINCOME and, even more so, FULL for a household is likely to change relatively little as its members grow older, compared with the level of FAMILY. There are several reasons for this. One is that family size varies systematically over the life cycle. At either end, families tend to be small—many are single people—and money income tends to be low. The period when family size is at its maximum also tends to coincide with the period when money income is high. Thus, application of an equivalence scale will tend to smooth out the age/income profile. We expect the greatest effect to be apparent when we switch from money income to full income. This is because full income incorporates items which have a different age profile from money income, such as home equity and non-employed time. The possibility of a different relation between age and the various measures of income has been allowed for by the inclusion in the analysis of a squared term for age. In the absence of a squared term for age, it is implicitly assumed that income rises steadily as age rises. The inclusion of a squared term implies that income rises at a diminishing rate with age and may even start to fall at some age. This term is expected to be negative.

The health variable is self-reported and combines the answers to two questions. One asks about absolute levels of health; the other asks about health relative to peers. The variable is coded so that higher self-assessed wealth is represented by higher values of the variable. We expect people with higher incomes to have better health. Thus, we expect to find a positive coefficient on the health variable.

Information was sought on whether and why marriages had ended and how the property had been divided up in the event of death, divorce or separation. We do not know the value of any property. Rather, respondents stated what proportion of the property of the marriage they received (all, more than half, half, less than half, none). This information has been coded on a scale of 1–5 to form the variable LOSSEND. We expect it to have greater significance for women than for men, and when the income variable is full as distinct from money income. High values of the variable imply a large loss of property.

Marital status is expected to be important in explaining the various forms of income for two reasons. One is that all the versions of income refer to family income rather than to individual income. The other is that marriage is not a random event. The men who stay single tend to not do quite so well in the labour market as do married men. Women who stay single do not have the chance to share in a husband's income and assets. The variable is expressed as a dummy, with the value 1 if a person is currently married, de facto or de jure, and 0 otherwise. We expect the coefficient on the variable to be positive, indicating that married people have higher incomes than do others.

• Results •

Two sets of results are presented. In the first, all the relevant variables have been included in their original form, without the use of instrumental variables. An ordinary least squares (OLS) regression procedure has been used. Women have been analysed separately from men in order to make it possible for the effects of any or all of the variables to differ between the sexes. In the second set of results, the variables which we judge to be endogenous have been replaced by their predicted values.

The choice as to which is the preferred approach is not clear-cut—hence, we present the results of them both. However, only the results of the two-stage least squares regression is presented in the text (Tables 3.3 and 3.4). The other results are to be found in Appendix 2.

It should be noted that the various measures of income are each calculated in a way which attributes similar levels to both members of a married couple. This makes the different coefficients for men and women particularly interesting. Of course, not everyone is married and the different experiences of men and women will be reflected in the incomes of single people. But 74 per cent are married, so the differences among singles will be greatly muted in the aggregate data. The coefficients on variables such as education and hourly earnings are different for women as compared with men. This implies that the sexes arrive at their outcomes by different paths.

Several variables which were initially included have not been reported in these results because they did not appear as significant in any of the equations: nor did dropping them from the equation affect the coefficient or t statistic of the remaining variables in anything other than a minor way. The dropped variables are school attended, number of siblings, and parents' migrant status. We infer that if these factors have an influence on a person's income, it is only in subtle and indirect ways.

Consider first the women. Their FAMILY income is reasonably well explained by the variables in the equation: the R^2 is 0.39. Healthy, young, educated, married women earning good wages have the highest family incomes. Note that for none of the versions of income is parent's class a significant predictor of daughter's outcome. Neither is migrant status from an English-speaking country. This is not the case with migrant women from non-English-speaking countries, who are disadvantaged on all four measures of income. We thus need to qualify the more optimistic conclusions for an open society that are suggested by the lack of predictive significance of the type of school attended and for parents' migrant status.

Table 3.3: *Two-stage least squares regression explaining the sources of different versions of income*

VARIABLE	EQUIVALENT INCOME COEFFICIENT		T STATISTIC		FAMILY INCOME COEFFICIENT		T STATISTIC	
	Males	Females	Males	Females	Males	Females	Males	Females
Constant	1098.487	-28932.000	0.099	-1.818	-17692.000	-29981.000	-1.423	-1.666
Parents' class	-746.042	218.572	-0.896	0.269	-351.674	341.001	-0.382	0.376
Migrant from Eng. speaking country	197.269	1186.746	0.173	0.990	528.425	1320.625	0.412	0.977
Migrant from non-Eng. speaking country	-1842.023	-2323.168*	-1.671	-2.023	-1351.344	-3738.731*	-1.108	-2.912
Loss on end of marriage	464.639	-509.389	1.465	-1.959	439.113	-503.629	1.228	-1.708
Health	899.858	1100.029	0.803	1.041	684.340	188.325	0.547	0.160
Married	400.417	2266.724	0.312	1.087	10924.000*	15676.000*	7.631	6.692
Age	114.435	542.681*	0.691	3.164	447.563*	1037.906*	2.443	5.412
Age squared	0.837	-4.108*	0.425	-2.360	-3.209	-9.759*	-1.478	-5.014
Predicted years of education	1011.472	1993.901*	1.020	2.259	2238.096*	1776.673	2.030	1.798
Predicted after-tax hourly earnings	784.924*	678.941*	7.151	8.386	1304.419*	1177.975*	11.296	13.083
Predicted currently unemployed	-6816.014	4098.473	-0.853	0.283	-17429.000	-16904.000	-1.944	-1.031
Predicted not in labour force	2472.142	1640.784	0.559	0.289	2405.493	12212.000	0.494	1.932
R2 (adjusted)	0.129	0.185			0.354	0.388		
Deg. of freedom	703.000	676.000			725.000	703.000		

Table 3.4: *Two-stage least squares regression explaining the sources of different versions of income*

VARIABLE	FULL INCOME COEFFICIENT		T STATISTIC		FULL INCOME NET GOVERNMENT COEFFICIENT		T STATISTIC	
	Males	Females	Males	Females	Males	Females	Males	Females
Constant	-41933.000*	-48030.000	-2.059	-1.505	-31847.000	-36519.000	-1.523	-1.188
Parents' class	-967.102	2142.588	-0.615	1.499	-892.799	2002.427	-0.589	1.455
Migrant from Eng. speaking country	-2861.026	-2042.158	-1.394	-0.962	-2823.423	-1968.579	-1.428	-0.963
Migrant from non-Eng. speaking country	-904.288	-4434.856*	-0.440	-2.178	-971.347	-4191.405*	-0.491	-2.137
Loss on end of marriage	-143.055	-1554.976*	-0.253	-3.400	-134.424	-1503.535*	-0.247	-3.414
Health	1477.720	1835.178	0.717	0.980	1562.587	1836.481	0.787	1.018
Married	969.135	5124.176	0.403	1.313	-1456.190	2239.533	-0.629	0.596
Age	711.150*	794.123*	2.238	2.684	575.904	622.253*	1.881	2.184
Age squared	-0.364	-3.129	-0.096	-1.039	1.020	-1.119	0.279	-0.386
Predicted years of education	3353.519	4876.623*	1.846	3.138	3017.680	4626.544*	1.724	3.091
Predicted after-tax hourly earnings	741.893*	1208.895*	3.425	8.712	622.275*	1112.409*	2.982	8.324
Predicted currently unemployed	-4598.177	-12953.000	-0.305	-0.413	-2410.582	-12556.000	-0.166	-0.415
Predicted not in labour force	11159.000	-1966.026	1.357	-0.205	9998.387	-3283.480	1.262	-0.356
	R2 (adjusted)		0.292	0.1857	R2 (adjusted)		0.177	0.283
	Deg. of freedom		491.000	499.000	Deg. of freedom		499.000	491.000

Women's education, age and earnings are significant predictors for all the variants of income, with the exception of education as apredictor of FULL. The differences lie with marital status, which is highly significant for FAMILY but not for the other income measures and, as expected, LOSSEND. The influence of this last measure is only picked up in the full income versions of income. That is, the loss of property on divorce does not affect money income greatly but, for women, it does adversely affect their material standard of living. The expectation about the effect of age is supported in the data. The squared term for age, which picks up any propensity for income *growth* to decline with age and even to be reversed, is significant only for FAMILY and for equivalent income. This implies that the age-income profile is flatter for the full income measures than it is for the FAMILY income measure. This is an important conclusion. While women *appear* on the basis of their income to experience a fall in their standard of living as they age, in fact, when standard of living is measured more comprehensively, it is apparent that they do not.

Marriage has least effect on women's equivalent income and most effect on their FAMILY income. Its effect on FULL income (both degree of significance and size of coefficient) is muted by the introduction of net government indirect taxes and benefits.

The picture for males is different. While the overall explanatory power of the models is consistently greater for men, the number of variables which are significant is in each case fewer. For both sexes the model is least satisfactory in explaining equivalent income and most successful in explaining family income. Only hourly earnings are significant in predicting all the forms of income for men. As with women, parents' class and English-speaking migrant status are nowhere significant. But unlike women, non-English-speaking migrant status is not significant for men. Again, as with women, the labour force status variables of unemployed and not in the labour force are not significant for men.

We conclude the following from the tables:
- Education, hourly earnings and health all significantly predict the various measures of income for both men and women, in the expected positive direction.
- The model explains family income and full income quite well, but is less satisfactory in explaining equivalent income.

• Being unemployed or out of the labour force is *not* significantly associated with lower income (in any of its varieties) for either women or men.

• Being older has a substantial positive effect on all forms of women's incomes and also on men's family and full incomes (but not on their equivalent income).

• Marriage has a large and highly significant positive effect on the family income of both men and women, but a non-significant effect on their equivalent income (either money or full income). This suggests that, on average, the higher incomes of married couples are absorbed in providing for children.

• There is little sign that high socio-economic status parents has a direct impact on the income of children.

• Migrant women from non-English speaking backgrounds have significantly lower levels of all the forms of income. However, there is no sign of significant disadvantage among the men.

• Health affects income through its impact on earnings, education and labour force status; it has no independent effect.

• For women, *but not for men*, the loss of property on divorce is a significant factor in reducing full income (but not money income).

• The predicted level of a person's *hourly* earnings has a strongly positive effect on all the forms of income for both men and women. Curiously, the size of the effect on full income is greater for women than for men.

NOTES

[1] For an account of the debate on this issue see Goldthorpe (1980, pp. 17–27)and Erikson and Goldthorpe (1992, p. 396).

[2] This income is before tax and includes government cash social welfare benefits.

[3] All the data are from the Australian Standard of Living survey, except the group of indirect taxes and benefits. This last group is taken from the 1988–89 Household Expenditure survey (ABS 1992). See Chapter 1 for a discussion of the calculation of full income.

4

MATERIAL WELL-BEING AND HUMAN WELL-BEING

In the Introduction, we explained why the primary focus of this book is material well-being. We then went on to foreshadow that we would take up in this chapter the question of how material well-being relates to the rest of life—what we have called human well-being. There are two reasons why we believe this is necessary. The first relates to the ever-present risk of what Whitehead has called 'the fallacy of misplaced concreteness' (Whitehead 1978). The second reason relates to a conception of justice according to which it is essential to preserve the separate meaning of the different spheres of life (Walzer 1985).

Whitehead defined the fallacy of misplaced concreteness as 'neglecting the degree of abstraction involved when an actual entity is considered merely so far as it exemplifies certain categories of thought' (p. 7). In a more general sense, 'it is the fallacy involved whenever thinkers forget the degree of abstraction involved in thought and draw unwarranted conclusions about concrete actuality' (Daly and Cobb 1989, p. 36).

An example of misplaced concreteness would be to take the theoretical construct we have used to define material well-being ('that aspect of human life which is affected by a change in produced goods and services') and conclude that a particular individual who is 'rich' in this sense is 'rich' in all aspects of life. A rather more insidious instance of the fallacy would be to conclude, at least implicitly, that there *are* no other pertinent aspects of life. This would be the case, for instance, if we concluded that full income is not only a good measure of material well-being, but that what it does not measure (for example, a sense of community) does not exist, or has no importance. What begins as a useful abstraction for particular analytic purposes, ends as being seen as reality.

One way of attempting to avoid misplaced concreteness is to resort to ever more expansive abstractions. For instance, 'wealth' may be defined not merely in terms of material well-being, but to include happiness, inter-personal relations, health, a sound relation to one's environment, and so on. If this sounds exaggerated, consider the 1947 definition of health adopted in the charter of the World Health Organization: 'a state of complete physical, mental and social well-being and not merely the absence of disease or infirmity' (Hetzel 1980, p. 16). Abstractions this general not only move even further from the concrete, but, in addition, are so broad as to be practically useless as theoretical constructs.

Our solution is to devote this chapter to the relationship between material well-being and some aspects of 'the rest of life' as an explicit reminder that the abstraction 'material well-being' covers only one aspect of human life. Since our aim is largely to illustrate the *manner* in which material well-being covers only one aspect of life, our purpose will be served if we broaden our horizon to three selected areas: happiness, health, and social participation. All three are facets of life where the relationship with material well-being has been widely discussed, and where abundant data are available. This discussion will be shown to have quite practical implications in Chapter 6, where we ask whether social welfare policy can be based on considerations of material well-being alone, or whether it should embrace wider aspects of life.

It is at this juncture that the second reason for this chapter emerges. In the Introduction we described Walzer's theory of justice according to which there are different spheres of life, involving different goods, with different meanings—consequently, there should be a plurality of principles of distribution. Thus, whereas the market-place is a highly appropriate means for the distribution of money and of commodities, most societies do not extend the principles of market-place to the sale of office, and none we know of to the sale of friends (Walzer 1985, pp. 3–30). In line with this reasoning, justice is infringed if any particular good has dominance—that is, if its possession determines one's standing in all other spheres of life. In a country such as Australia, the most likely candidate for a dominant good is wealth. With this in mind, we will examine in this chapter the extent to which wealth, or material well-being, dominates three crucial areas of life: happiness, health, and social participation. Our findings will have major implications for the discussion of public policy.

MATERIAL WELL-BEING AND HAPPINESS

Few would claim that happiness can be identified directly with material well-being. Economists, who would probably omit this chapter entirely, start from a strong philosophical commitment to the primacy of individual preferences, and an assumption that human well-being rises as the options open to people increase. Material resources are important in that they expand the range of options. If accurately measured, they are direct indicators of command over resources, and consequently are seen as proxy indicators of the welfare of the nation and of the individual. This does not, however, equate material resources with happiness.

If material well-being is not the same as happiness, how well does it serve, then, as a proxy? Not very well, it would seem. In cross-sectional studies, rich people invariably declare themselves to be happy more often than do poor people, but not by a large margin. Figures 4.1 to 4.6, based on the Australian Standard of Living study (ASL), show two ways of thinking about the relationship between happiness and material well-being. In Figures 4.1 to 4.3 the

119

Figure 4.1: Happiness and material well-being, age 20–29

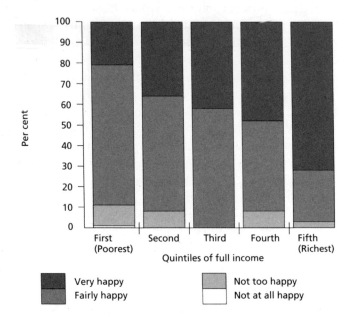

Figure 4.2: Happiness and material well-being, age 30–54

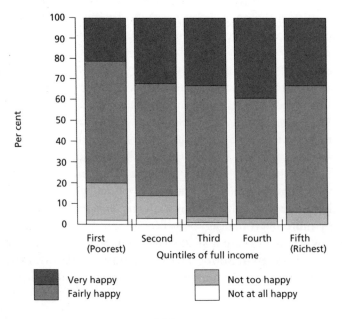

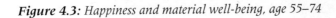

Figure 4.3: *Happiness and material well-being, age 55–74*

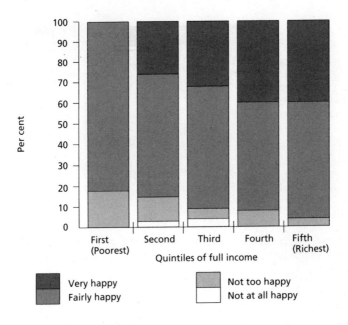

similarities in scores are more apparent—the vast majority at every level of material well-being rate themselves as either happy or very happy. In contrast, Figures 4.4 to 4.6, based on the same data, accentuate the differences—in each age group, the rich invariably score higher than the poor. These kinds of findings are remarkably consistent across countries.

Duncan found that 90 per cent of variation in satisfaction scores occurs for respondents with the same income, and only 10 per cent is associated with income differences (Duncan 1975). One does not have to accept the precise accuracy of these numbers in order to conclude that variance in income at least, and probably also variance in broader material well-being, does not translate closely into differences in happiness. Furthermore, the static picture of the rich being happier than the poor within a given country does not translate clearly into rich countries having greater average levels of happiness than poor countries. In a 1960s study of happiness in fourteen countries with widely differing levels of GNP, ten had average scores falling within a very narrow band: Nigeria, Philippines, Egypt, Panama, Brazil, Yugoslavia, Japan, Poland, Israel and West Germany

Figure 4.4: *Happiness and material well-being, age 20–29*

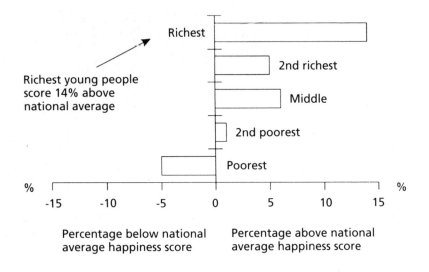

Figure 4.5: *Happiness and material well-being, age 30–54*

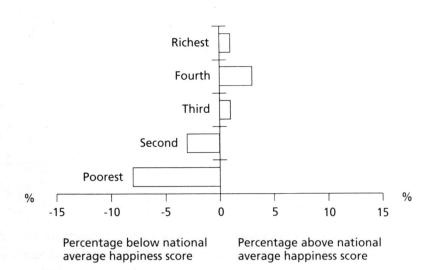

Figure 4.6: *Happiness and material well-being, age 55–74*

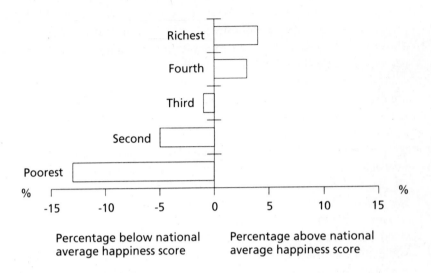

Percentage below national average happiness score

Percentage above national average happiness score

(Easterlin 1974, p. 106). As for changes over time within the one country, what little evidence is available suggests that a rise in real income *for all* has little effect on levels of happiness (Easterlin 1974; Duncan 1975). The most plausible explanation seems to be that material aspirations and tastes vary with national income, and that the frame of reference people use in judging their situation is a national one. Buying power matters less than having more money than others (Diener et al. 1985; Easterlin 1973; Wachtel, 1983). Is there a level at which one's relative wealth ceases to matter, and is no longer associated even weakly with greater happiness? If there is, it was not evident among a sample from the *Forbes* list of wealthiest Americans, who showed the usual small but significantly greater level of happiness than their less wealthy compatriots (Diener et al. 1985).

The low correlation between indicators of material well-being and those that focus on subjective states such as happiness and life satisfaction has produced sharply differing conclusions. What might be called the 'objective' school notes the low correlation, and concludes that since subjective indicators merely show how people adapt to their surroundings, so much the worse for subjective indicators.

These researchers see little theoretical interest in studies that tell us of 'the forbearance of the poor and the discontent of the rich' (Johansson 1976). This is the position of Scandinavian researchers in particular, and also those who follow in the British tradition of Titmuss, with his emphasis on command over resources over time (Erikson and Uusitalo 1987; Titmuss 1962).

Among those who use subjective indicators of well-being there are divergent schools. The first agrees with the proposition that sub-jective (self-assessed) well-being does indeed reflect the gap between aspirations and current situation, and in any stable situation the gap is small, since people adjust their aspirations to reality. Their more psychologically oriented rivals query the explanatory power of this model, and find more plausibility in theories such as the human *sense of relative superiority*. Fully 86 per cent of Australians, for instance, rate themselves as 'above average' in performance of their main job (Headey and Wearing 1988; Headey 1989). In this view, subjective well-being is enhanced by perceiving oneself as being ahead of the pack. Thus, though the explanation is still in terms of adaptive responses, there is disagreement as to the nature of the adaptive mechanism.

Where users of subjective indicators tend to agree is in their con-clusion that since material indicators tell us so little about life satis-faction, that is a very good reason to prefer the subjective indicators.

At one level, we are probably dealing here with a genuine differ-ence in values as to 'whether factual living conditions or satisfaction is the core of welfare' (Erikson and Uusitalo 1987, p. 191). However, there are many instances where it is not a question of choosing *either* objective *or* subjective indicators. A useful analogy may be drawn from the debate on the role of expert and lay opinion in environmental issues. If a population is being poisoned by environ-mental pollution, that fact is surely of interest, whether the victims are aware of it or not. But in a different context, an equally valid question is whether a location is perceived as peaceful, exciting, frightening or depressing—judgments that can only be made on the basis of subjective, lay opinion (Eyles 1990). Similarly, the choice between objective or subjective indicators will depend largely on what issues are being addressed. Our point in this chapter is that despite our obvious interest in objective indicators, it would be an error to bracket out all other aspects of reality.

• Sources of Happiness •

To this point, the argument has been that there is a low correlation between material well-being and happiness, and that some kind of adaptive mechanism seems to be at play whereby people come to terms with their situation, either by lowering their aspirations, or by comparing themselves to others who are worse off. We can throw further light on this relationship by asking what things *do* contribute to happiness? One serious scholar of this subject goes so far as to say, 'The issue is that commodities themselves, and the income to purchase them, are only weakly related to the things that make people happy: autonomy, self-esteem, family felicity, tension-free leisure, friendships' (Lane 1978, p. 815). In the same vein, Knight (1923) claims that 'happiness depends more on spiritual resourcefulness, and a joyous appreciation of the costless things of life, especially affection for one's fellow creatures, than it does on material satisfaction'.

A strong argument can be made that these non-material sources of happiness would, in fact, cease to bring the happiness they do if they were to become marketable commodities. One could imagine a society in which money could literally buy everything that was a source of satisfaction. Then income would be perfectly correlated with what passed for happiness. As we pointed out in our discussion of Walzer in the Introduction, the conversion of all human experience into market relations would be a radical transformation of the meanings of these other 'spheres' of life, and probably cause the destruction of their capacity to bring happiness—at least as we know it. Thus, friendship is a major source of happiness, but 'bought friendship' would cease to be friendship and become some other kind of instrumental relationship.

A further limitation on the capacity of markets to deliver happiness has been developed by Hirsch in relation to positional goods (ones that are scarce in some absolute sense or are subject to congestion or crowding). In the words of the tourist whose visit to an exotic country was made possible only by cheap charter flights, 'Now that I can afford to come here I know that it will be ruined' (Hirsch 1977, p. 27). Using a different metaphor—this time de Tocqueville's analogy of the marching column—with the rich always ahead of the poor, but all moving on so that the poor eventually get to where the rich had been, Hirsch points out that where positional goods are concerned, there is a basic weakness. 'What is neglected is that by the time the sought-after ground is reached by the rear column, that ground will have been affected by the passage of the column itself' (Hirsch 1977, p. 167).

Markets are also competitive, and have been likened by Knight to a sporting contest in which the 'greater virtue is to win; and meticulous questions about the methods are not in the best form, provided the methods bring victory' (1923). Knight goes on to point out that competition—while enjoyed by winners and those with a good prospect of winning—is hostile to a sense of community and co-operation.

> *A strong argument for cooperation, if it would work, would be its tendency to teach people to like each other in a more positive sense than can ever be bred by participation in a contest—certainly in a contest in which the means of life, or of a decent life, are felt to be at stake (Knight 1923).*

To sum up, the association between material well-being and happiness is positive but weak—rich people are more likely to be happy than poor people, but only by a small margin. If all get richer together, self-reported happiness does not necessarily rise, or rise by much. In terms of life satisfaction, the chief advantage of having more money is that it gives greater control over one's life. However, if money really could buy everything, many spheres of life would lose their present meaning, and their present ability to bring happiness. There are positional goods that can indeed be bought, but can be enjoyed only by limited numbers. There are a finite number of desert islands for would-be Robinson Crusoes. Finally, the market relations of competition and quid pro quo, while productive of material wealth, are inimical to the happiness that comes from relating to people in co-operative and charitable ways. Thus, for the individual and for the nation, there may even be a trade-off between material wealth and life satisfaction.

• Sources of happiness: some Australian evidence •

The ASL survey contains several questions about people's levels of satisfaction with their lives. These include a four-level response to the questions 'How happy are you these days?' and 'When you think of the things you want from life, how would you say you are doing?'. We use these responses to examine the factors which are associated with high as distinct from low levels of satisfaction on these two questions.

An important issue is the contribution made by income to high levels of satisfaction: is it either necessary or sufficient to have a high income (variously measured) in order to feel happy and that one is doing well out of life? A tentative hypothesis is that income is not strongly associated with self-rated levels of happiness. The explanation for this is two-fold. One is that people adapt to their conditions, as discussed earlier in this chapter. The other is that it is not *levels* of income but *changes in levels* which induce feelings of happiness or unhappiness: it is precisely the human capacity to adapt which means that when a level of income has been experienced for a while it will cease to be a direct source of happiness. The argument is that feelings of pleasure or pain are generated directly by income in two circumstances (leaving aside incomes which are so low that life can barely be sustained). One is a change in the absolute level of a person's income, with feelings of pleasure or happiness when income rises. The other is a change in a person's income *relative* to the people with whom the person usually compares him or herself (Wachtel 1983). A crude test of this hypothesis is possible with the ASL data (refer to Tables 4.1 and 4.2 below), since they include a question on whether the respondent is currently better or worse off than they were previously.

The most notable feature of Table 4.1 is that in no equation is the income variable significant. While this is consistent with our earlier hypothesis, it *is* unusual to find that it has a negative sign. If taken literally, a negative sign implies that higher incomes are associated with lower levels of happiness. (Perhaps the sixteenth century English proverb 'Riches bring oft harm, and ever fear' has contemporary relevance.) We do not actually believe that higher incomes make people miserable, and note that in the 'snapshot' pictures reported above (Figures 4.1 to 4.6), there is a weak but positive association between happiness and income. Consistent also with the Wachtel hypothesis is the result that people who reported being worse off now than they were three years ago are significantly less happy.

The overall explanatory power of the equations is not very high, at an R^2 of about 0.21. Variation in the income measure between

Table 4.1: *Sources of happiness*

DEPENDENT VARIABLE: HAPPY	COEFFICIENT		T STATISTIC	
Variable	Males	Females	Males	Females
Constant	3.835*	2.292	6.097	1.829
Social support from friends	0.178*	0.159*	2.880	2.240
Class 1, 2 or 3	-0.100*	-0.027	-2.431	-0.638
English-speaking migrant	-0.030	-0.132	-0.391	-1.540
Non-English speaking migrant	-0.118	-0.321*	-1.560	-3.864
Own home	0.126	0.069	1.894	1.049
Worse off than 3 years ago	-0.215*	-0.118*	-3.758	-1.970
Loss on end of marriage	0.042*	-0.013	1.959	-0.727
Health	0.345*	0.191*	4.838	2.505
Marriage	0.398*	0.243	4.240	1.472
Age	-0.015*	-0.002	-3.193	-0.439
Can just get by on income	-0.092	-0.140*	-1.559	-2.230
Ratio of debts to income	0.213	0.102	1.558	1.131
Problem paying bills	-0.031	-0.113*	-1.017	-3.838
Predicted education	0.028	-0.054	0.541	-1.204
Predicted unemployed	-0.428	1.033	-0.745	0.771
Recently unemployed	-0.076	0.039	-1.001	0.494
Predicted not in labour force	-.962*	0.448*	-3.952	1.149
Full income	-0.000002	—	-1.0410	—
Equivalent income	—	-0.000003	—	-1.2490
R2 (adj.)	0.2003	0.2226	0.2128	0.2276
Degrees of freedom	488	481	625	600

Table 4.2: *Sources of sense of achievement*

DEPENDENT VARIABLE: DOING	COEFFICIENT				T STATISTIC			
Variable	Males		Females		Males		Females	
Constant	3.6921*	3.5305*	2.5075*	2.3440*	5.6640	6.0640	1.9790	2.3860
Social support from friends	0.2697*	0.2484*	0.2221*	0.2626*	4.2140	4.5220	3.0980	4.0360
Class 1, 2 or 3	-0.1078*	-0.0938*	-0.0839*	-0.0111*	-2.5330	-2.5180	-1.9850	-2.6060
English-speaking migrant	-0.0030	-0.0382	-0.1530	-0.0716	-0.0380	-0.5380	-1.7600	-0.9270
Non-English speaking migrant	-0.0331	-0.0703	-0.1389	-0.0853	-0.4230	-1.0030	-1.6520	-1.0970
Own home	0.0572	0.0663	0.1681*	0.1848*	0.8300	1.0840	2.5230	2.9680
Worse off than 3 years ago	-0.2275*	-0.2535*	-0.2460*	-0.2793*	-3.8330	-4.7930	-4.0650	-5.1020
Loss on end of marriage	0.0053	0.0091	-0.0215	-0.0099	0.2420	0.4380	-1.1600	-0.5890
Health	0.2632*	0.3197*	0.2255*	0.2230*	3.5600	4.8350	2.9300	3.1690
Marriage	0.2557*	0.2504*	-0.0248	-0.0449	2.5910	2.8520	-0.1480	-0.3110
Age	-0.0064	-0.0015	-0.0042	-0.0053	-1.3620	-0.3530	-0.8850	-1.1920
Can just get by on income	-0.1270*	-0.1847*	-0.2229*	-0.2568*	-2.0720	-3.3990	-3.5210	-4.4290
Ratio of debts to income	0.0961	-0.0115	0.0981	0.0531	0.6800	-0.1270	1.0760	0.5860
Problem paying bills	-0.1264*	-0.1240*	-0.1535*	-0.1607*	-3.9890	-4.4510	-5.1350	-5.7520
Predicted education	-0.0214	-0.0004	-0.0825	-0.0214	-0.4010	-0.0090	-1.8100	-0.5200
Predicted unemployed	-0.5864	-0.9674	1.1359	0.9586	-0.9850	-1.8420	0.8380	0.9370
Recently unemployed	0.0132	-0.0747	0.0764	0.0536	0.1680	-1.0550	0.9660	0.7160
Predicted not in labour force	-0.4806	-0.3287	-0.0854	-0.2847	-1.9060	-1.4710	-0.2170	-0.7720
Full income	0.000004	—	0.000005*	—	1.881	—	2.549	—
Equivalent income	—	0.000001	—	0.000002	—	0.498	—	0.579
R2 (adj.)	0.2669	0.2931	0.3936	0.3773				
Degrees of freedom	488	625	481	600				

full income and equivalent money income has little effect on either the explanatory power of the equation or the variables which are significant at the five per cent level.

Women are least happy when they do not have support from friends or family when they are ill, need someone to talk to about problems or need company (social support from friends); when they do not have good health; when they have trouble paying the bills, when they are migrants from a non-English speaking background; and when they report not having enough income to get by on or only just having enough to get by on. None of the other variables is significantly different from zero at conventional confidence intervals.

The picture is broadly similar for men but with some interesting differences. For men, being married is a source of happiness in a way that is not apparent for women. Older men and men who are predicted not to be in the labour force are, unlike women, less happy. This gives a picture of relatively unhappy single, aged men, where the lack of happiness is not arising from low income but from some other source. Lack of social support from friends and family and being worse off and in relatively poor health also contribute, as with women, to lack of happiness. None of this is surprising. In contrast with the women, the men do not report an association between stress in paying the bills and happiness.

The equations reported in Table 4.2 have been estimated in the same manner as in Table 4.1. Note that, especially for women, the overall explanatory power of the models is rather higher for DOING than it is for HAPPY. Once again, equivalent income is not significantly associated with how people say they are doing in terms of what they want from life. There *is* some association, however, with full income, especially for women. Overall, the factors which are associated with feeling one has done well from life are similar to those which are associated with feeling happy. One exception is own class. For both men and women, being in a higher socio-economic class is significantly associated with doing well, but not with being happy. For women there is another interesting difference, and that is the significance of owning their own home. This does not feature for men. Age, while something of a barrier to happiness for men, does not diminish their sense of having obtained what they wanted from life. As with happiness, marriage is important to men but not to women.

The conclusions we have drawn from Tables 4.1 and 4.2 must be tentative. The overall explanatory power of the equations varies from satisfactory (DOING for women) to small (HAPPY for men). We do not have a robust model on which to base the selection of variables, so there is a risk that the coefficients are biased by the existence of omitted variables. None the less, the story is quite strong and consistent: in terms of self-assessed contentment, once there is enough to get by, money and possessions are not very important—avoidance of stress arising from shortage of cash, is, however. Non-material dimensions of life, such as support and company, health, social standing, marriage and not being worse off than previously, are all important. In no case did education, being unemployed or having recently experienced unemployment or having a high ratio of debts to income show up as affecting people's feeling of doing well or being happy.

MATERIAL WELL-BEING AND HEALTH

As with material well-being and happiness, there is an apparent association between material well-being and health. Yet the interpretation of this relationship is complex. We will begin with what appears to be the straightforward association, and then go on to discuss how this might be interpreted.

There is evidence of a positive association between material well-being and health in Australia, whether material well-being is measured by way of the proxy of income (Australian Institute of Health 1987) or the proxy of social class as estimated by occupational prestige (McMichael 1985). For instance, McMichael used a four-rank Social Class Scale based on occupational prestige to compare the age-standardised mortality ratios for Australian males aged 15 to 64 between 1970 and 1977. Class A includes doctors, dentists and lawyers; Class B includes teachers, scientists, administrators, managers and farmers; Class C includes technicians, mechanics, carpenters, hairdressers; Class D includes timber workers, builder's labourers, storemen, council labourers, and domestic workers. Table 4.3 shows the clear inverse relationship between the occupational prestige scale and mortality ratios. However, the relationship is less clear when we move to selected causes of death.

Respiratory diseases and traffic accidents are traditionally seen as 'diseases' of poverty, and they show the expected gradation. However, colon cancer is more a diet-related disease of 'affluence'. Diabetes mellitus shows minimal gradation—despite a strong inverse relation with class in Britain, while the relatively weak relationship between class and ischaemic heart disease may well point to different risk factors operating in opposing directions (McMichael 1985).

Table 4.3: Age-standardised death rates (per 100 000 per annum) for selected causes of death, by social class: Australian males aged 15 to 64, 1970–77

CAUSE OF DEATH	SOCIAL CLASS			
	A (high)	*B*	*C*	*D (low)*
Respiratory disease	14.8	23.9	27.0	42.0
Traffic accidents	20.9	50.0	51.1	95.5
Colon cancer	15.9	15.5	12.3	11.3
Ischaemic heart disease	240.6	271.1	237.7	287.4
Diabetes mellitus	8.0	10.0	8.0	9.4

Source: McMichael 1985, Table 4

• Australian Standard of Living Study •

A complicating factor in studies of the relationship between material well-being and health may be that material well-being is not adequately measured. To reduce this problem we turn to the ASL data, which has rich detail on standard of living, especially as measured by full income. To summarise the description of full income given in Chapter 1, it is based on after-tax family income, adjusted for family size, and includes also the value of selected assets and of free time. As we argued in Chapter 1, it enables us to rank people on an index that gives a much more accurate indication than income alone of people's material circumstances. The health indicator used is self-assessed health, on a range of excellent, good, fair and poor.

In Figures 4.7 to 4.12 we follow a similar procedure to that used in Figures 4.1 to 4.6—that is, the same data are presented in two ways, with Figures 4.7 to 4.9 tending to emphasise the similarities in self-assessed health, and Figures 4.10 to 4.12 focusing on the differences. Not surprisingly, age is a major influence on health. Within each age-group, self-assessed health also improves with level of material well-being. In fact, the richest older people have marginally better health than the poorest group among the twenty-year-olds (Figures. 4.10 and 4.12). As with happiness, there is a positive but weak link between health and material well-being.

• Interpretation of the Apparent Links between Health and Material Well-being •

Figures 4.7 to 4.12 take the measurement of health as unproblematic. That is an heroic assumption—the difficulties in measuring or even defining health are, in fact, considerably greater than those we encountered in measuring material well-being. It is not surprising, therefore, that there should be major controversy as to how apparent associations between material well-being and 'health' should be interpreted.

Figure 4.7: Self-assessed health and material well-being, age 20–29

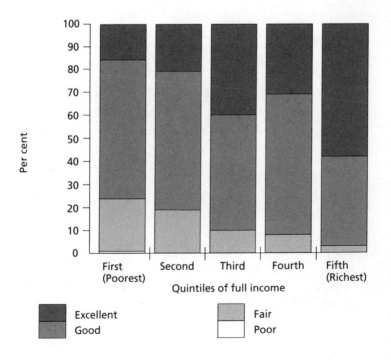

Figure 4.8: *Self-assessed health and material well-being, age 30–54*

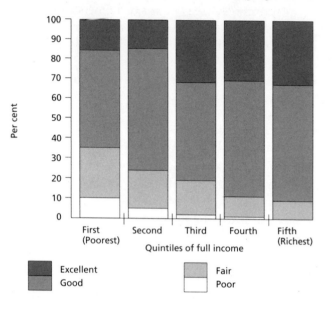

Figure 4.9: *Self-assessed health and material well-being, age 55–74*

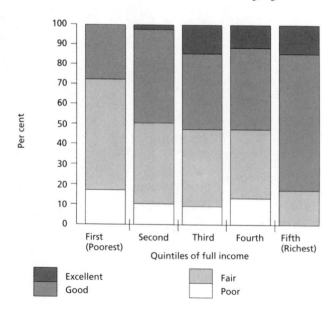

Figure 4.10: *Self-assessed health and material well-being, age 20–29*

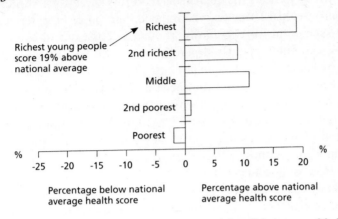

Figure 4.11: *Self-assessed health and material well-being, age 30–54*

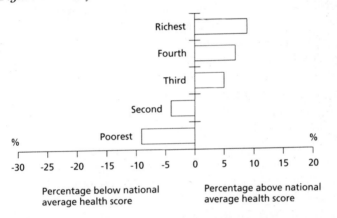

Figure 4.12: *Self-assessed health and material well-being, age 55–74*

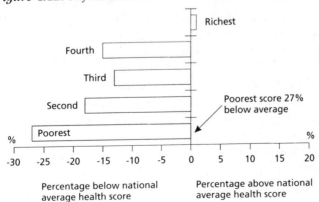

Health is frequently measured in terms of self-assessment, whether in global terms (excellent, good, fair, poor) or in terms of specific symptoms or conditions. Though self-assessment certainly tells us something about self-perception, it will be strongly influenced by cultural factors. Similarly, use of services may tell us more about their availability and the social propensity to use them than about health status (Illsley 1990). Medical diagnosis by experts appears to add a degree of objectivity, but the 'medical model' is strenuously rejected by many, especially proponents of preventative medicine, and by those who wish to define health in positive terms rather than as the absence of ill-health.

Given the lack of agreement on what constitutes 'health', it is not surprising that there is frequent debate as to the validity of indicators—that is, whether they 'really' measure health. One way around this problem is to side-step it, and to define health as a set of 'characteristics'. The 'characteristics' approach might select functional capacity (ability to walk a certain distance), pain, emotional state, or anything else deemed relevant (Culyer 1983, p. 7). The relativistic nature of the measures is apparent. But the question of whether they measure 'true' health does not arise: by definition, the indicator measures health or ill-health. However, users of a 'characteristics' approach still have to face the question of whether a particular bundle of characteristics is appropriate, a question whose answer will vary with time and place. For all these reasons, blunt instruments such as mortality and life expectancy are often preferred, at least for cross-cultural comparisons.

Probably the best-known modern study of the relationship between health and material well-being is the British Department of Health and Social Security survey known as the Black Report (DHSS 1980). There, very extensive use was made of mortality rates correlated by class. Its principal finding was that the class difference in health as measured by mortality rates between Class I (professional workers and their families) and Classes IV and V (partly skilled and unskilled manual workers and their families) had actually widened between the 1950s and the 1970s. The Report called for a massive increase in spending to redress this growing inequality.

The Black Report had been commissioned by a Labour government in 1977, but when it was published in 1980 it was accompanied by a Foreword by Patrick Jenkin, the Secretary of State for

Social Services in the newly elected Conservative government, dismissing out of hand its spending recommendations. Though Jenkin expressed doubt that the recommendations of the Report would have been effective in countering the growing inequalities, he did not question the finding of increasing inequality. Much of the subsequent and continuing debate has centred on the extent, or even the existence, of the claimed rise in inequality. A second stream of debate has accepted that there are growing class-related disparities in mortality rates, but focused on whether the cause lies in life style rather than in 'materialist' explanations.

• Rising Health Inequalities: an Artefact? •

The Black Report's evidence of growing class-related disparities in mortality rates was based on so-called *achieved* class—that is, class based upon current occupation, usually that of the male breadwinner. Yet the period covered by the Report was one of very high social mobility. The central issue for those who say the growing inequalities are an artefact is whether and how health affects one's chances of mobility. If we assume that the chances of upward mobility are greater for those in good health, and the chances of downward mobility are greater for those with poor health, then we would *expect* to find more ill-health in the lowest class (Stern 1983). In other words, the causal direction is not from class to ill-health, but from ill-health to class. What is more, the greater the rate of social mobility, the greater would be the health disparities.

Stern's argument rests crucially on the assumption that mobility into the most privileged classes is positively associated with good health, and that the converse is true of downward mobility. The assumption seems plausible. What remains at issue is how much of the observed disparities in mortality rates can be explained in this manner. Longitudinal data on health differences at ages 7 and 23 confirm that health is associated with mobility, particularly good health in the case of the upwardly mobile. However, this factor is not sufficiently large to explain all self-reported health differences (Fogelman, Fox and Power 1989). Furthermore, even if the apparent increase in disparities based on achieved class are shown to be an artefact, that leaves open the question of whether people born into a lower social class or income group have a higher probability of ill-health than people born into a higher social class or income group

(Stern 1983). What little information exists from longitudinal studies suggests that they do, though the disparities are less pronounced than when people are ranked by achieved class (Fogelman, Fox and Power 1989).

• Materialist Versus Lifestyle Explanations •

The Black Report made much of the distinction between materialist and lifestyle explanations of health inequalities, and, although it conceded that it was a rather slippery concept, in the end opted for 'some form or forms of the "materialist" approach' (DHSS 1980, Chapter 5). At one level, 'materialist' can be understood in a manner similar to our concept of 'material well-being'. On this understanding a 'materialist' explanation of health differences would be one that examines the manner in which differences in produced goods and services affect health. One would thus focus on income and all that income could buy—including education and medical services. However, there are also much broader versions of the 'materialist' approach, where the concept goes far beyond what we understand by material well-being to include the whole way of life and cultural patterns associated with a given class position. At this stage, 'materialist' and lifestyle approaches tend to shade into each other and the debate becomes one over the appropriate level of abstraction. In other words, adherents of materialist explanations do not deny that excessive alcohol, defective diet, and tobacco can harm health; what they query is whether it makes sense to examine lifestyle in isolation from the material circumstances of life. Users of 'lifestyle explanations' are similarly aware of material and social constraints on individual behaviour, and of the risks of blaming the victim. Yet their emphasis is, none the less, on individuals' ability to influence their own prospects of health and longevity, even if it is a question of 'making a start' rather than of taking total responsibility for their health (Hetzel and McMichael 1987).

Some would claim that the materialist/lifestyle distinction makes rather more sense in relation to specific causes of disparities in mortality. Traditionally, there have been clear socio-economic gradients both within and between countries in relation to infant mortality and to deaths from infections. Spectacular reductions in these causes of death have resulted from measures such as clean water supplies, improved sanitation, better nutrition, and better medical care. Yet major causes of death such as lung cancer and ischaemic heart disease are not very responsive to treatment or physical enivironment, but rather are closely related to lifestyle (Wnuk-Lipinski and Illsley 1990). It is claimed that precisely because lifestyles are changeable, the relationship between these diseases and socio-economic circumstances change over time.

The change in the lifestyles associated with wealth and poverty means that the 'diseases of affluence' and the 'diseases of poverty' are acquiring new meanings. For instance, although the poor in Hungary have poor health, so, increasingly, do the well-off. Some 70 to 75 per cent of income earners have a second job, and relative affluence has been paid for at the price of overwork, alcoholism and poor health. Life expectancy for most social groups is actually falling; in the case of male manual workers, it has reverted to the levels of the 1930s (Orosz 1990). In fact, a general feature of the non-market economies of Eastern Europe and what was until recently the Soviet Union has been a worst-of-all-worlds scenario in which the same groups simultaneously experience the older poverty-related diseases *and* the newer lifestyle and environmental diseases that might once have been associated with affluence (Wnuk-Lipinski and Illsley 1990).

On the whole, we regard the materialist–lifestyle debate on the determinants of health as one that is not particularly fruitful. The ambiguity of the 'materialist' concept and the false choice between 'materialist' *or* lifestyle explanations lead into blind alleys. We believe we can gain more insight into the association between material well-being and health that we noted in Figures 4.7 to 4.12 from a seemingly unlikely source: research on low mortality in poor countries.

• Low Mortality in Poor Countries •

We stated above that the principal aim of this chapter is to avoid the fallacy of misplaced concreteness—that is, forgetting that an abstraction made for one purpose necessarily ignores many aspects of reality, and then drawing unwarranted conclusions from the abstraction. The abstraction we are most concerned with in this book is material well-being, defined as that aspect of life that can be affected by a change in produced goods and services. More specifically, we are considering material well-being at the individual level. We do not ask how a particular distribution came about, but take the actual distribution as given. Though we use a relatively rich indicator of material well-being—full income—we do not consider the nature of the health-insurance system, or the availability, the accessibility and the quality of services. Now all of this is defensible, even necessary, if we are not to be swamped by more information than we can cope with. None the less, in keeping with the aim of this chapter as a reminder of what is *not* covered by our particular abstraction from reality, we turn to the experience of differing mortality rates among countries that have one thing in common: extreme poverty.

From the time of Malthus, there has been concern that the ultimate constraints on mortality decline are those of material resources (Caldwell 1986). Malthus took issue with Adam Smith's optimistic claim that an increase in the wealth of the nation would result in an improvement in the condition of the poor. Malthus predicted that, on the contrary, the fixed laws of nature would result in an increase in population that would necessarily outstrip any rise in food production (Malthus 1960, pp. 100; 109; Himmelfarb 1984, p. 109). Subsequent history has been kinder to Smith than to Malthus: there is indeed a correlation between an increase in the wealth of the nation and declining mortality. However, an examination of countries with very low per capita income shows some remarkable exceptions to the general rule of high mortality and low income going hand-in-hand, and this in turn throws light on the complex relationship between material well-being and health.

Caldwell made a detailed examination of the situation of Sri Lanka, Costa Rica and Kerala (South India), three countries or regions with exceptionally low per capita income, but with mortality rates on a par with rich, industrialised countries. Of the seven crucial determinants of low mortality identified by Caldwell in all three countries, five would come within our definition of material well-being (considerable inputs into both health and educational services; health services accessible to all; egalitarian food distribution; universal immunisation; high quality antenatal and postnatal services), while two would not (female autonomy; a political setting where popular pressure ensured services worked efficiently). If we go further, and ask what the common circumstances in which these seven factors occur are, the answer is largely in terms of social and cultural patterns. In all three places, there was a long tradition of relatively egalitarian attitudes, open political systems, and a strong emphasis on education, including education for women. In these circumstances there was both a strong demand for good health services and, consequently, there was also the political will to deliver them. Though Caldwell is confident that *all* countries today have sufficient resources to achieve low rates of mortality, he is less sanguine about the universal transferability of the social and cultural ethos found in Sri Lanka, Costa Rica and Kerala. At the other end of the spectrum, for instance, the oil-rich Gulf states demonstrate that high per capita income alone can be a poor indicator of mortality decline (Caldwell 1986).

One of the lessons to be drawn from the health experience of these poor countries is the extent to which the material well-being of individuals may diverge from the global picture portrayed by indicators such as average per capita income. An analogy may be drawn here with the experience of a rich country confronted by the economic upheaval of war, and the manner in which policy measures served to avert the decline in health that might otherwise have occurred. Titmuss points out that during World War II in Britain, rationing of food by price continued to operate as it always had done, but, in addition, there was rationing by coupons. This meant a fairer distribution of what was available. Furthermore, policy measures were taken to improve the quality of food, especially bread, and particular attention was paid to the health of mothers and of infants. From about 1943 there was evidence of an improvement in civilian health, rather than the expected decline (Titmuss 1950, pp. 523–32).

The example of World War II in Britain is particularly interesting, not so much because it shows a tenuous link between material well-being and health, but as a reminder that average per capita income can be a poor indicator of material well-being. In this instance, policy intervention in the form of rationing, regulation of food quality, and the provision of services reduced the link between income and material well-being at the individual level. The context of these policy interventions was a sense of community highlighted by the common experience of war. It was a time when policy makers were already extending their vision to the kind of society they wished to live in after the war. '[A]bolition of want just before this war was easily within the economic resources of the community; want was a needless scandal due to not taking the trouble to prevent it' (Beveridge 1942, p. 445).

According to this reading, material resources not only matter, but matter to an enormous extent. The very poor countries that achieved such amazing reductions in mortality devoted a relatively large proportion of their meagre resources to that end. Yet even this would have been insufficient without an educated and autonomous female population who could take advantage of the resources and knowledge that were crucial to achieving a breakthrough in terms of mortality. Moreover, a commitment to education, health and female autonomy does not fall out of the sky, but is related to social and cultural history. Finally, the example of British policy during World War II is a reminder that the level of specific material resources available to individuals need not reflect the state of the economy, and that consequently there is no paradox in the health of the poorest sections of the population actually improving during times of economic dislocation. Low mortality is achieved not so much by high *average* levels of resources as by the specific uses which are made of those resources. Policy can ensure that the specific requirements for low mortality—good sanitation, good nutrition, educated women and access to medical services—are distributed among the population more equally than is income.

To sum up, our argument is that to discuss the link between material well-being and health in terms of 'materialist' versus lifestyle approaches is misleading. The issue is not so much one of materialist versus lifestyle factors, but rather one of the interaction between cultural and material inputs into health, and of the social circumstances that make an egalitarian distribution of these inputs possible. This account of low mortality in poor countries and in a rich country in time of war has relevance also for high mortality in a rich country—specifically, the case of Australian Aborigines.

• High Mortality in a Rich Country: Australian Aborigines •

The health of Australian Aborigines as reflected in life expectation and in death rates is strikingly worse than that of the total Australian population. In terms of life expectation at birth, there is surprisingly little variation in this low expectation among Aborigines in different regions of Australia. In the best regions, life expectation at birth for Aborigines is 12 to 15 years less than for all Australians, comparable to that of Kerala, but well below that of Sri Lanka and Costa Rica. The worst levels are some 20 years lower than for the total Australian population, and comparable to India and Papua New Guinea (Thomson 1991; UNDP 1990; Caldwell 1986). Thomson points out that the lower expectations of life at birth for Aborigines largely reflect the extremely high mortality of young adults, as shown in Table 4.4 (Thomson 1991).

Table 4.4: *Aboriginal and total Australia age-specific death rates and rate ratios, 1985*

| Age group | MALES | | | FEMALES | | |
	Aborigines	Total Australia	Rate ratio	Aborigines	Total Australia	Rate ratio
0–4	9.5	2.7	3.5	9.2	2.2	4.3
5–9	0.6	0.3	1.9	0.2	0.2	1.0
10–14	2.2	0.3	7.7	0.4	0.2	2.5
15–24	3.2	1.4	2.4	2.7	0.5	5.7
25–34	10.1	1.3	7.7	3.3	0.6	5.9
35–44	18.7	1.8	10.5	6.9	1.0	6.8
45–54	26.8	5.1	5.2	22.5	3.0	7.4
55–64	58.3	15.0	3.9	38.3	7.6	5.0
65+	94.8	61.0	1.6	75.9	45.6	1.7

Source: Thomson 1991, Table 2.8

Note: *Aboriginal figures represent the combined data from the Queensland communities, Western Australia and the Northern Territory.*

One of the few areas of improvement in recent years has been a decline in Aboriginal infant mortality from 80 to 100 per 1000 live births in 1971–73, to a rate of about 30 in 1981, and as low as 21.3 for Queensland communities in 1986 (Thomson 1984; 1985; 1991). To place this in context, the Aboriginal rate is superior to that of Kerala, similar to that of Sri Lanka, and about three times that of Costa Rica and of Australia as a whole (UNDP 1990, p. 147; Caldwell 1986). Unfortunately, even taking account of the limited nature of data from the past, the progress with regard to infant mortality is not reflected in the older age-groups, where there is almost certainly a deterioration (Thomson 1991).

In terms of material well-being, the Australian Aboriginal population experiences high rates of many of the factors known to be associated with a low level of income: large families, a large proportion of single-parent families, and, above all, very low rates of employment. Aboriginal and non-Aboriginal families where no one is employed have similarly low levels of income. But more than 50 per cent of Aboriginal families with children contain no employed adult, compared to fewer than 20 per cent of non-Aboriginal families (Ross and Whiteford 1990; Ross 1990). Low income, however, tells only part of the story regarding material well-being, which, using our definition, also encompasses facilities such as health services. The mere existence of a medical service does not mean that it is culturally appropriate, or acceptable to Aborigines. Aboriginal-controlled medical services (AMSs) which began in the Sydney suburb of Redfern in 1971, and now number over sixty, were set up in recognition that issues intimately bound up with Aboriginal culture were at stake (Saggers and Gray 1991, p. 399; Reser 1991, p. 231). Not only are cultural issues such as identity and relationship to the community and to the land of decisive importance, but the culture itself is faced with problems 'which have no precedent and for which there exists no ready wisdom' (Reser 1991, p. 279). Among these relatively recent problems for Aboriginal communities are binge drinking, youth gangs, suicide, and faltering social control systems.

In these circumstances, it would be ludicrous to see the issue only as one of material well-being, that could in turn stand proxy for a relatively simple concept of health.

It is important for those who wish to understand 'the Aboriginal experience' as a Fourth World nation to see contemporary patterns of ill-health as shadows on the wall of the cave cast by events on a broader horizon. Morbidity and mortality statistics reflect an inheritance of loss and social upheaval that remains a central feature of Aboriginal consciousness today. The rhetoric of the struggle for land rights is a language for expressing and engaging broader concerns, and the activities and activism of the Aboriginal medical services encompass more than 'illness' or 'health' as they are commonly understood (Reid and Lupton 1991, p. xxi).

The accounts of low mortality in poor countries and of high mortality among Aborigines in rich Australia have in common the interaction of material resources with cultural, social and historical factors. Low mortality in poor countries demonstrates how a happy combination of cultural, social, and historical factors can make it possible for meagre resources to be used to achieve surprisingly high life-expectation. The Aboriginal experience shows that material resources are only one element needed to redress the legacy of 200 years of dispossession.

Let us return to our interpretation of Figures 4.7 to 4.12, all of which show an apparent small but positive association between income and health. Our subsequent discussion has qualified this in the following ways. Material well-being in the sense we have defined it ('that aspect of life which can be affected by a change in produced goods and services') is closely related to health, but only part of the story is captured by a measure such as full income, and even less by current income. It would be unwarranted to conclude from Figures 4.7 to 4.12 that a boost to average income (either current income or full income) would translate directly into better health. Our examples of good health in poor countries, and of the experience of the command economies and of Australian Aborigines, demonstrate that what is of central importance is the interaction between the average level of material resources, the specific uses to which those resources are put, and cultural, historical and social factors. This cannot be reduced to a choice between 'materialist' and lifestyle explanations of health differences.

MATERIAL WELL-BEING AND SOCIAL PARTICIPATION

In the Introduction we cited Aristotle's dictum that it is impossible or difficult to do fine things without resources. Participating in the community life, sharing with friends, and enjoying leisure—all activities that require some resources—are among those 'fine things'. Walzer points out that some early examples of welfare provision were not so much aimed at meeting material needs as enabling the poor to participate in community life. Thus, the Athenians distributed public funds to enable artisans and farmers to miss a day's work to attend the Assembly or to sit on a jury. Schools were not subsidised, but the great dramatic festivals were. In contrast, medieval Jewish communities did subsidise schools, above all to permit maximum participation in the religious life of the community (Walzer 1985, pp. 69–74). These examples can be seen as embryonic attempts to ensure that community life was not dominated by wealth.

With Walzer's examples in mind, we now ask how much material well-being tells us about this further aspect of life. We are interested to know if the positive but small association between wealth and happiness, and between wealth and health, that we noted earlier in this chapter also holds good for wealth and social participation. In particular, we want to know if those on the bottom of the scale in terms of material well-being are in some sense excluded from social activities.

• Exclusion from Social Activities •

Some scholars claim that not only is there a link between material well-being and social participation, but that poverty should be defined in terms of social exclusion. For instance, Townsend and Gordon define poverty as 'the point on a ranked income scale where deprivation grows disproportionately to falling income, and at which people withdraw from fulfilment of some if not all of their social roles and from participation in social customs, and are multiply deprived materially and socially' (1991, p. 48). Townsend and Gordon go on to define social deprivation in extremely broad terms, covering six fields:

- rights to employment
- family activities
- integration into community
- formal participation in social institutions
- recreation
- education.

Based on these six fields, Townsend and Gordon drew up a list of indicators of social deprivation which, together with their indicators of material deprivation, make up a total of seventy indicators of deprivation. They then used discriminant analysis to separate two groups: one that is multiply deprived on the index, and the other that is less deprived. Income is correlated with deprivation thus defined, and the poverty line was set at ' the income level at which these two groups can best be separated objectively' (1990, p. 49).

Given this methodology, poverty is not merely highly correlated with social and material deprivation, it is identical to it. In this chapter, we take a different approach, and ask how people's ranking in terms of material well-being correlates with social participation. The point of this question is to examine both the overall correlation between wealth and social activities, and the more focused question of whether those with least wealth are in some sense excluded from social activities.

• Index of Social Participation •

Drawing on the ASL data, we have constructed an index of social participation consisting of the following twelve variables:

1 CINEMA—frequency of going to cinema
2 THEATRE—frequency of going to theatre, concerts, museums
3 EATOUT—frequency of going to restaurants
4 PLAYSPORT (participant)
5 WATCHSPORT (watches live)
6 PUB,CLUB—frequency of going to pub or club
7 VISITS—visits friends
8 VISITED—receives visits
9 HELPSICK—someone to turn to (other than partner) when sick
10 COMPANY—someone to turn to (other than partner) for company
11 CONSOLE—someone to turn to (other than partner) with problems
12 HOLIDAY—away from home in past year.

Variables 1 to 8 were scaled according to frequency of activities, and variables 9 to 11 were scaled on a three-point scale of 'Always', 'Sometimes', 'Never'. The conversion of the twelve variables into a single scale was done using the United Nations Human Development Programme's HDI methodology described in Chapter 1. In brief, each person is given a score on a similar scale for each item, and the final score is simply the average of the twelve separate scores. As we commented there, and will later in this chapter where we apply the HDI itself, this methodology has the strength of being simple and intelligible, but it is weak in its rationale as to why each item should carry the same weight. It has the strength of giving a ranking of all on the one scale, but it can be subject to the criticism that a ranking on such disparate items has little meaning. Moreover, it should be kept in mind that such an index is an *ordinal* scale. Its only claim is that it ranks people in the sense that a higher score is greater than a lower score. It does not tell us the size of the gap between two rankings. For instance, while a score of .8 is greater than a score of .4, one cannot say that the first score is double the second.

Because of the strengths and weaknesses of the aggregated scale, we present the findings in two versions: one using the aggregated index ACTIVITIES, combining all twelve variables, and one with ACTIVITIES broken down into four subsets. We used factor analysis to arrive at the four subgroupings:

SUBGROUP:	VARIABLES:
YUPPIE	CINEMA
	THEATRE
	EATOUT
	HOLIDAY
OCKER	PLAYSPORT
	WATCHSPORT
	PUB,CLUB
FRIENDLY	VISITS
	VISITED
SUPPORT	HELPSICK
	COMPANY
	CONSOLE
ACTIVITIES	All 12 variables

• Material Well-being and the Aggregated Index of Social Participation •

In Figure 4.13, we present the summary results of the relationship between material well-being measured by full income and ACTIVITIES, the twelve-variable aggregated index of social participation. Figure 4.13 suggests a similar story to that already told about the relationship between wealth and happiness, and between wealth and

Figure 4.13: *Activities and material well-being*

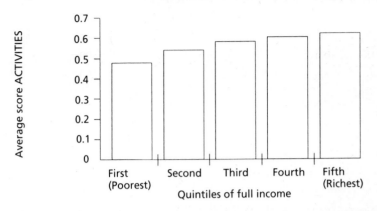

health—namely, that the association is positive, but small. The rank order correlation between full income and ACTIVITIES is only .29.

Is there support for the claims of authors such as Townsend that there is an income threshold below which social participation falls away rapidly? In the first place, the concept of a threshold only makes sense if we have interval level scales—that is, ones where there is a common metric, so that, for instance, we can say that the difference between a score of .1 and .2 is the same as that between .6 and .7. Neither Townsend's participation scales nor ours has that property, unless we make quite heroic assumptions. But let us assume, for argument's sake, that our index ACTIVITIES really has the properties of an interval scale. On this assumption, we tested the association between full income and ACTIVITIES and found no significant deviation from linear homogeneity. In other words, we found no threshold. At every level of income, social participation tends to increase slightly with a rise in income. While the links between income and ACTIVITIES is statistically significant, its explanatory power is very weak. Ninety-three per cent of the differences in scores on ACTIVITIES are associated with factors other than income.

• Material Well-being and Subgroups of Activities •

Since it could be objected that the aggregated index ACTIVITIES mixes chalk and cheese, we now examine the association between material well-being and each of the four subgroups of activities.

Figure 4.14: *OCKER and material well-being*

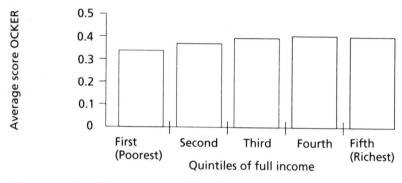

Figure 4.15: *YUPPIE and material well-being*

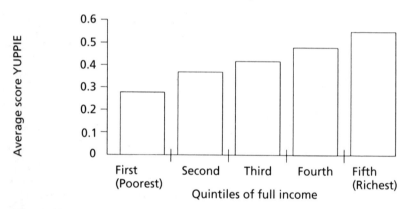

Figure 4.16: *FRIENDLY and material well-being*

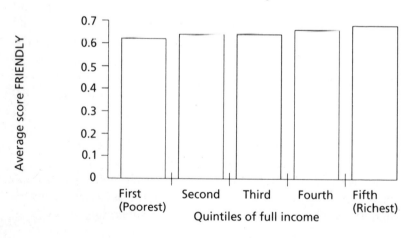

Figure 4.17: *SUPPORT and material well-being*

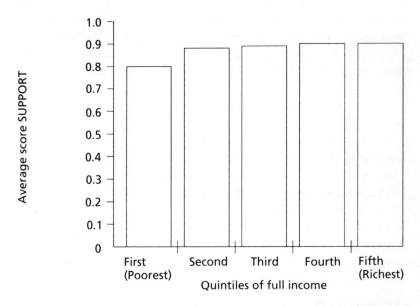

Once again, we present the results first in summary form in Figures 4.14 to 4.17.

Figures 4.14 to 4.17 already suggest what the statistics tell us with greater precision. There is a statistically significant rank order correlation between full income and all four indices, but in the case of FRIENDLY, OCKER and SUPPORT it is a very weak .077, .095 and .129 respectively. The association between YUPPIE and full income is relatively stronger, but still with a rank order correlation of only .415.

This breaking down of the composite index ACTIVITIES into four subgroups has been useful in telling a story with greater nuance than one that says simply that more money means a *slightly* greater tendency to take part in social activities. That account masks the modest association between material resources and the kind of activities included under YUPPIE, and the non-existent or extremely weak association with the remaining types of social participation. The link between income and YUPPIE activities—going to the cinema, theatre, restaurants and away on holidays—is about what we expected to find. However, in view of the claim that loneliness and social isolation are among the chief characteristics of low income

(Mack and Lansley 1985, p. 154), we were pleasantly surprised to find such weak relationships between material well-being and OCKER, FRIENDLY and SUPPORT. None the less, it is still possible that those on low income suffer a different kind of disadvantage— that is, the tendency to be *multiply deprived* in terms of the four different types of social activity. We examine this possibility next.

• Multiple Social Deprivation •

We define social deprivation as scoring in roughly the bottom 20 per cent of an index—since some of the indices are lumpy, it was not possible to select precisely 20 per cent in each case. On this definition of a 'problem', people could score between 0 and 4 problems, with the higher the score implying greater social disadvantage. The average scores for each quintile of full income are given in Figure 4.18. This time there is a small but negative association between income and multiple problems—that is, the higher the income, the fewer the problems. As usual, the association is not strong, with a rank order correlation of just .229. At the extremes of income, the

Figure 4.18: *PROBLEMS and material well-being*

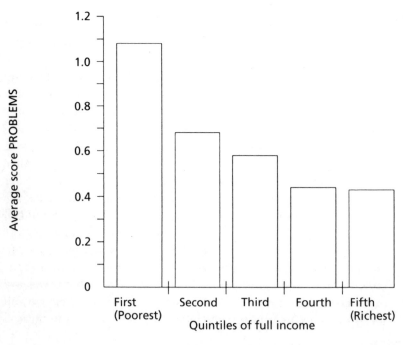

Figure 4.19: *PROBLEMS and material well-being*

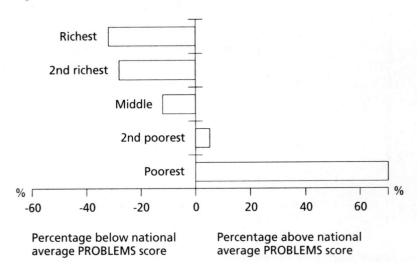

Percentage below national average PROBLEMS score

Percentage above national average PROBLEMS score

differences are more pronounced, as shown in Figure 4.19. One way of summarising this is to note the difference between the relative chances of the top and the bottom 20 per cent of full income having more than one problem. The bottom 20 per cent are five times as likely as the top to have multiple problems. This is despite the fact that 70 per cent of those on the bottom do *not* have multiple problems.

The relationships we have examined between material well-being and social participation all suggest that, for Australia, it would be too strong a statement to say that low levels of material resources *exclude* the poor from participation in normal social activities. There is, however, a greater probability of poor people being multiply deprived.

• Accumulated Misery •

In this chapter we have examined the relationship between material well-being and three aspects of 'the rest of life': happiness, health and social participation. In each case there was a significant but weak link with material well-being. We conclude by asking to what extent the same people fare badly in happiness, health and social participation, and how this relates to material well-being. As in the previous section, we define faring badly as scoring in roughly the bottom 20 per cent of the appropriate index. Since we have three

Figure 4.20: *MISERY and material well-being*

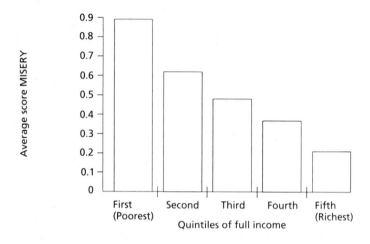

Figure 4.21: *MISERY and material well-being*

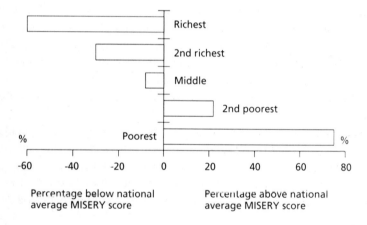

indices, scores range from 0 to 3 'problems', on the index MISERY. Figure 4.20 gives the summary picture of MISERY and material well-being. Overall, there is a low association between the number of problems in health, happiness and social participation, and full income (correlation .30). But once again, the extremes of full income tell a somewhat different story, as portrayed in Figure 4.21. Those in the bottom 20 per cent of full income are eleven times as likely as the top 20 per cent to have multiple problems. In fact, there are negligible chances of those in the top 20 per cent of full income having more than one problem in happiness, health, and social participation.

An examination of who the people with accumulated misery in this sense are is revealing. Low full income, low equivalent income, age greater than 55, Class VI–VII (skilled and unskilled manual workers and their families), and being a widow (female), divorced or separated are all associated with multiple problems.

To sum up this section on social participation and material well-being, let us return to our original questions: does the small but significant association between wealth and happiness, and between wealth and health, also hold good for social participation? Does a low level of material well-being result in some form of exclusion from social activities? The answer to the first question is yes, especially when it comes to activities where money is directly involved, such as attending the theatre or restaurants. However, we were surprised to find an extremely low association between material well-being and such activities as visiting friends and receiving visits, playing sport, and going to a pub or club. With regard to the second question, we could not detect a threshold of income below which social activities fell away so markedly that one could speak of 'exclusion'. However, there is certainly a greater *probability* of experiencing problems in social participation at the bottom of the income scale. At the other end of the scale, the very well-off are well insulated against social isolation.

We can conclude that a question raised by Walzer's work—whether community life is dominated by material resources—can be answered with a qualified 'No'.

- As with happiness and health, there is a positive, but small, association between the level of material well-being and that of social activities.

- That summary statement can be modified by distinguishing between various sets of activities. The association varies from moderately strong to trivial as we move from activities such as visiting restaurants to those such as visiting friends.

- A further modification is needed if we look at the extremes of income. At the bottom of the income scale, though the majority lead typically active lives, the chances of a low level of social activity increases markedly, while the chances of a low score on social activity are very small indeed at the top of the income scale.

A similar story emerges if we look at the chances of a low score not only in terms of activities, but also on an index of happiness and of health.

CONCLUSION

What have we learned in this chapter from our discussion of the relationship between material well-being and happiness, health and social participation? It will be recalled that for Walzer, a society where the distribution of all goods mirrored the distribution of material resources would be an unjust one, even if the distribution of material resources was itself relatively egalitarian. His basic objection is that if money dominates to this extent, the very meaning of the other goods would be perverted. If public office, justice, Divine Grace and friends can all be bought, the remedy is not to equalise people's buying power, but to cut the link between money and these other spheres of life. In fact, we have found that in each of the three cases we examined, the distribution of goods was only weakly related to income, and to the richer measures of material well-being such as full income. In Walzer's terms, this is a welcome finding. Yet there are many more facets of life than the three we have considered here: happiness, health and social participation. Moreover, there are other reasons than those raised by Walzer for shaping public policy. We draw these issues together in the final chapter: on the public policy implications of our discussion to date.

NOTES

[1] Table 4.1 is a two-stage least squares regression with the answer to the question 'Taken all together, how would you say your life is these days?', (HAPPY, scored 1 to 4) as the dependent variable. Table 4.2 is a two-stage least squares regression with the answer to the question 'In terms of the things you hoped to achieve out of life, how are you doing?', (DOING, scaled 1 to 4) as the dependent variable. The equations have been estimated using two-stage least squares procedures. The dependent variable is better characterised as categorical rather than as continuous; i.e. while a score of 4 implies greater happiness than a score of 2, it cannot be said to imply twice as much happiness. For this reason a multinomial probit technique may be more appropriate than ordinary least squares. In fact, in terms of the variables which appeared as significant, the two procedures produce the same result. We therefore prefer to report the OLS (ordinary least squares) results because it is easier to interpret both their coefficients and the degree of explanatory power. A two-stage procedure is used because it is preferred on theoretical grounds, since endogeneity is expected among some of the variables. Only a small amount of explanatory power was lost as a result of using this less efficient procedure, compared with use of simple OLS. Again, the variables which are significant are little affected by the choice of technique.

5

POVERTY IN AUSTRALIA

In this chapter we examine how poverty is measured in Australia, and what story this produces. We discuss the strengths and weaknesses of specific ways of measuring poverty, and whether, for all their faults, the commonly used poverty lines remain a useful device. In order to understand the issues we begin with an examination of the *concept* of poverty. The way we conceive of poverty will decide whether we think it can be measured at all; if it can be measured in concept, whether it is feasible to do so in practice—and, if it is feasible, how we should go about the task.

POVERTY IS AN ETHICAL CONCEPT

Philosophers speak of 'thick' or substantive ethical concepts that have descriptions of what the world is like built into them, as well as valuations of the situation (Williams 1985, pp. 129; 140; Donnison 1991, p. 43). Examples are treachery, promise, brutality, courage, gratitude. Scholars brought up in the English-speaking world since the time of Hume tend to be uncomfortable with such concepts. They do not give rise to analytical propositions of the kind $2+2=4$; they are not simply empirical statements dealing with 'facts'; they *do* imply statements of value, statements that generations of students have been taught to regard as not belonging in scientific discourse. Yet such concepts are useful, and they guide our actions. In fact, one of their chief characteristics is that they do provide reasons for action.

Poverty is such a 'thick' ethical concept. It describes situations such as hunger, lack of shelter, clothing or some other material resources. It also contains at least an implicit evaluation of those situations, and gives reasons for action. The public policy evaluation (as distinct from the ascetic) is almost invariably negative, implying some kind of claim for relief, but the reasons given as a basis for action, and the consequent urgency of the action vary widely. At one extreme, for instance, we have the thirteenth century teaching of St Thomas Aquinas that human necessity takes precedence over laws regulating property ownership. The poor always have a contingent claim on what is held by others in 'superabundance'. He argued that since the poor are so numerous that not all can be relieved, it is normally up to the individual to decide how the wants of the sufferers should be met. But Aquinas admitted exceptions to this rule:

> If, however, there is so urgent and blatant a necessity that the immediate needs must be met out of whatever is available, as when a person is in imminent danger and he cannot be helped in any other way, then a person may legitimately supply his own needs out of another's property, whether he does so secretly or flagrantly. And in such a case there is strictly speaking no theft or robbery (Aquinas 1974, p. 81).

It will be noted that for Aquinas, the claims of those in necessity are based on characteristics of the poor themselves, not on the effect poverty has on the non-poor. In sharp contrast we find Rowntree some six centuries later basing his pioneering work on poverty lines on the consequences of poverty for employers. Rowntree found that labourers supporting a family on minimum wages were, quite simply, underfed, and as such would be inefficient workers (Rowntree 1902, p. 221).[1] While both Aquinas and Rowntree are using extreme poverty in a 'thick' ethical sense—each uses it both as a description and as a ground for action—the *reasons* for action differ markedly.

Other reasons for relieving poverty are also advanced. Poverty is a form of avoidable pain and human suffering (Donnison 1991, p. 58); a decent sympathy for the poor is one of our shared values (Joseph and Sumption 1979, p. 27). In terms harkening back to Aquinas, Goodin points out that even if those of the poor who are very old, blind, very young or disabled are unlikely to present a physical threat to the non-poor, the *moral* basis of private property is insecure in the face of desperate need (1988, p. 163). Goodin's argument thus appeals to the interests both of the poor and of the non-poor.

These differing reasons for action clearly point to differing kinds of action. A claim based on the efficiency of workers is a claim for adequate nourishment, whereas one based on the removal of avoidable pain is more open-ended.

If the reasons for relieving poverty can thus differ, so can the urgency of the claims of the poor. We saw how for Aquinas, the sheer impossibility of relieving all poverty meant that, at least in the normal run of events, considerable discretion remained with the non-poor as to how they should distribute their 'superabundance'. For most of human history, poverty was, like the weather, an unalterable fact of life. This perspective only changed with the increased affluence arising from the Industrial Revolution. 'Only when its eradication became possible did poverty become a problem' (Cannadine 1985). Now that the alleviation of poverty is feasible, the implicit ethical claim for action takes on added urgency.

• Living Decently •

T. H. Marshall observed, 'It is often said that the poor must be given a chance to live "decently", a blessed word which conveys exactly what is meant and evades the need to put it in precise terms' (1981, p. 44). We agree, but the imprecision of this blessed word leads to ambiguity. It might refer to a life that is respectable or proper. It might also refer to a tolerable or 'good enough life', or even to a full life. Both usages are found, for instance, in a much-quoted passage from Adam Smith, where 'decency' refers both to a 'necessary of life' and to proper conduct:

> *By necessaries I understand not only the commodities which are indispensably necessary for the support of life, but what ever the custom of the country renders it indecent for creditable people, even of the lowest order, to be without. A linen shirt, for example, is, strictly speaking, not a necessary of life. The Greeks and Romans lived, I suppose, very comfortably though they had no linen. But in the present times, through the greater part of Europe, a creditable day-labourer would be ashamed to appear in public without a linen shirt, the want of which would be supposed to denote that disgraceful degree of poverty which, it is presumed, nobody can well fall into without extreme bad conduct. ... Under necessaries, therefore, I comprehend not only those things which nature, but those things which the established rules of decency have rendered necessary to the lowest rank of people (Smith [1776] 1976, pp. 351–2).*

These two meanings of living decently were also implicit in the notorious distinction between 'indigence' and 'poverty' in the Poor Law Report of 1834: 'indigence' was the state of a person unable to labour, or unable to obtain, in return for labour, the means of subsistence; 'poverty' was the state of one, who in order to obtain a mere subsistence, was forced to have recourse to labour (British Parliamentary Papers: *Poor Law* 1834, vol. 8, p. 143).

Under the new Poor Law, subsistence would be assured, but only following a test of moral probity by means of the rigours of the workhouse. This concern for the moral probity of the poor remained at the centre of debates on poverty throughout the nineteenth century, especially in the writings (and actions) of the Charity Organisation Society:

> *[The life of one man I know] ... has been spoiled by this easy-going condonation of faults of character ... Of course, the more chances were given the more were wanted, and now it has come to this, that his wife and daughters go out to work while he sits at home and minds the baby. A little wholesome starvation at the beginning of his*

*career might have taught this man a lesson he would never have for-
gotten, and enabled him to preserve his manhood; but hunger is now
accounted a greater evil than any loss of self-respect or moral degra-
dation (Dendy 1895).*

In this context, where 'moral' refers exclusively to proper conduct, and 'a little wholesome starvation' becomes a useful means to
that end, it is hardly surprising that the ethical or moral dimensions
of 'decent living' should fall into disrepute.

• Poverty Lines and the Quest for 'Objective' Measurement •

One of the chief purposes of the impersonal techniques employed by
poverty researchers from Booth (1902) and Rowntree (1902) to the
present has been to sidestep moral judgments, both in the analysis of
who is poor, and in the remedies proposed—such as higher wages,
or pensions administered without regard to individual worth
(Williams 1969).

In the first of the great poverty surveys Charles Booth was only
partially successful in focusing on 'the facts', without indulging in
the moralising that he found so distasteful in his contemporaries. He
had been inspired to action by an inquiry conducted by F. D.
Hyndman for the Social Democratic Federation, whose sensational
findings were extensively debated in the *Pall Mall Gazette* in 1886.
Hyndman's inquiry became even more contentious when it was
rumoured that a riot among unemployed in the West End had been
incited by him (Simey and Simey 1960, p. 69). Booth resolved to
conduct a scientific inquiry where the facts could speak for themselves, without either the incendiary pleading of socialists, or the
moralising of the 'experts' on poverty of the Charity Organisation
Society.

Booth's actual method of counting poverty was a mixture of the
impersonal and the moralising. Though his 'line of poverty' was
based primarily on income, it was closely linked to a class schema in
which the eight classes ranged from A (the poorest) to H (the richest).

*The divisions indicated here by 'poor' and 'very poor' are necessarily
arbitrary. By the word 'poor' I mean to describe those who have a*

sufficiently regular though bare income, such as 18s to 21s per week for a moderate family, and by 'very poor' those who from any cause fall much below this standard. The 'poor' are those whose means may be sufficient, but are barely sufficient, for decent independent life; the 'very poor' those whose means are insufficient for this according to the usual standard of life in this country. My 'poor' may be described as living under a struggle to obtain the necessaries of life and make both ends meet; while the 'very poor' live in a state of chronic want (Booth 1902, p. 83).

Thus far, Booth is typical of the modern poverty researchers in his use of income to distinguish the poor from the not-poor. His moralising becomes more evident in his class schema. Class A (the lowest class of occasional labourers, loafers, semi-criminals) and B (casual earnings) make up the 'very poor', while Class C (intermittent earnings) and D (small regular earnings) make up the 'poor' (p. 83). Class A is tiny, no more than a quarter per cent. Booth has the lowest opinion of this group, but concludes triumphantly: 'The hordes of barbarians of whom we have heard, who, issuing from their slums, will one day overwhelm modern civilization, do not exist. There are barbarians, but they are a handful, a small and decreasing percentage: a disgrace but not a danger' (p. 39).

He is little more enthusiastic about Class B: 'Class B, and especially the "labour" part of it [i.e. as distinct from artisans], is not one in which men are born and live and die, so much as a deposit of those who from mental, moral, and physical reasons are incapable of better work' (p. 44). His solution is startling. First, he puts to one side consideration of Class A where there is a question of 'disorder' rather than poverty, and focuses on Class B (p. 131). 'The poverty of the poor is mainly the result of the competition of the very poor. The entire removal of this very poor class out of the daily struggle for existence I believe to be the only solution of the problem' (p. 154). With Class B out of the labour market, their entire earnings could go to Class C, who would then 'be immensely better off' (p. 154). He is adamant that the issue of the desire of the 'true working classes' for a larger share of wealth is a quite different one from the plight of those who suffer poverty. It is agitators and sensational writers who conflate the large numbers of the first with the small numbers of the poor (p. 155). The key to the solution is to focus on Class B. They would be sent to compulsory labour settlements, separated from the rest of society, where men and women would be taught skills and the discipline of work while their children were raised under strict supervision. Failure would lead them to the workhouse; rehabilitation would permit them to re-enter civilisation. Once Class A was no longer confounded with Class B, Class A 'could be gradually harried out of existence' (p. 169). 'Thorough interference on the part of the state with the lives of a small fraction of the population would tend to make it possible, ultimately, to dispense with any socialistic interference in the lives of all the rest' (p. 167).

Booth's empiricism, his attempt to 'let the facts speak for themselves', was thus heavily qualified by his moral judgments on the character of Classes A and B, and the moralistic policy prescriptions that followed from them.

A far more clear-cut attempt to avoid moral judgment was made by Rowntree in 1899. In his first survey of York, he used an extremely strict definition of primary poverty: 'Families whose total earnings are insufficient to obtain the minimum necessaries for the maintenance of merely physical efficiency' (Rowntree 1902, p. 86). The strength of this definition was that it permitted him to avoid the question of whether a family were good managers or of good character. The whole point of choosing such a strict definition was to be able to say that no matter how efficient the family was, its income was so low that it must be underfed (p. 135).

Even using this definition, 10 per cent of the population of York were poor. In addition, a further 18 per cent were in 'secondary poverty'—that is, their incomes were above the strict poverty line, but they were judged by observers to be in poverty (pp. 87; 115). Rowntree himself left open the question whether those in secondary poverty were at fault, but his critics did not. In particular, the Charity Organisation Society and *The Times* leader-writer were quite unsympathetic to his findings. This was in part because his critics saw secondary poverty as self-inflicted, but also because of his implicit demand for state action (Briggs 1961, p. 35).

The Charity Organisation Society (COS) was, in fact, implacably opposed to the very concept of measuring poverty in terms of lack of resources, rather than in terms of social habit. Not even an extraordinarily low poverty line could convince them otherwise. In the words of the long-time secretary of the COS:

> *Everywhere one may see people of similar means living under similar conditions, some successfully and usefully, some with failure and social inutility. The difference, it is clear, lies not in the difference of resources, but in social habit. Hence, not the relative riches or poverty of the classes, or of the individuals that compose them, are primarily of material importance, but their social habit (Loch 1910, pp. 386–7).*

Loch's views were in perfect accord with the so-called New Poor Law of 1834, where the distinction was made between 'indigence', which merited relief, and 'poverty', which did not.

> *But in no part of Europe except England has it been thought fit that the provision, whether compulsory or voluntary, should be applied to more than the relief of indigence, the state of a person unable to labour, or unable to obtain, in return for his labour, the means of subsistence. It has never been deemed expedient that the provision should extend to the relief of poverty; that is, the state of one, who in order to obtain a mere subsistence, is forced to have recourse to labour. (British Parliamentary Papers: Poor Law, 1834, vol. 8, p. 143)*

The solution of the New Poor Law to the problem of distinguishing between indigence and poverty was simple. The condition of the pauper—that is, one who receives relief—should be made 'less eligible' than that of the independent labourer of the lowest class. In other words, the conditions for receiving relief would be so harsh that none but the truly destitute, the indigent, would apply. Loch was perfectly correct in his perception that Booth and Rowntree were not merely measuring poverty in a manner of which he disapproved, but were defining it in a manner that would have radical consequences for the entire Poor Law tradition.

Rowntree's attempt to make operational an absolute poverty line is generally in disfavour today, with some notable exceptions such as Joseph and Sumption:

> *But these are all arguments for providing an absolute standard of living to which the poorest and most incapable shall be entitled. An*

absolute standard means one defined by reference to the actual needs of the poor and not by reference to the expenditure of those who are not poor. A family is poor if it cannot afford to eat. It is not poor if it cannot afford endless smokes and it does not become poor by the mere fact that other people can afford them. A person who enjoys a standard of living equal to that of a medieval baron cannot be described as poor for the sole reason that he has chanced to be born into a society where the great majority can live like medieval kings' (1979, p. 27).

One reason why the concept of absolute poverty is not in favour today is that, with the increase in absolute levels of affluence during this century, such an approach soon defines poverty out of existence. In his second survey of York in 1936, Rowntree arbitrarily upgraded his 1899 poverty line by 43 per cent in real terms, and used this as the basis for the final survey in 1950. Even using this higher line, only 1.66 per cent were below the line by 1950 (Rowntree 1942, p. 451; Rowntree and Lavers 1951, p. 31). This is, of course, a notable achievement, and we shall later advocate the use of measures constructed in such a way that just such progress (or decline) over time can be documented. Of itself, it is not a decisive argument against the use of absolute measures.

The more basic objection to defining poverty only in terms of physical efficiency is that it truncates needlessly what is captured by Marshall's phrase 'living decently'. It is one thing to remove ambiguities—such as the Poor Law overtones of the phrase. But it is going too far to restrict a decent, 'good enough' life to mere physical efficiency. Recall that Rowntree's poverty line was pitched so low to make the point that even with heroic virtue and supreme management skills, those below it *must* be underfed. Rowntree was well aware that the custom of the day demanded far more for decent living than could be attained on his meagre poverty line (Rowntree 1902, pp. 133–4). His choice was basically a strategic one, in that it enabled him to present a powerful argument to his fellow industrialists that despite the extreme conservatism of the poverty line, there were still 10 per cent below it, most of whom were in full-time employment. He does not avoid a value judgment by defining poverty in these terms, any more than Joseph and Sumption avoid it when they use a similar definition today. But whereas Rowntree's strategy was then both defensible and credible, it would be neither today. Such a strategy that defined poverty out of existence would simply not be credible, precisely because it ignores what the custom of the country regards as living decently.

• • •

To sum up, our argument is that the concept of poverty has a strong ethical content that should not be masked behind the seemingly technical exercise of setting a poverty line. Given both the extreme nature of the poverty they were investigating, and the highly moralistic climate of the day, it is understandable that early researchers such as Booth and Rowntree should have sought so strenuously to concentrate on 'facts' such as malnourishment. Our argument is that this will not do today.

FROM POVERTY TO INEQUALITY

We have seen how what is regarded as a necessity of life changes over time, and this has the puzzling consequence that poverty is defined in 'relatively absolute' terms (Marshall 1981, p. 43). Since the mid 1960s, some have gone much further and resorted to the concept of 'relative poverty'. For its best-known advocate,

> *Individuals, families and groups in the population can be said to be in poverty when they lack the resources to obtain the types of diet, participate in the activities and have the living conditions and amenities which are customary, or are at least widely encouraged or approved, in the societies to which they belong. Their resources are so seriously below those commanded by the average individual or family that they are, in effect, excluded from ordinary living patterns, customs and activities (Townsend 1979, p. 31).*

Townsend correctly points out that, according to his definition, there may be more poverty in a rich country than in a poor one (ibid.). We may go further, and observe that this would be true, even if there were widespread starvation in the poor country, provided the starvation was equally shared. But as Sen points out, 'there is an irreducible core of *absolute* deprivation in our idea of poverty, which translates reports of starvation, malnutrition and visible hardship into a diagnosis of poverty without having to ascertain first the relative picture' (Sen 1982, p. 17).

The trouble with the concept of relative poverty is that it conflates two separate ideas. One is the minimum necessary for living decently (which changes with time, place and, as we shall see, reference group); the other is the concept of inequality—that is, that some have less than others. Inequality *may* imply that one cannot live decently, and conversely, the inability to live decently, or to live at all, *may* coincide with inequality, but it need not.

Questions about inequality can be asked of all communities or nations, the richest and the poorest, the most egalitarian and the most unequal. In purely relational terms, there are unpleasant features in being on the bottom of the scale. If I am the only millionaire on Billionaires' Row, I may well complain that I feel excluded from their company, that I am not invited to their parties, and that their children will not play with my children. I have a relative disadvantage, but while I am unequal, I am not poor. Another person may not only be unequal, but also suffer hunger, cold and lack of shelter. Of itself, information as to who is on the bottom of the scale tells us nothing at all about their actual material circumstances, beyond the relative statement that they have less than the rest.

We argue that questions of inequality and of poverty should be kept separate, and we propose a method for doing this. But first, let us see how poverty is currently measured in Australia.

POVERTY MEASUREMENT IN AUSTRALIA

Although there is no official poverty line in Australia, there is something very close to one. A poverty line devised by Professor Ronald Henderson and his associates for their 1960s Melbourne study (Henderson, Harcourt and Harper 1970) was later developed and used nationally in a massive federal government Commission of Inquiry into Poverty (1975). The Commission of Inquiry into Poverty received a great deal of publicity during its public hearings, and its findings generated intense interest. Since this period, the 'Henderson poverty line' has been institutionalised at both a policy and popular level, and also in academic debate. The original poverty line is updated every quarter by the Institute of Applied Economic and Social Research of the University of Melbourne, and also by the National Institute for Economic and Industry Research, Melbourne.

The first discussion paper issued by the Commonwealth Social Security Review used the Henderson poverty line to show changes in the number and the composition of 'people in poverty', and it went on to cite these changes as one of the principal reasons for the Review (Cass 1986). Legal Services Commissions throughout Australia use the Henderson poverty line in determining eligibility for legal aid. Though the Hawke government's 1987 election pledge that 'by 1990 no child will need to live in poverty' (Australian Labor Party 1987) made no explicit reference to the poverty line, it was universally understood to imply a poverty line by commentators, the media and academics. A major academic analysis of the Hawke promise has used the Henderson poverty line to assess the impact on child poverty of the package of measures introduced by that government to implement its promise (Saunders and Whiteford 1987). At a popular level, the quarterly updating of poverty lines is usually carried in the press, as are regular feature articles on 'people in poverty' based on the Henderson line.

Despite these indications that a quasi-official status has been given to the Henderson poverty line, governments regularly cite its non-official status when dismissing claims based upon it by lobby groups such as the Australian Council of Social Service and the Brotherhood of St Laurence. There is also a growing body of academic criticism of most features of the construction of the poverty line (Richardson 1979; Stanton 1980; Social Welfare Policy Secretariat 1981; Richardson and Travers 1989). In fact, the lament has been made that a disproportionate amount of effort has been put into criticism of the existing line rather than the development of an alternative (Saunders and Whiteford 1989). Our own approach will be to describe how the line is constructed and discuss briefly the criticisms, before passing judgment on whether poverty lines are redeemable. We will conclude that they are not, but we will propose an alternative form of measurement with which to examine poverty in Australia.

The Henderson poverty line is based on income, and like all income-based lines, it nominates a point on the income-scale below which one is said to be in poverty and above which one is deemed not to be in poverty. The income in question is current (annual) after-tax money income, adjusted for family needs—generally known as 'equivalent income'. The technical details of the calculation of equivalent income were discussed in Chapter 1, but the key assumption behind it is that people with similar levels of equivalent income have a similar standard of living. Actual income is 'adjusted' by an 'equivalence scale' that attempts to take into account such things as the costs of working, and the economies of scale involved in living as a family rather than alone. For instance, if the equivalence scale for a couple (not working) is 1, and that of a single person is .7, it means that the single person needs 70 per cent of the income of the couple to reach the same standard of living. Thus, a couple on $214 per week after-tax *actual* income and a single person on $150 *actual* income have the same *equivalent* income of $214 ($214 ÷ 1 for the couple; $150 ÷ .7 for the single person).

We also discussed in Chapter 1 the disadvantages of relying on current income as a measure of standard of living when we described our own preferred measure, full income. These arguments also apply when it comes to measuring poverty. In brief, the chief ones are, first, income gives us only one perspective on poverty, yet people on similar incomes may be quite different in other ways, for instance, their future prospects. Second, income does not tell us what other resources people have access to, such as the entire range of government services. Third, current income fluctuates over a lifetime, and tells us less about poverty than would a measure that takes into account savings and assets built up during times of prosperity. Fourth, income is notoriously difficult to measure accurately, and errors abound even in the best surveys.

Once a decision is made to use equivalent income as the measuring stick, the next task for the traditional poverty researcher is to draw a line, or cut-off point, that distinguishes the poor from the non-poor. Henderson sought a commonly accepted community standard to set the original cut-off point—namely, the Melbourne basic wage, plus child endowment, for a family consisting of a working husband, a wife at home and two children. The belief was that this would lessen the arbitrary element since the basic wage originally represented some sort of community judgment of 'the normal needs of the average employee, regarded as a human being living in a civilized community' (Higgins 1907). However, by 1966 Justice Higgins' 1907 standard had long since been modified by assessments of industry's capacity to pay (Richardson 1979). Moreover, in the 1930s the Commonwealth Court of Conciliation and Arbitration said explicitly that the basic wage was no longer needs-based. In other words, its use as the basis for the poverty line is arbitrary. That is not the same as saying that it was an indefensible choice. If one were charged with setting an arbitrary poverty line in Australia in 1966, this would be a defensible choice. Our objection is to presenting it as other than arbitrary.

The next task is to decide on how the poverty line should be updated. The original poverty line for the standard family was the equivalent of 56.5 per cent of seasonally adjusted average-weekly-earnings (AWE) in 1966. The Commission of Inquiry into Poverty used this figure to set the 1972/73 line: at 56.5 per cent of AWE. Since 1981 it has been the practice to update the line with reference to changes in *disposable* income—that is, income after payment of income tax—rather than AWE. Consequently, the poverty line is now updated with reference to per capita household disposable income. This has, in fact, risen much faster than inflation, so that the poverty line in 1990/91 was 18 per cent higher in real terms than in 1973/74.

In the light of our discussion of absolute and relative poverty lines, how should the Henderson poverty line be described? The original line bore some resemblance to an absolute line, with its reference to the 1907 decision of Justice Higgins. But, as we have seen, that was essentially an arbitrary choice. The method of its updating is purely relative: as the nation's income changes, the poverty line is adjusted to match the changes. It thus has the merits and defects of a relative poverty measure. People whose income had remained exactly on the poverty line since its inception would, by definition, have had an income that always bore the same relationship to national per capita income. Their standing relative to the community would not have changed. However, because of the 18 per cent rise in their real income, they would have greater ease today in buying a 1973/74 basket of 'necessities'. What we do not know is how they would cope buying a 1990/91 basket of 'necessities', since the approach of the Henderson poverty line does not attempt to take into account changes over time in what counts as necessities, nor changes in their cost, if these differ from the average rate of change of prices. To be precise, it assumes that the cost of necessities will vary with national per capita income.

• Poverty in Australia According to the Henderson Poverty Line •

The chief purposes of a poverty line are to enable us to know how many people are in poverty, who they are, and whether the situation is changing over time. The story as told by the application of the Henderson poverty line is found in Table 5.1 on pp. 172–3. When interpreting this table it should be kept in mind that, whereas the results for 1981/82 and 1985/86 are based on actual surveys of the Australian Bureau of Statistics, those for 1989/90 are only estimates, based on microsimulation techniques, and hence are not as reliable as the earlier data.

First, who is most likely to be poor? Clearly, single parents fare worst in all three periods. By 1989/90, 44.3 per cent of single parents were estimated to be in poverty, though they make up only 15 per cent of all the poor. Single people are less likely to be poor (17 per cent), but their total numbers are much larger—62.5 per cent of all the poor. Among the single, the aged fare worst, with 28.3 per cent poor in 1989/90. Couples without children have a very low poverty rate, but those with large families are much worse off.

When it comes to change over time, there has been a general deterioration since 1981/82, but a slight improvement since 1985/86 for all groups except single persons. Overall, the poverty rate has risen by 39 per cent between 1981/82 and 1989/90.

What are we to make of these results? On the face of it, there has been a notable deterioration. But it will be recalled that the poverty line has been increasing in real terms in recent years. If the poverty line is held constant in real 1982/83 terms, there was actually a *decline* in poverty over this period to around 7 per cent, rather than the sharp rise to 12.8 per cent (Saunders and Matheson 1991). It would be difficult to find a more striking illustration of the crucial importance of one's concept of poverty. If poverty means not being able to keep up with sharply rising community affluence, then there has been a significant rise in poverty during the 1980s. But if poverty means being able to buy in 1989/90 what one could buy in 1981/82, then there has been a significant fall in poverty during the 1980s.

One of the reasons why the level of poverty is so sensitive to precisely where the poverty line is pitched is its close relationship to social security pension and benefit levels. For instance, in June 1991

Table 5.1: The incidence and structure of poverty by income unit type

	1981–82			1985–86			1989–90		
	Number of IPUs ('000) in poverty(a)	Poverty rate (%)	Composition of the poor (%)	Number of IPUs ('000) in poverty(a)	Poverty rate (%)	Composition of the poor (%)	Number of IPUs ('000) in poverty(a)	Poverty rate (%)	Composition of the poor (%)
Single people:									
aged under 25	88.6	11.0	17.9	82.8	11.4	12.5	97.3	12.0	12.6
aged 25 to 44	41.3	6.7	8.4	54.3	7.5	8.2	69.5	8.4	9.0
aged 45 to 60/65	55.3	15.8	11.2	77.2	20.9	11.7	92.2	22.4	11.9
aged 60/65	55.8	7.9	11.3	136.4	18.7	20.6	224.1	28.3	29.0
All Single People	**241.0**	**9.7**	**48.8**	**350.7**	**13.8**	**53.0**	**483.1**	**17.0**	**62.5**
Aged couples	19.8	4.8	4.0	23.5	5.0	3.6	24.9	4.9	3.2
Non-aged childless couples	26.1	3.2	5.3	38.8	4.3	5.9	39.6	3.9	5.1
All Childless Couples	**45.9**	**3.8**	**9.3**	**62.3**	**4.5**	**9.5**	**64.5**	**4.3**	**8.3**
Couples, 1 child	17.7	4.0	3.6	20.9	4.6	3.2	19.3	4.0	2.5
Couples, 2 children	32.4	5.2	6.6	47.1	7.7	7.1	40.0	6.3	5.2

Table continues on next page

Couples, 3 children	23.9	8.6	4.8	40.9	16.6	6.2	33.7	13.8	4.4
Couples, 4 children	14.5	20.8	2.9	13.7	21.8	2.1	10.6	17.3	1.4
Couples, 5 or more children	8.7	33.0	1.8	8.5	36.9	1.3	6.3	29.3	0.8
All Couples with Children	**97.2**	**6.7**	**19.7**	**131.1**	**9.4**	**19.9**	**109.9**	**7.6**	**14.3**
Sole parents, 1 child	43.9	30.8	8.9	50.9	38.2	7.7	51.9	36.1	6.7
Sole parents, 2 children	37.6	48.1	7.6	43.8	52.8	6.6	43.4	49.3	5.6
Sole parents, 3 children	21.1	64.9	4.3	18.0	71.7	2.7	17.4	70.1	2.2
Sole parents, 4 or more children	7.3	85.8	1.5	4.0	62.9	0.6	3.9	60.2	0.5
All Sole Parents	**109.9**	**42.0**	**22.3**	**116.7**	**47.2**	**17.6**	**116.6**	**44.3**	**15.0**
All Aged	**75.6**	**6.8**	**15.3**	**159.9**	**13.3**	**24.2**	**249.0**	**19.1**	**32.2**
All Non-aged	**418.4**	**9.8**	**84.7**	**500.8**	**11.4**	**75.8**	**525.1**	**11.0**	**67.8**
All Income Units	**494.0**	**9.2**	**100.0**	**660.7**	**11.8**	**100.0**	**774.1**	**12.8**	**100.0**

Notes: [a] Income position units

These estimates exclude income units whose current employment status is self employed and juvenile income units aged 16 to 19 or 20 without dependants and living with their parents.

Source: Saunders and Matheson 1991, Table 5

a single adult pensioner, not eligible for rent assistance, received $150.80 per week, while the poverty line was $150.95. Clearly, even a slight change either in the pension level or the level of the poverty line, could result in an entire category of pensioners moving into or out of measured poverty. Pension rates are indexed to inflation, but in addition, for many years it has been federal government policy for pension rates to be adjusted broadly in line with movements in average earnings, with the aim of the single rate attaining 25 per cent of average male weekly earnings. Though the poverty line is adjusted on a different basis (per capita household disposable income) the two tend to move roughly in tandem. Thus, the close relationship between pension levels and the poverty line is likely to remain. This is especially the case for aged pensioners (both single and couples) and sole parent families (Bradbury and Saunders 1990). This is a serious problem, since these are precisely the groups for whom we wish to be able to answer the question, 'Is poverty rising or falling?'. Can anything be done to counter this problem? One solution is to use the so-called 'poverty gap' rather than merely counting the numbers below the poverty line. However, this does not solve a separate issue, the sensitivity of equivalence scales. We will examine each in turn.

• The Poverty Gap •

We have seen that one problem with poverty lines is that when they are used in their traditional form—that is, to count how many are 'in poverty' in the sense that they have incomes below the poverty line—poverty is an all-or-nothing concept. In the extreme case we cited, a few cents a week is enough to place single pensioners in or out of poverty. Unfortunately, this is not a hypothetical case but one that involves tens of thousands who rely on government income support. One way around this is to think in terms of the poverty gap—the total amount of money required to lift all poor people, or an entire category of poor people, above the poverty line. In the example cited of single pensioners who are a few cents a week below the poverty line, the amount to close the poverty gap for this group would be minimal. This would give a more accurate picture of their situation than would the usual 'headcount' measure that tells us that all are either poor or not poor. A further advantage is that the poverty gap takes account of *any* move, rather than only being sensitive to moves to either above or below the poverty line. Thus, the poverty gap detects an improvement of a group from being, say, $40 per week below the poverty line to $20 per week below. This is particularly helpful when examining the impact of policy changes, such as the 1987 Family Package that was intended to move towards the elimination of child poverty (Saunders and Whiteford 1987).

Unfortunately, a difficulty with the poverty gap approach is that its very strength, its sensitivity to changes in income distribution at *any* point below the poverty line, is also its weakness. The measurement of income is a rough-and-ready process and always contains errors. Using the headcount procedure, the only errors that count are ones that place someone on the wrong side of the poverty line. But the poverty gap method is much more sensitive to errors (Saunders and Whiteford 1989). For instance, suppose single parents are incorrectly estimated to receive $2 per week more than they do. This *may* affect the headcount method if it happens to move some single parents to just above the poverty line, but it *must* affect all single parents below the poverty line if one uses the poverty gap method.

• The Sensitivity of Equivalence Scales •

Equivalence scales present one of the most intractable problems affecting poverty lines. We described their technical construction in Chapter 1 and gave a concrete illustration above, where we said that an equivalence scale of 1 for a couple and .7 for a single person is the same as saying that if the couple needs $214 to reach a certain standard of living, the single person needs $150 per week to reach the same standard of living. But how do we know that a single person needs 70 per cent of the income of a couple to reach a similar standard of living? And if we decide instead that they need 65 per cent or 75 per cent, does it make much difference to poverty calculations? The short answer to the first question is that all methods of calculating equivalence scales contain largely arbitrary elements. The short answer to the second question is—yes and no: the choice of one scale rather than another makes huge differences in the relative standing of some categories, though not of others.

The best illustration of where equivalence scales are and are not sensitive is offered by the Luxembourg Income Study (LIS) database, where painstaking efforts have been made to produce comparable data for ten countries. This is no small task, since income surveys frequently use different definitions of families and of income. The LIS data can be taken as comparable, and give us the most accurate picture yet of the situation in the ten countries around the years 1979/83, when the surveys were carried out. Four different equivalence scales are applied to the same data, using in each case the same poverty line, namely, a purely relative poverty line set at half the median disposable income in each country (see Table 5.2).

The least sensitivity to equivalence scale is in the case of single mothers. For instance, whichever scale is used, Australia ranks highest of the ten counties in its rate of poverty, and the absolute rate of poverty is also high. Poverty among couples with no children is also relatively insensitive, with Australia ranking in the middle of ten countries in each case. The most dramatic differences occur in the case of people aged 60 or more. For single women, the poverty rate for Australia varies from 54.4, among the highest of ten countries, to 5.0, one of the lowest, with almost as much variation in the case of an aged couple. From these data, one can conclude unambiguously that single parents in Australia fare very badly compared to those in other rich countries. But one cannot draw any sensible conclusion regarding the aged. It is scarcely very helpful to say that the aged in Australia are somewhere between the best-off and the worst-off among ten rich countries, and have somewhere between very low and very high absolute rates of poverty.

• A Better Poverty Line? •

Some of the problems we have discussed could be avoided if we abandon some of the conventions used in the Henderson poverty line. This has been done in an important paper by Harding and Mitchell (1992), using data from 1981/82, 1985/86 and 1989/90 income surveys of the Australian Bureau of Statistics. Following the conventions of international research, Harding and Mitchell use a purely relative poverty line, set at a percentage of equivalent disposable median family income. To avoid the problem of the sensitivity to where the line is set, they give three different versions: 40, 50 and 60 per cent of the median. Their definition of a family differs from that used by Henderson. For the purposes of poverty measurement, all children living at home are counted as part of their parent's income unit. In addition, elderly people living with their children

Table 5.2: *Poverty rates among different family types in ten countries, using alternative equivalence scales: Luxembourg Income Study[a]*

FAMILY TYPE & EQUIV. SCALE	AUS	CAN	GER	ISR	NL	NOR	SWE	SWI	UK	USA
Sole mother, one child										
SUBJ	45.3	38.7	15.4	21.1	14.8	22.5	8.4	18.2	32.5	44.6
CONS	43.9	37.1	13.2	15.8	9.6	21.8	8.0	17.0	30.1	42.9
PROG	42.5	35.2	9.2	5.3	9.7	17.0	8.0	15.7	22.9	39.7
STAT	39.8	33.5	9.3	5.3	14.3	14.3	7.5	15.7	21.3	37.5
Couple, no children										
SUBJ	4.5	5.1	2.3	4.7	6.3	4.5	3.2	2.3	2.8	5.4
CONS	3.8	4.6	2.3	4.8	6.3	4.5	2.9	2.4	2.4	5.0
PROG	2.7	4.0	2.2	2.9	6.1	4.1	2.6	2.0	1.7	4.2
STAT	2.3	3.7	2.2	3.7	6.3	3.7	2.3	1.7	1.6	4.0
Single woman, 60 or over										
SUBJ	54.4	52.9	40.1	52.5	11.0	58.4	21.2	42.7	65.8	52.2
CONS	50.0	49.5	31.4	48.1	7.5	45.7	11.6	32.4	61.6	48.2
PROG	26.1	35.3	17.4	35.0	6.2	7.3	2.8	19.1	41.1	38.1
STAT	5.0	16.2	10.2	30.5	5.9	5.6	0.0	11.3	12.9	30.5
Couple, 60 or over										
SUBJ	27.4	17.9	11.4	29.3	4.2	5.9	1.9	7.4	37.0	17.4
CONS	19.7	14.7	9.9	26.6	4.3	4.3	2.0	7.2	32.9	16.0
PROG	8.4	10.3	7.9	22.0	4.3	3.1	1.5	6.1	23.8	14.5
STAT	7.1	8.8	6.7	21.3	4.1	2.4	1.5	4.9	13.5	13.5

[a] *The poverty line used is half the median disposable income in each country. SUBJ (subjective) is derived from the 'attitudinal' approach; CONS (consumption) is derived from actual consumer expenditure; PROG (programme) is the scale implicit in administrative programmes; STAT (statistical) based on experts' analyses of family budgets.*

Countries listed: Australia, Canada, W.Germany, Israel, Netherlands, Norway, Sweden, Swizerland, UK, USA.

Source: Buhmann, Rainwater, Schmaus and Smeeding 1988, Table 12.

are counted as part of their children's income unit. This is a sensible move. The alternative approach classifies both older children and aged relatives as separate income units, and thus inflates the number of 'poor' single families. Finally, Harding and Mitchell offer results based on two sets of equivalence scales: the OECD scale and the Whiteford scale, which averages 59 different sets of scales. Results of this approach are shown in Table 5.3.

Table 5.3: *Poverty rates in Australia in the 1980s, using three levels of poverty line, and two equivalence scales*

POVERTY LEVEL	OECD EQUIVALENCE SCALES	WHITEFORD EQUIVALENCE SCALES
40% of median income		
1981/82	6.1	4.0
1985/86	6.9	4.9
1989/90	5.3	4.7
50% of median income		
1981/82	11.0	9.1
1985/86	11.6	10.7
1989/90	9.5	9.9
60% of median income		
1981/82	18.7	15.3
1985/86	20.8	18.2
1989/90	18.5	17.6

Source: Harding and Mitchell 1992, Table 3

Table 5.3 shows a clear picture of a rise in poverty in the early 1980s, and a decline in the latter half. Using the OECD scales, poverty is lower is at the end of the 1980s than at the beginning at whichever level the poverty line is set. The Whiteford scales tells a story that is closer to that of the Henderson poverty line (Table 5.1), with a rise in poverty between 1981/2 and 1989/90.[2] Apart from repeating what we have said about the intractable problem of equivalence scales, there is a further factor to keep in mind in interpreting these results. As Harding and Mitchell point out, something odd happened between 1985/86 and 1989/90. Real wages fell in that period, but the income of society as a whole (on which poverty lines are based) rose sharply owing to the rise in labour force participation rates of married women: half a million single-income families became two-income families. To have reduced poverty rates during this period when the level of the poverty line itself rose so rapidly is a remarkable achievement.

We are broadly sympathetic to the approach taken by Harding and Mitchell, with the important qualification that we would not call it a measure of poverty, but a measure of inequality. In fact, its very strength lies in its unashamedly relativistic basis: it tells us neither more nor less than how things are changing over time at the bottom end of the income distribution, relative to the prosperity of society as a whole. That is very important information, and we will advocate a similar approach *as one stage in the process* of measuring poverty. It is only one stage in the process since, of itself, it tells us nothing about what life is like at bottom of the income scale. We will argue later in this chapter that it makes no sense to talk of poverty unless know *how* people are living.

• Alternative Approaches to Measuring Poverty •

We have seen that some of the problems associated with poverty lines can be removed by approaches such as that of Harding and Mitchell, together with the rather more radical surgery we advocate of calling them measures of inequality rather than measures of poverty. That still leaves us with the issue of equivalence scales.

The problems relating to the sensitivity of equivalence scales are of a different order from any other. When we find that the aged in Australia are doing either very well or very badly depending on which equivalence scale is chosen (Table 5.2), or that poverty either rose or declined during the 1980s depending on which equivalence scale is chosen (Table 5.3), we simply do not know what to make of it. Unfortunately, the problems we face here are not peculiar to one particular type of income-based poverty line, but to *all* income-based approaches. In the light of all we have said in this book about the defects of current income as a measure of material well-being, this should come as no surprise. The question then arises whether we can sidestep at least some of these problems by resorting to other types of measurement.

The most important attempts to avoid the problems of income-based measures of poverty have involved the direct measurement of standard of living. An income-based measure assumes that everyone needs so many dollars to cover the expenses of food, clothing, shelter, transport and so one. If one can bypass the income question and ask directly how people fare in terms of food, clothing, shelter, and transport there are some obvious advantages. For instance, the problems inherent in equivalence scales are due above all to differing assumptions about economies of scale in the household, about sharing, and about costs of work. If we can gain direct access to information on people's diet, transport and so on we can avoid all or most of those assumptions.

Perhaps the most imaginative attempt at direct measurement of poverty is the British study of Mack and Lansley (1985). The methodology was simple. Respondents to a survey were shown a list of thirty-five items relating to standard of living, and asked first to divide them into two groups, those that are necessary and which all should be able to afford and not have to do without, and those which may be desirable but are not necessary. Next they were asked if they had each of the items; if they did not have one, they were asked whether this was by choice (Mack and Lansley 1985, pp. 293#7). The result of this 1983 survey of the British public's perception of necessities is given in Table 5.4.

The next stage was for the researchers to decide what degree of consensus should count for an item to be listed as a necessity. They decided to accept as necessities those items that were designated as such by at least 50 per cent. This resulted in 26 'necessities'. If people lacked three of more necessities other than by choice, they were defined as poor. The decision that the lack of three necessities should constitute poverty was not entirely arbitrary. The researchers observed that relatively fewer people on high incomes lacked that many, and few who lacked three necessities indulged in high spending in luxury areas (p. 176). The inclusion of some items as necessities immediately gave ammunition to critics (for example, a roast meat joint once a week) (Mack and Lansley 1985, pp. 196; 276). *The Times* showed it had progressed since its 1902 reflections on Rowntree to the extent of accepting television as a necessity, but drew the line at colour television (*The Times*, 16 April 1987, p. 19).

Table 5.4: *The public's perception of necessities—Britain, 1983*

	Standard of living items in rank order	% saying item a necessity
1	Heating to warm living areas of the home if it's cold	97
2	Indoor toilet (not shared with another household)	94
3	Damp-free home	96
4	Bath (not shared with another household)	94
5	Beds for everyone in the household	94
6	Public transport for one's needs	88
7	A warm water-proof coat	87
8	Three meals a day for children	82
9	Self-contained accommodation	79
10	Two pairs of all-weather shoes	78
11	Enough bedrooms for every child over 10 of different sex to have his/her own	77
12	Refrigerator	77
13	Toys for children	71
14	Carpets in living rooms and bedrooms	70
15	Celebrations on special occasions such as Christmas	69
16	A roast meat joint or its equivalent once a week	67
17	A washing machine	67
18	New, not second-hand, clothes	64
19	A hobby or leisure activity	64
20	Two hot meals a day (for adults)	64
21	Meat or fish every other day	63
22	Presents for friends or family once a year	63
23	Holiday away from home one week a year, not with relatives	63
24	Leisure equipment for children, e.g. sports equipment or bicycle	57
25	A garden	55
26	A television	51
27	A 'best outfit' for special occasions	48
28	A telephone	43
29	An outing for children once a week	40
30	A dressing gown	38
31	Children's friends round for tea/a snack once a fortnight	37
32	A night out once a fortnight for adults	36
33	Friends/family round for a meal once a month	32
34	A car	22
35	A packet of cigarettes every other day	14

Source: Mack and Lansley 1985, Table 3.1

Mack and Lansley were well aware that even though people say they do not have some item by choice, that may reflect limited aspirations rather than genuine preference. They therefore provided two sets of data, one on the assumption that the choice was genuine, and the other assuming the choice itself was constrained by low expectations (p. 182).

One final decision was made on an arbitrary basis by the researchers. People in the top half of the income distribution who lacked three or more necessities were excluded from the poverty count (p. 176). In other words, even this determined effort to use direct measurement of poverty still used income as a filter. The numbers were not small: among adults, 8 per cent of households in the 6th and 7th deciles and 4 per cent in the 8th to 10th deciles said they lacked three of more necessities because they could not afford them (Mack and Lansley 1985, Table 4.7).

The Mack and Lansley approach is certainly of interest, both because it attempts to measure poverty directly rather than via the proxy of income, and because it uses the so-called 'consensual approach'. That is, it seeks to avoid the usual prescriptive approach to poverty measurement in which experts define what is a necessity or how much money would be required to purchase necessities. Instead, it uses a consensual or democratic approach in the sense that it asks 'the people' their views. The consensual method has been developed by Goedhart et al. (1977) and Van Praag et al. (1982). More recently, Walker (1986) has put forward useful suggestions as to how the consensual approach might avoid the obvious dangers inherent in seeking answers to highly complex questions by means of standard survey techniques. Mack and Lansley's approach is being used in Australia by the Australian Institute of Family Studies in their survey of families with children in twelve regions of Australia (Brownlee 1990).

There is some appeal in avoiding the prescriptions of experts in deciding what constitutes poverty. However, we have noted that it is not easy to avoid these entirely, and arbitrary decisions on the part of experts remain. In particular, the researchers drew up the list of possible items for designation as necessities; they decided that 50 per cent agreement designates an item as a necessity; they decided that the lack of three or more necessities constitutes poverty; and they decided that an income filter should exclude from poverty those in the top half of the income distribution, even if they did lack three necessities.

The fact that judgments on the part of researchers, even arbitrary judgments, still play a major role even in a highly 'democratic' survey such as Mack and Lansley's does not surprise us. We argued earlier that poverty is a 'thick' ethical concept in the sense that it contains both a descriptive element (for example, how many people lack a telephone) and an action-directing judgment (this is/is not tolerable). We saw how Rowntree sought to avoid such ethical judgments by restricting his appeal to such propositions as, 'Underfed labourers are inefficient'. In more recent times, Townsend has sought an 'objective' method of defining poverty in terms of a statistical threshold at a point on the income scale when participation in common activities falls away significantly. The consensual approach does not face the ethical issue directly, and a consensus that the poverty line should be set at a certain point is by no means a consensus on what is tolerable. It gives us no inkling, for instance, as to how citizens will react as tax-payers (Piachaud 1987). Moreover, one could well query the value of an off-the-cuff response to a question on what is the minimum amount for a family of a certain size to make ends meet. At the very least, one should heed Walker's advice (1987) and use in-depth qualitative group-discussion that gives people the opportunity to discuss the issues critically, hear contrary opinions, and possibly change their minds.

At the end of the day, there is another type of democratic judgment that every poverty survey must pass, and that is whether the public regards the results as credible. Those who do not regard 'a roast meat joint or its equivalent once a week' as a necessity are unlikely to be convinced by the finding that 67 per cent of respondents in a national survey say that it is. In the next section, we will argue for the use of both an income-based measure (full income) and direct measures. We are not particularly troubled if they involve arbitrary judgments by researchers, provided the researchers make clear what they are doing. What would trouble us would be any attempt to mask ethical or arbitrary judgments under the guise of 'science', or by presenting poverty measurement as a purely technical exercise.

A PREFERRED APPROACH TO POVERTY MEASUREMENT

The first question is whether we should even try to measure poverty. After examining all the pitfalls to poverty measurement we have discussed to this point, it might seem that a reasonable conclusion would be to abandon the whole enterprise, or at least to treat it as a matter of minor importance. In the Nordic countries, a conclusion along these lines appears to have been taken in practice. Contemporary Swedish analyses of living conditions, for instance, show far more interest in inequality than in poverty. Typical questions are to do with changes over time in inequality in such areas as income, social mobility, conditions at work, health and educational opportunities (Erikson and Åberg 1987). Similarly, comparative studies of living conditions in Nordic countries tend to be in terms of changes in inequality over a wide range of aspects of life, and over time, with no discussion at all of poverty (Vogel 1991).

The degree of emphasis on poverty measurement is certainly related to how public policy is understood. If the purpose of public policy is to secure *only* a basic minimum, as is argued by the New Right, then the study of poverty is crucially important to ensure that benefits are sufficient and go only to those in greatest need. Poverty measurement remains important even for those who seek rather more expansive intervention to ensure that *at least* those in distress are assisted (Goodin 1988, p. 19). It is only when one moves in the direction of universal provision of services and to pension entitlements based on grounds other than need, that the importance of poverty measurement diminishes. It is no accident that in countries such as Australia, where targeting of benefits is ubiquitous, that poverty measurement is given such prominence.

In the next chapter, we propose some public policy measures where poverty is not the basis for pension entitlement, and these would have the effect of lessening the importance of poverty measurement. We go further in the case of the traditional poverty line: we think it should be abandoned. Even those who agree with most of our criticisms of poverty lines have usually hesitated to abandon them. There are two reasons. First, the concept of poverty has a long and hallowed tradition which cannot be collapsed into that of inequality. Second, it is claimed there is no alternative. We agree on the first point, but disagree that there is no alternative. There is indeed a place for poverty *measurement*, as we now describe, but it is a type of measurement that lacks the simplicity and neatness of a poverty *line*. First we need to sort out just what it is that we are seeking to know.

• Key Questions •

Our argument that poverty is a 'thick' ethical concept is analytically inconvenient since controversy is inescapable with thick ethical concepts.

The most contested aspect of the measurement of poverty in affluent countries is the establishment of the characteristics which would justify an individual or group being labelled 'poor'. Should such a label require that people be malnourished, or is it sufficient that they be restricted from joining in the normal activities of the community in which they live? Should people who are deprived because they use their resources inexpertly thereby be excluded from the category? Should people who have opportunities to increase their material resources but do not make the most of them be included among the poor? Should people be classified as poor only if their productivity as a human resource is thereby diminished, or are they poor if they experience avoidable pain and suffering as a result of their low material resources? These are all moral questions. What we wish to avoid, however, is that any conclusions about the extent and nature of poverty are acceptable only to those people who share the ethical position and moral vision of human beings of the researcher who produced the conclusions. We argue that this can be done to a useful extent by unpacking the idea of poverty to identify the different types of information which people seek to obtain from it.

• *Unpacking poverty* •

The questions that poverty measurement is most commonly used to answer are:

- Who and how many are on the bottom in terms of material well-being?
- What are their actual material circumstances?

- How much mobility into and out of poverty is there across a lifetime and between generations?
- How do all the above compare with other countries, and with Australia in other periods?
- Is this an affront to our notions of decent living?

Of these, only the last embodies the controversial judgments which we have listed above. The remainder are much 'thinner' concepts, and may be separated analytically from the final stage of moral judgment.

We begin our 'unpacking' by separating the idea of inequality from the idea of poverty. Inequality[3] is a more neutral term than is poverty and we take advantage of this in the design of an alternative approach to the measurement of poverty which eschews the use of a poverty line. We advocate a careful distinction between issues of inequality and issues of poverty and the use of analysis of inequality where ever this will suffice.

The strategy we advocate is as follows:
- rank income units (defined according to purpose) by some measure of material standard of living
- select the percentile(s) or other criteria that define the bottom group on which attention will be focused, such as the 10th or 20th percentile or half the median income
- examine the material resources of this bottom group relative to the whole population, using various inequality measures
- describe how the bottom group (and selected subsets) is living, both in absolute terms and relative to some appropriate reference group (for example, extent of ownership of cars, houses, consumer durables, ability to pay bills, holidays away from home)
- perhaps reflect upon, but do not claim expertise in, judging whether the circumstances described, both relative and absolute, constitute living decently.

This strategy sees the role of research as providing widely acceptable information as the basis for the formulation of judgments and the taking of action by others. The researchers may well participate in the judgment and action phase, but they would do so as informed citizens, not as experts.

We emphasise that this approach is designed for reasonably affluent countries. We agree with Sen that some situations involve the 'irreducible core of absolute deprivation', such as malnutrition, that always translate into poverty, without reference to the relative picture. Then the sequence of steps and the self-denial advocated above are unnecessary: we can conclude without further examination that people in these circumstances are poor.

Our approach differs greatly from that of Rowntree, Booth and subsequent poverty researchers who sought to find an income line that would of itself not only define who was on the bottom, but also describe life on the bottom and judge that it was not a decent life. It is our intention to deal separately with these three steps. Several aspects of the approach we advocate warrant expansion and comment.

First, the criterion used to define the bottom group is explicitly arbitrary and its exact specification is unimportant, unless the characteristics of the bottom group are sensitive to this.[4] Poverty lines could in principle be used for this purpose, since they also are essentially arbitrary (within some plausible band). This is particularly so when manifestly relativistic lines such as those used by Harding and Mitchell (1992) are used. However, we do not advocate this strategy, at least as long as they are called 'poverty lines' rather than 'inequality lines', since they have the disadvantage of appearing not to be so. The controversy and scepticism which surround the selection of a poverty line is avoided in our approach because at this stage we seek only to establish inequality: we avoid the claims a) that there is a threshold in the distribution of income such that below it one is poor and above it one is not, and b) that those below the selected cut-off are unable to live decently and thus have a claim on the resources of others. The difference can be illustrated by reference to the recent international comparative study reported above (Table 5.2). This table concludes that, using a variety of different assumptions, sole parents are concentrated on the bottom of the income scale to a much greater extent in Australia than in ten other rich countries. This information tells us something about the *relative* situation of sole parents in Australia compared with elsewhere, but nothing about how their *actual* material circumstances compare with those of sole parents elsewhere, nor whether they are poor.

Second, once the bottom group has been delineated, it is then possible to see whether this group is commanding a greater or smaller share of total resources than previously or in other countries. This can be done by using the tools of inequality analysis. To do this, we need only identify the bottom group and then examine the characteristics of the people who fall within it. We do not need, at this stage, to decide whether this bottom group is also poor.

Third, to know anything at all about the actual material circumstances of those on the bottom of the scale, we need a different kind of measure from the purely relational ones. We already know the bottom decile have *less* than others. But does that mean merely that they have, say, smaller mansions than others, or does it mean they have no shelter at all? We need measures that describe actual circumstances. These kinds of measures are sometimes called absolute measures, but since they are absolute in a very unusual sense (they change with differences in customs over time and place) in this context we will refer to them simply as direct measures.

Knowledge of the actual (and not just the relative) material circumstances of those on the bottom is essential if a conclusion is to be drawn about whether or not they are poor. But only if poverty is seen as purely relative can this conclusion be derived simply from information about the distribution of income: and then inequality and poverty become indistinguishable. If we observe the 'irreducible core of absolute deprivation' then we can, without further enquiry into the situation of the rest of the population, conclude that these people are poor. Absolute poverty of this sort is rare in affluent countries and it is for this reason that more generous concepts of minimum acceptable living standards are used. A description of actual living circumstances then becomes a necessary but not a sufficient requirement for classifying people as poor or not poor. This necessary step can be accomplished without the 'thick', evaluative judgment involved in the next step—of deciding whether the conditions so described constitute poverty. We thus propose that the two steps be separated: the first may command widespread acceptance whereas the second most likely will not.

Fourth, the issue of mobility, which is of great interest to those concerned with the openness of the society and the degree of equality of opportunity, is entirely an inequality rather than a poverty concept.

Fifth, comparisons across countries or time may refer to inequality, to poverty or to both. We claim simply that comparisons which focus on the differing pictures of inequality will be much less contested than comparisons of the extent and character of poverty.

Finally, we are left with the value-laden question inherent in all judgments about poverty: does the situation which has been described constitute an affront to some standard of decent living? For affluent countries the answer requires qualitative judgments about what constitutes 'decent living', about appropriate reference groups and about acceptable differences in material circumstances within a reference group. Researchers have no monopoly of wisdom in making such judgments. We see their role, rather, as providing excellent information on which others, including the researchers acting as citizens, can base such judgments.

• The Data •

We now illustrate our approach, using data from the Australian Standard of Living study (ASL).

• *The relational questions* •

There need be no great mystique in drawing a line and saying, 'Below this line is what we regard as being on the bottom of the scale of material well-being.' The examples we give use a rich measure, full income, that tells us more about material well-being than does income alone. However, if such an indicator were not available, income would mostly serve well enough.

• *Who is on the bottom?* •

First, we need to draw a line. Since this decision is purely arbitrary, 10 per cent from the bottom, 20 per cent, half the median, or the Henderson poverty line would all serve equally well. The advantage of the first three is that since they are so obviously arbitrary choices, it is perfectly clear what we were doing. As we explained above, while poverty lines are also arbitrary, they *appear* not to be so. In Figures 5.1 and 5.2 we use two such arbitrary low-income lines, the bottom decile (10 per cent) and the bottom quintile (20 per cent) of full income.

Once the bottom groups have been defined, the 'who?' question can then be answered. Following a tradition that goes back to Rowntree (1902, p. 137), we use life-cycle categories, such as couples with and without children, single people, and the aged. In addition, we have *a priori* reasons for thinking that other groups may be faring badly. In particular, we would wish to check on the situation of social security recipients and Class VII, that is, unskilled workers and their families.

Figure 5.1: *Percentage of each category in the bottom decile and the bottom quintile of full income for the whole population*

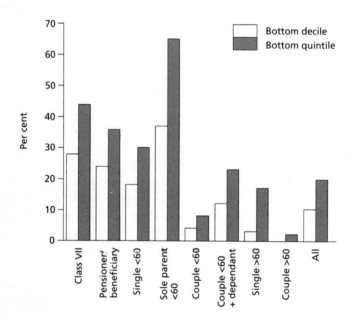

Figure 5.1 shows that there are some modest changes in the probability, relative to the community average, of being below the low-income line as we move from the bottom decile to the bottom quintile. Single parents, for instance, are 3.8 times as likely as the community average to be in the bottom decile, and 3.2 times as likely to be in the bottom quintile. The one exception is the sharp rise from 0.2 to 0.9 in the probability for single aged.

Figuress 5.2: *Percentage in the bottom decile and quintile of full income who are in each category*

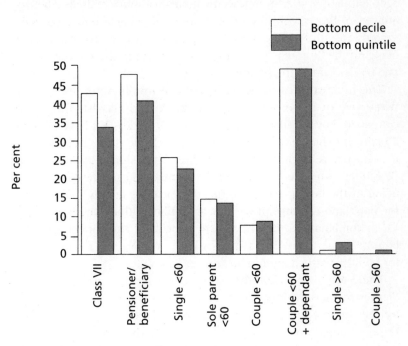

*Categories are not mutually exclusive, and percentages do not sum to 100

Figure 5.2 shows the make-up of the low-income group. In other words, instead of answering the question 'What percentage of sole parents are below each line?', Figure 5.2 answers the question 'Of those below each line, what per cent are single parents?' Again, the picture is generally stable, with the exception of the single aged. Even then, though the probability rises sharply (from 0.08 to 0.3), the absolute numbers are very small in both cases.

Who, then, are those on the bottom? The largest categories are pensioners, Class VII (people who were unskilled blue collar workers in their current or last job, and their families) and families with children, each comprising roughly between 40 and 50 per cent of the low-income category. (The categories overlap, and the one person may be in all three.) Of the categories listed here, those with the smallest representation in the bottom group are the aged, especially aged couples, and also non-aged couples without children. About a quarter of those with low income are single people under 60. Sole parents are numerically not a large group. However, their *chances* of being on the bottom are very high: 37 per cent in the bottom decile, and 65 per cent in the bottom quintile.

The highest odds of being below the low-income lines occur when two or more of the characteristics we have listed here are combined. For instance, both pensioners and Class VII have about a 25 per cent chance of being in the bottom 10 per cent. But this rises to a 40 per cent chance if one is both a pensioner *and* Class VII. Pensioners who are *not* Class VII have only a 15 per cent chance of being in the bottom 10 per cent—that is, only slightly higher than the population at large. If we look at families with children and Class VII in combination, they have a 34 per cent chance of being in the bottom 10 per cent. This contrasts with only an 8 per cent chance for families with children who are *not* Class VII.

There are, of course, other social characteristics not included in Figures 5.1 and 5.2 that might be found to typify those at the bottom of the low-income scale. Some we did examine produced surprises. Women are only slightly more likely than men to be in the bottom group of full income. Part of the explanation is that the low-income group where women most certainly predominate—sole parents—is small in absolute numbers. Another reason is that for most of the components of full income, we assume sharing among couples. For instance, a couple living in a $100 000 home are assumed to share equally in the services provided by the home. A further reason is that we place a value on time not spent in the paid workforce. If we use equivalent income (which does not include assets or time, but does assume income is shared), with the Henderson poverty line as the low-income line, there is a significant female/male difference, with females having a 20 per cent probability of being below the line, and males a 14 per cent probability.

Being a migrant is, if anything, a small (but non-significant) advantage when it comes to avoiding being in the low-income group. Having a low education means one is more likely to be in the low-income group, but not by a significant margin. Being an unskilled worker (Class VII) is a far stronger indicator of disadvantage.

Our choice of the bottom 10 and 20 per cents to define the low-income groups means that the numbers in these groups are predetermined. To obtain a feel for how the incomes of our bottom groups compare with the rest of the community we report several relevant statistics.

In our data, the person located at the 10th percentile had a full income that was 49 per cent of median full income and 45 of mean full income. For the 20th percentile, the respective numbers are 66 and 61. The bottom decile receive 3.5 per cent of total full income, and the bottom quintile 8.8. The ratio of the top to the bottom quintile is 2.6:1. The Gini coefficient index for the total distribution is .26.

Inequality within the bottom group can be measured similarly, but with the aggregate now confined to those in the lowest quintile. Thus, on our data, the Gini coefficient within the bottom quintile is .15; the ratio of the 10th of percentile full income to the 20th percentile of full income is .74; and the bottom half of the quintile (for example, the bottom decile of the total distribution) receive 39 per cent of the quintile's total income.

To obtain an accurate picture of change over time, we would need at least a periodic repetition of surveys, and ideally a longitudinal survey of the same people over an extended period of time. We do not yet have these for full income, but even if we did, that would tell us nothing about the concrete circumstances of those on the bottom. For that we need direct measures which serve in effect to interpret the significance of the purely relational measures. The results of some direct measures are shown in Figures 5.3 to 5.6.

• Direct measures •

The chief function of the direct measures is to enable us to know how bad it is to be on the bottom: what are the actual material circumstances of those at the bottom of the scale? To answer that, we use four different direct indicators of deprivation. 'NCASH MARGIN' indicates that a person could not raise $1500 within a week from any source in an emergency.

NBASICS means a person lacked any *one* of the following: a washing machine (3.2); a refrigerator (0.8); a telephone (5.6); an indoor lavatory (7.1); a colour television (3.6).[5] NHOME indicates not owning or buying a home; and NCAR not owning a car. We have deliberately chosen a range of items to cover life-style variations. For instance, for people with children, a car may be much more of a necessity than for, say, a single aged person. The four direct measures are applied to the categories used in Figures 5.1 and 5.2, though the 'aged' are excluded because of their negligible numbers.

Figures 5.3 to 5.6 show that the bottom decile of full income is indeed a strikingly homogeneous group in terms of the direct indicators of deprivation. This is only in part because some items (home-ownership in particular) play a role in the calculation of full income. There is even greater homogeneity in the case of NCASH MARGIN ('can't raise $1500'), which is not included in the computation of full income. This means that full income is doing what it was intended to do—namely, serve as a summary indicator of people with roughly similar levels of material well-being. It does not follow, however, that we need make no further use of the direct indicators: we will still need to *interpret* those numbers that suggest a broadly similar standard of living for all groups.

Figure 5.3: *Direct indicators of deprivation: NBASICS*

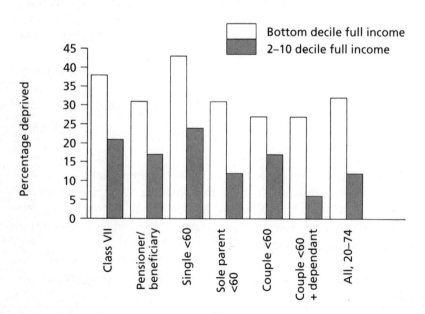

Figure 5.4: *Direct indicators of deprivation: NCash Margin*

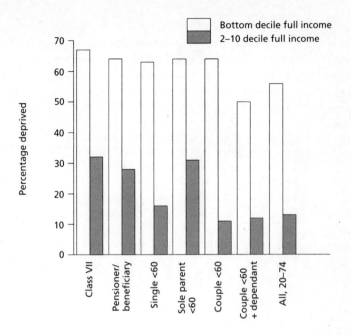

Figure 5.5: *Direct indicators of deprivation: NCAR*

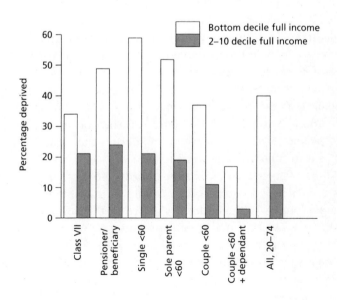

Figure 5.6: *Direct indicators of deprivation: NHOME*

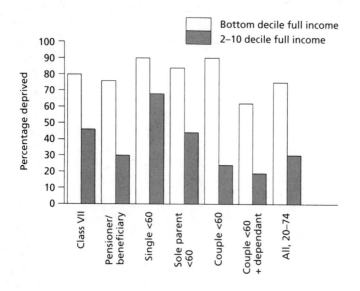

The issue is this. What is our reference group when we say the various categories in Figures 5.3 and 5.6 have roughly similar degrees of deprivation? We would conclude they are similarly deprived if we compared them either to all in the bottom decile, or to all adults. But it is not obvious that these are the correct reference groups. Let us take the example of couples with children. On the face of it, they are the least deprived of all, especially when it comes to car-ownership and home-ownership. But surely an argument can be made that the correct reference group when considering the deprivation of couples with children in the bottom decile is not single people, or couples without children in the same decile, but couples with children in deciles 2 to 10.

We discover in Figure 5.5 that outside the bottom decile, car-ownership is close to universal for couples with children. Compared to them, couples with children who are in the bottom decile are twelve times as likely not to be car-owners. If we take the case of single people and home-ownership, Figure 5.6 suggests much greater disadvantage for them than for couples with children. However, home-ownership is low for *all* single people under the age of 60. This means that if our term of reference for single people and for couples with children in Figures 5.4 and 5.5 is in each case their richer peers, then it is couples with children who are the more deprived group.

In other words, to interpret the significance of the data in Figures 5.3-5.6, we need in every case some reference point for 'decent living' when we conclude that a category is or is not poor.

These examples are sufficient to illustrate why our final conclusion is against the use of poverty lines: over and above all the technical problems, they hide ethical judgments. Even when we have isolated a group such as the bottom decile of full income, who have in common similarly low scores on indicators such as owning basic goods, a car, a house, and being able to raise $1500, we still do not know what this means in terms of necessities of life until we have made a further series of judgments, and ones that will be heavily influenced by qualitative judgments as to what constitutes living decently. In terms of car-ownership, couples with children in the bottom decile are faring slightly better than average (when compared to all in the bottom decile); they have a 2:1 disadvantage (when compared to all adults); or they have a 12:1 disadvantage (when compared to other couples with children). We think a good case can be made that it is the third comparison that makes most sense. But that is more a political judgment than a research finding. This leads us to the final question involved in making judgments on poverty: the ethical judgment about what is tolerable, and who it is who makes this judgment.

• From Description to Judgment •

We have argued throughout this chapter that poverty is a concept that involves both description and ethical judgment. Material living standards are described, a judgment is made that they involve a lack of the necessities that permit one to live decently, and it is implied that action should be taken to correct this. We think that kind of decision is best made by citizens in the course of the political process. Researchers can assist citizens in this by providing the kind of material we have shown in Figures 5.3 to 5.6, and drawing attention to the elevated risk of some groups who lack items that have near universal ownership among others. If we were to take the next step and identify this as 'poverty', it would be on the basis of no special expertise beyond that of citizens engaging in the political process.

There are other situations, however, where the question of the appropriate reference group does not arise. The lack of food or of shelter constitute poverty, irrespective of the circumstances of others. As researchers, we would have no hesitation in declaring such a finding to constitute poverty, without waiting to hear community opinion on whether hunger or lack of shelter are 'tolerable', or, worse still, tolerable for a particular category of people.

Researchers could well provide further useful information, such as public opinion on what constitutes decent living, which groups people in fact compare themselves with, and how they themselves regard their situation. However, the question of what one should make of such information would still remain . As we pointed out in Chapter 1, Sen has alerted us to the deeply conservative bias in basing one's calculus of standards of living on inner states such as happiness or utility. People adapt to the most appalling conditions, and take some joy from small mercies (Sen 1990).

In this chapter, the methodology we have proposed does not attempt to identify each poor individual. The focus is, rather, the identification of *groups* with a high risk of, say, homelessness, or whose risk is deteriorating relative to the rest of the community. The assumption behind this is that while any particular individual may have uncommon tastes (for example, to sleep under bridges, dress in sackcloth, or live on locusts and wild honey), groups of people are less idiosyncratic in their behaviour. If an entire group or category behaves thus, we are likely to be witnessing poverty. For most public policy purposes, this is all the information we require. Suppose widespread malnutrition is found among old-age pensioners. In any individual case, there may be a variety of explanations for this that are not related to poverty. But this is so unlikely at the group level that one would have no hesitation in declaring that the malnutrition of this group denotes poverty, and in seeking remedies for it. However, there is no reason why researchers favouring, say, an individual case-study methodology might not attempt to identify poor individuals.

To sum up, we think poverty is a concept that should be retained, even in rich countries such as Australia, and we think poverty research is a worthwhile endeavour. Our objection to traditional poverty lines is that they are asked to carry too heavy a burden, they confuse issues of inequality with issues of the ability to live decently, and seek a degree of precision which is greater than can be given. Our alternative measures involve the imprecision of concepts such as 'living decently'. Researchers can provide quite precise information of the kind we have gathered in this chapter, but judgments on whether this adds up to a lack of what is required to live decently are better left to citizens acting through the political process.

NOTES

[1] As we shall see, Rowntree's personal abhorrence of poverty had a much broader base than issues of efficiency.

[2] An important difference between Tables 5.1 and 5.3 is that Table 5.3 is based on actual survey data for 1989/90, whereas Table 5.1 is based on a simulation for that year.

[3] We are here using inequality in its 'thin', descriptive sense. Like poverty, inequality can also be used in a thick sense, with the moral judgment based on notions of justice rather than living decently.

[4] It is necessary to be on guard for such sensitivity: it will occur, for example, where the cut-off is located near some peak in the frequency distribution such as the level of eligibility for the old age pension.

[5] The numbers in parenthesis are the percentage of people aged 20 to 74 who lack each item.

ONE NATION OR TWO?

INTRODUCTION

In the course of this book, we have examined material well-being in Australia using a method that is more comprehensive than is normally followed. The outcome of this approach is a picture of Australian society that is quite positive. We have found little evidence, for instance, to suggest that Disraeli's portrayal of Britain in 1845 as 'Two Nations' is an apt description of Australia today.[1] Nor do we see signs of a more modest division of society into 'insiders and outsiders'. This conclusion is in accord with Mishra's recent study of Australia and five other advanced capitalist societies.[2] Though Mishra's methodology and focus are different from ours, he too finds cause for guarded optimism in the resilience of Australian institutions in the face of the crises that have affected all market economies since 1973 (Mishra 1990, p. 88). However, like Mishra, we do not claim that the situation we have documented is necessarily stable. An examination of the bases of our positive findings suggests they are under threat, and we make no claim that a survey taken ten years from now would replicate our optimistic snapshot of Australia at the end of the 1980s. We do claim, however, that there are policy options that would increase the chances of the situation we have described continuing beyond the present. It is to these policy proposals that we now turn.

• The Grounds for Optimism •

We have argued at length that too high a price is paid when simple measures such as current income are used to measure material well-being. Our overall message has been one of stressing the *complexity* of the measurement of material well-being, and, even more so, the complexity of measuring poverty. This is despite our commitment to an exercise of simplification and quantification; that is, we think such things can in fact be measured, and should be.

Thus, we discussed a variety of indicators in Chapter 1, and developed one of these, full income, in some depth. Full income is our preferred measure. Its use substantially alters our understanding of the situation of some groups, most notably the aged. Chapter 2 asks what picture the various measures present and concludes that, comparing Australia with the past and with other countries, the picture is of a relatively egalitarian society. Chapter 3 examines the reasons for this. In Chapter 4 we looked at other aspects of life that are not covered even by the 'complex' measures of material well-being. Finally, Chapter 5 describes in some depth how we would advocate coming to grips with one question of extreme importance, the measurement of poverty.

Our study has detected little that would justify the gloom about inequality, poverty and general misery in Australia that is a favoured theme of many editorial writers, welfare lobbies and some academics.[3] On the contrary, we have observed many strong features in the Australian version of capitalism as modified by the welfare state. In particular, we found that inequality in money income and inequality in other components of full income (for instance, home-ownership) tend to offset each other. The use of full income does not produce a more egalitarian picture of Australia than does current income, but it does show that there is little *compounding* of disadvantage when the broader aspects of material well-being are considered. Those who are weak in one resource (income) are often strong in another (housing or non-employed time).

Similarly, we found only a weak tendency for disadvantage in material well-being to spill over into other aspects of life, such as social activities, happiness, health and a general sense of optimism.

If we recall Walzer's (1985) conception of a just society as one in which the various spheres of life (such as health, education, money and commodities, participation in the life of the community, free time and access to justice and to office) are relatively independent, Australia emerges rather well. Though advantage and disadvantage in different spheres show *some* tendency to be cumulative, the tendency is weak.

In addition, we drew on the findings of recent studies that show Australia to be a highly mobile society in the sense of having low levels of inheritance of privilege and disadvantage across generations (Erikson and Goldthorpe 1992). Though Australia is similar to other industrial societies in its overall patterns of social mobility, it is at the outer limits of these patterns in the sense that the tendency for either privilege or disadvantage to be passed on to one's children is *weaker* in Australia than in practically any other country.

Our story covers only some aspects of Australian society, and to this point it looks to the recent past rather than to the future. There is always a lag between the collection of the kind of data we have used and its analysis and publication. Our own ASL survey was carried out at the end of 1987. The most recent work of the ABS we have used (ABS 1992) is based on a 1988–89 survey. Our account of Australia is thus based on evidence from the 1980s, and already, in the early 1990s, it is clear that several of the foundations of that story are under threat.

When thinking about the future there is, of course, a large element of speculation about how things will actually transpire. However, we can identify four areas that were decisive in the past, and are likely to remain decisive in the future. The four areas relate to: 1) employment; 2) the social security system; 3) home ownership; 4) the communal provision of other goods and services.

EMPLOYMENT

Of the four areas we have identified, employment is of such over-arching importance that it is of a different order from the other three. Any proposals for the design of a welfare state will depend on whether or not the aim of something approaching full employment is seen as realistic. One could put this even more strongly and say that there are no examples of a modern welfare state functioning with very high levels of unemployment over a long period of time.[4] The proposals that follow are based on the assumption that one of the principal goals of the Australian welfare state is to continue its historical aim of achieving full employment.

Unemployment in Australia was high, in terms of Australia's post-war experience, in the 1980s, and even higher in the early 1990s. Just over one-quarter of all respondents to the ASL survey had experienced at least one month's unemployment in the previous three years. However, in the case of our older respondents, any unemployment they experienced was likely to have come *after* they had established themselves in terms of home-ownership—by far their most important asset. The picture of high levels of affluence in terms of commodities which we have documented, especially among old-age pensioners, would be unlikely to be repeated if people experienced a pattern of moving into and out of unemployment during much of their working lives.

During the period 1945 to 1973, Australia enjoyed extremely low rates of unemployment, usually in the range of 1.0 to 1.5 per cent of the work-force, with an average of 1.4 from 1955 to 1968 (Jones 1990, p. 146). It is difficult to exaggerate either the importance of this phenomenon in understanding the present level of affluence, or its corollary, the impact that sustained levels of high unemployment would have in the future.

In the turbulent years since 1973 Australia has been far less successful in avoiding unemployment, and has moved from being consistently below to being consistently above the average OECD rate (Jones 1990, p. 149). There is no single explanation for this, but one plausible argument is that the more successful countries were those that designed welfare states that assisted rather than impeded industrial restructuring (Katzenstein 1985, p. 48; Scharpf, 1991).

We see a two-way link between a 'good' welfare state and full employment. A welfare state assists full employment by increasing the willingness of citizens to accept the costs of structural change that is, in turn, essential for full employment in a dynamic world. The welfare state assists with the costs of transition by guaranteeing income, by increasing the security of housing ownership or tenancy by paying some of the costs of retraining, and by assisting with relocation to new jobs. It will be noted that we are stressing how a welfare state can *assist* in the aim of full employment. It does not, of course, guarantee it. Moreover, these kinds of policies become prohibitively costly if high levels of unemployment do in fact eventuate. Until recently, the most successful example of a welfare state being used in this way, as an instrument of industrial restructuring, has been Sweden. Yet it is a model that would be impossible to sustain if anything like Australia's recent levels of unemployment occurred there (Esping-Andersen 1990, p. 28). At the end of 1992, the Swedish welfare state was facing just such a crisis, as its unemployment rate surged to a level close to the OECD average. Despite the current experience of both Sweden and Australia, we are not convinced that the continuation of these high levels of unemployment is inevitable. It is precisely with that in mind that we make the present proposals.

We first turn to the income maintenance side of the Australian welfare state and ask how well it is performing, and how well placed it is to assist in moving towards the goal of full employment.

THE INCOME MAINTENANCE SYSTEM

Australia has the *reputation* of being a classic 'Poor Law' welfare state. By this we mean that there is heavy emphasis on self-reliance through the market, with social security provided only through means-tested payments to those who fall below some standard of minimum income. There are certainly grounds for this reputation, as can be seen from the government's own rhetoric in the following statement of purpose of the social security system:

> The Australian social security system is designed to assist people in
> economic hardship by providing income support to groups at risk
> because they are unemployed or are not expected to work because of
> age, invalidity, sole parenthood or similar factors. Lower and middle

*income families with children also receive support, in recognition of
the additional costs they face. Veterans and their dependants can
qualify for both income support and in-kind benefits under the repatria-
tion system as compensation for war service.*

*Assistance provided under this function is intended to encourage
self-help and financial independence, as well as being targeted
towards those most in need. (Australia, Budget Paper 1, 1990–91,
p. 3.134)*

It should be noted that the Poor Law features were notably
strengthened by the addition in 1990–91 of the final paragraph, with
its ominous references to 'self-help', 'independence' and 'greatest
need'. The designation 'Poor Law welfare state' is usually intended
to be pejorative, and the welfare states of Europe can be understood
as a reaction against precisely this kind of regime. The arguments
against the Poor Law model generally decry the following: its punitive features; its inadequacy in terms of levels of benefit; its constant
risk in terms of legitimacy; its failure to deliver owing to low take-up
rate of means-tested, stigmatised benefits; its failure to recognise the
potential role of welfare states in assisting rather than impeding
industry restructuring; and its tendency to divide society into insiders and outsiders. This book has added a major new argument:
the difficulty of identifying need.

The Poor Law model of the welfare state assumes that it is not
problematic to propose that assistance should be 'targeted towards
those most in need'. Our argument throughout this book has been
that this is in fact highly problematic, and will always be a contested,
political activity. Even within the anonymous framework of a
research project, we have encountered difficulties in identifying who
is in greatest need. A great deal more information than just money
income is needed in order to establish whether one family has a
higher level of need for material assistance than does another. There
is a yet higher order of difficulty when we are dealing with *entitlements* based on 'greatest need'. The more one goes down the track of
improving on measures of material well-being in order to identify
the 'truly needy', the stronger the risk of intrusive investigation that
is likely to accentuate the division of society into insiders (who enjoy
steady employment and the accompanying respect and entitle-

ments) and outsiders (who have to demonstrate need in a way which cultivates a sense of paternalism and irritation on the one hand and dependency and resentment on the other).

As we have shown, it requires a great deal of information about a person's assets, family relationships, receipts in kind, and income before her or his material well-being can be identified with any accuracy. The social welfare system is thus faced with a dilemma. On the one hand, it can seek only such information as is readily available and quantified without too much difficulty, such as weekly money income and number of dependants. The consequence of doing so is that people will not be reliably classified according to need, either in an absolute sense or in terms of a ranking among themselves. Welfare support in a system which focuses on those in greatest need will either have to be denied to some who are in real difficulty, or paid to some who are not in real difficulty. (Note that we were unable to find any substantial group in the population for whom equivalent money income was a good proxy for material well-being). On the other hand, if, in order to receive benefits, people are required to provide detailed information on their material and family circumstances, of the sort which is needed for an accurate identification of their standard of living, then they will be being treated as second class, needy, incompetent people. There will be an implicit signal that such people are not entitled to the ordinary levels of privacy and respect which are due to first-class citizens. These are the conditions which aggravate, if not create, a divided society.

Fortunately for the Australian social security system, the reality is far more complex than the official rhetoric implies, reflecting several divergent strands and rationales. Even the official statement of purpose of the social security system cited above includes elements that do not fit the Poor Law model. The payments for the *extra expenses* incurred by families with children, and for *compensation* for veterans and their dependants, reflect other, more complex rationales for communal provision of cash assistance.

The welfare states of continental Europe have long been based on a set of rationales designed to *prevent* poverty, rather than the Poor Law rationale of *relieving* poverty. These systems are almost invariably insurance-based,[5] and provide payments in the face of special expenses; for loss of earnings; for the fact of disability (over and above earnings loss); and as compensation to those who are either not permitted or not expected to work. These payments are usually *not* means-tested. The only means-tested payments are for a residual category who 'fall through the cracks' and are not covered by the insurance-based schemes (Barry 1990), or who have exhausted their insurance-based entitlements. The overall rationale for this approach is that those who suffer through no fault of their own have a valid claim against the more fortunate (Barry 1990). It is very much a 'One Nation' rationale, where all could stand equal, as creatures subject to risk (Baldwin 1990, p. 2).

On the face of it, the European approach to the welfare state is much stronger than the Australian version when it comes to avoiding a Two Nations, or an insider–outsider division. However, neither the European nor the Australian model is what it appears to be: the Europeans are faring worse, and the Australians are faring better, than might be expected from their rhetoric or even from their structure.

In the case of the European states, the number 'falling through the cracks' of the insurance-based systems is very large indeed, and will remain large as long as high levels of unemployment persist. Moreover, the insurance models were based on what has been termed the 'Standard Employment Relationship' (SER). The SER implied full-time work, and included heavy 'non-wage costs' such as employer social security contributions. The proliferation of irregular working patterns in recent years (part-time, casual work; interrupted careers; fixed-term contracts; 'false self-employment') poses serious challenges to a social security system based on the standard employment relationship. Though the new working patterns do not *necessarily* negate the effectiveness of an insurance-based system, longitudinal studies in Germany show a strong insider–outsider tendency. This is especially the case when irregular working patterns are accompanied by periods of unemployment (Hinrichs 1991, 115–18; Esping-Andersen 1991).

For the purposes of this discussion, the crucial point is that, though an insurance-based system such as West Germany's appears capable of covering contingencies, such as unemployment and new forms of work relationship, in a manner that avoids an insider–outsider division of society, the reality is that a large and growing proportion of the unemployed have either exhausted their entitlements or never had any, and must rely, as in Australia, on means-tested assistance.

Until recently, Australia has not faced the kind of insider–outsider divisions that now plague the insurance-based welfare states, with the insiders receiving generous, non-stigmatised payments as a matter of entitlement based on prior contributions, and outsiders relying on means-tested assistance. In fact, there is something of a paradox that the much-derided Australian Poor Law model of the welfare state was, at least until the late 1980s, avoiding this particular problem rather well (Travers 1991).

The Australian version of the welfare state has always relied overwhelmingly on non-contributory, means-tested schemes. In 1900 the labour movement in particular was insisting on a non-contributory old-age pension on the grounds that the pension should be a right based on prior contribution to the wealth of the nation, not a form of charity. A contributory system such as Germany's was rejected on the grounds that it would penalise the sick, the feeble and women. Moreover, a large proportion of the Australian work-force was engaged in casual, seasonal labour, and would not be able to make regular contributions (New South Wales Parliamentary Debates, 14 November 1900, pp. 4968, 4973, 4991). In the event, both the early state pension schemes and the federal Invalid and Old-Age Pensions act of 1908 were non-contributory, but for pragmatic fiscal reasons were also means-tested. This set the pattern for future cash payments.

There have been several attempts to introduce insurance-based schemes. In 1938 a National Insurance Act was introduced by the conservative government, and was passed and proclaimed. It was to cover old-age pensions and disablement, medical and sickness benefits, though not unemployment. It was bitterly opposed by a diverse array that included various interests and ideologies, among them the Labor Party, unions, the medical profession, communists and anti-socialists (Watts 1987, p. 16). In the face of this opposition, and with war looming, the Government lost heart and abandoned the project.

The Whitlam Labor government appointed a committee of inquiry into national superannuation in 1973 (the Hancock Committee) which advocated a national superannuation scheme in its final report in 1976 (Hancock 1976). Its proposal to abolish the means-test was not supported by the Australian Council of Social Service, the Brotherhood of St Laurence (a leading welfare agency), or by the Chairman of the concurrent Committee of Inquiry into Poverty (ibid., p. 15). The Liberal government in power in 1976 rejected its recommendations outright, mainly on the grounds of cost.

The opposition of the welfare lobby to a non-means-tested scheme is curious. It is typical of a strong strand of thought that rapidly gained ground in the 1980s, and argues that the focus of the welfare system should be on the relief of poverty, to the exclusion of all other considerations. What is curious is that an argument that in most countries is associated with the far Right should in Australia come from the Left. It also comes from the Right, of course. Both sides of politics now concur that benefits should be targeted to those in 'greatest need', and the only points of contention today are the levels of benefit and the definition of 'greatest need'.

While need is increasingly the sole basis for entitlement for government income-maintenance schemes, there are once again moves towards a form of insurance. National insurance-based schemes are out of favour, but occupationally-based schemes are very much alive. The Hawke government's Social Security Review stated categorically that the opportunity for introducing a national superannuation scheme had passed, despite a guarded commitment to the 'consideration' of such a scheme in the 1983 Accord between the Labor Party and the Australian Council of Trade Unions (Foster 1988, pp. 183, 205). The thrust of the labour movement in this area since 1985 has been, rather, towards *occupational* superannuation. When it became impossible to sustain an earlier commitment to wage-indexation, the union movement accepted a 'wage–tax trade-off', and payments for increased productivity taking the form of employer-funded superannuation, to the equivalent of a 3 per cent wage rise. This was extended to 4 per cent in 1992, with the intention that it should be raised to 9 per cent by the year 2002.

What this adds up to is that income maintenance in the Australian version of the welfare state is losing its distinctive character. In 1980 some 80 per cent of those eligible in terms of age actually received the old-age or veterans' pension. Unemployment benefits were open-ended in duration, and unemployment was for the most part a short-term experience.[6] Australia had one of the most comprehensive safety-nets in the world.

Our argument is that since 1983 the reality of the Australian welfare state has come to match its rhetoric much more closely. In other words, it really is moving towards a Poor Law welfare state. The growth of compulsory occupational superannuation is explicitly intended to cut the ranks of those on means-tested payments. The insider–outsider divisions that are such a feature of the European systems are likely to be much more apparent in Australia in the future. This tendency is even more evident in the superannuation policy of the Liberal and National Parties, which emphasises the move from compulsion to 'choice and incentive' (Hewson and Fischer 1991, p. 118).

• The Future •

Barr concludes his comprehensive survey of the myriad versions of social insurance with the sobering observation that all have disadvantages. Their attempts to counter the inherent weakness of private insurance in the fields of unemployment compensation, the indexation of pensions, and medical risk have always resulted in trade-offs among desirable goals.

> *Given the inevitable tradeoffs, even if equity issues have been resolved, the problem is to choose the disadvantages which are least burdensome for the society in question. The search for better cash benefit and health care institutions continues; completely efficient institutions, however, are a Holy Grail (Barr 1992, p. 794).*

We argue that Australia can do better, particularly with regard to avoiding a division of society into two nations, or into one of insiders and outsiders. Our argument has been guided by two considerations: first, a good income maintenance system assists in achieving the goal of full employment, which we view as the most important step in avoiding a divided society. Second, an income maintenance system is itself a system of stratification—that is, it orders social relations in a particular fashion.

In terms of the first consideration, we have seen that a supposedly weak feature of the Australian model—the relatively low level of benefits—is compensated for in many instances by extremely high levels of home-ownership. The lack of any link between unemployment benefits and prior work-history has mixed effects. For middle and high income earners, unemployment may mean a catastrophic drop in income. On the other hand, those with only intermittent prior work-history benefit from precisely this lack of a link between work-history and level and duration of benefits.

Under the second consideration, our judgment of the Australian welfare state is that it has taken an unfortunate direction in the late 1980s. As Australia increasingly follows a Poor Law model, with its emphasis on 'genuine need' as a condition for entitlement, and 'independence and self-help' as the goal, the nation is stratified into the independent and the needy. Each group is governed by a different set of laws, and is accorded different social status. The greater the divide under this heading, the more such a system becomes an impediment to the first aim—namely, facilitating the restructuring that is a condition of full employment. Furthermore, the more tightly the welfare system is targeted on the 'needy', the more important it becomes to assess need accurately. As we have shown, to do so requires considerable information, of a sort which can only be acquired by intrusive procedures. Intrusive, detailed questions and a tight definition of need invite deception on the part of those who are seeking to establish their eligibility.

The first step in reversing this trend is to acknowledge clearly that there are several reasons for the welfare state, of which poverty alleviation is only one. Other important goals for the welfare state include the provision of insurance against contingencies which markets fail to provide, and income redistribution. This last is in part to reflect and to reinforce the sense of community and common citizenship among all members of society.

The market failure argument provides a basis for the welfare state which is founded on economists' notions of efficiency (rather than on the more usual grounds of fairness, compassion, social solidarity etc.). There is a strong case that the private market will fail to provide certain forms of insurance, even if there is an effective demand for that insurance. The grounds for this market failure are: a) adverse selection; b) moral hazard; c) unpredictable probabilities (that is, uncertainty rather than risk, in Knight's sense);[7] d) interdependent probabilities; and e) probabilities close to unity.[8] Protection against complete income loss from unemployment, protection of the real value of retirement incomes and protection against large medical expenses are examples of contingencies which experience these problems to a major degree. The first two grounds arise from information asymmetries: the insuree has more information about his or her risk and actions taken to reduce the risk than the insurer is able to have. Barr concludes that these 'information failures provide both a theoretical *justification of* and an *explanation for* a welfare state which is much more than a safety net—because it does things which private markets for technical reasons would either do inefficiently, or would not do at all' (Barr 1992, p. 754).

Of course, the fact that the market will not produce the most efficient result does not entitle us to conclude that the government will do better. But it does *make it possible* for the government to do so. The problem of adverse selection (where only the worst risks are insured) can be overcome by government requirement that insurance be compulsory. The problem of moral hazard—where people adopt more risky behaviour if they are insured against some of the consequences—is less easy for government to deal with. None the less, governments can impose conditions of receipt of payment— such as the job search test—which it would be difficult for a private insurer to enforce.

Obstacles c), d) and e) arise from sources other than asymmetric information. In each case, the fact that government-provided protection against specific contingencies need not be actuarially fair enables it to overcome at least some of the impediments which face private insurers.

Since the early debates on the welfare state in Australia, the European interest in maintaining social cohesion and a sense of shared community have rarely been a part of the rationale for welfare provision.[9] Despite this, as was noted, the Australian system has in fact had this effect, partly because of the very high rate of eligibility for the old-age pension and partly because of the relatively low rates and duration of unemployment. Both these things are now changing, and the emergence of a substantial set of second class citizens is a real risk which deserves explicit attention.

To sum up our thinking about the design of a social welfare system, we find it helpful to consider the five objectives identified by Barr (1992).

The first is efficiency. A social welfare system can help to get the right total level of support for people who do not receive income from employment. Part of this support comes from their own efforts at saving, insurance and borrowing; part comes from private charity (including family support) and part comes from government provided or mandated support. The efficiency argument claims that the non-government levels of support will be below the amounts which people would choose were markets to operate perfectly. A second efficiency task is to get the allocation between the different types of welfare right; while a third is to minimise adverse impacts on private behaviour in labour supply, self-insurance, saving and risky behaviour.

The second goal is to support living standards. This may be limited to the relief of poverty or may also embrace income-smoothing over the lifetime, whereby income is transferred not necessarily from high income to low income people but from the one person when he or she has a high income to the same person when he or she has a low income (for example, tax a person when in employment and provide income support if the job is lost).

A third task for a social welfare system is the reduction in inequality. This is usefully divided into vertical equity, whereby income is redistributed from people with high (current or lifetime) incomes to those with low incomes, and horizontal equity, whereby people with similar levels of need are treated similarly and irrelevant characteristics, such as race and gender, have no influence.

A fourth objective, and the one which features least in Australian debate, is social integration. This includes the maintenance of dignity. It also embraces the idea of social solidarity. Social solidarity requires the same system for all (for example, a health system which is used by people from all levels of society), and that the levels of support are sufficient to permit people to participate fully in the ordinary life of that society.

Finally, an important objective is administrative economy. Any system should be easy to understand, cheap to operate and not open to abuse.

These different objectives, of course, may be in conflict and part of the public policy debate should be about the relative priority to give to each where this is the situation. A familiar example is the conflict between horizontal equity—which calls for criteria to distinguish different levels of need—and simplicity and transparency in administration.

The design of a social welfare system will depend importantly on the relative weights given to the objectives listed above. Our argument is that the Australian system is increasingly being slanted towards the objective of efficiency (and a narrowly-conceived understanding of efficiency at that), to the detriment of the other goals.

HOME-OWNERSHIP[10]

We have already said that it was the low levels of unemployment over the lifetime of most of our respondents that made home-ownership a realistic option for the vast majority. In addition, home-ownership was assisted by high minimum wages in a centralised wage-fixing system, and such policy measures as the rental-purchase of government housing that permitted even low-income earners to buy a home. The rental-purchase scheme was in turn made possible by commonwealth–state agreements that facilitated its financing.

The impact of high levels of unemployment on home-ownership can be particularly severe.

As a form of saving, housing has two major drawbacks. One is that it is not very liquid. Forced sale of a house incurs substantial transactions costs (agents fees, possible capital loss etc.), together with possibly even greater indirect costs of a form that cannot readily be quantified. The more that owning one's own home is a source of security, identity and productive use of non-employed time, the more damaging will it be to have to sell it and return to tenant status.

The other major drawback is that the credit foncier system (wherein a constant monthly payment is made for the life of the loan) of home financing results in large monthly payments being required early in the life of the loan, which usually comes at a time when people have few other assets and, frequently, the expenses associated with small children. Increases in nominal interest rates have a disproportionate impact on the size of the monthly payment in the early stages.

These two aspects of home-ownership make it a very risky business for people who are at real risk of episodes of unemployment. A spell of unemployment will make it impossible to continue to pay the monthly mortgage. This is especially true for young couples with families who, partly *because* they are paying a mortgage, will not have been able to accumulate other forms of saving which may be drawn on to meet the mortgage when income falls. The *risk* of unemployment is thus a deterrent to home-ownership, even for people who currently have jobs.

Home ownership serves two important functions. It gives immediate benefits to those who are in the process of buying a home, and it serves as a most effective form of superannuation for old age.

In our computation of full income, we have taken into account a portion of the value of services people receive from owner-occupied housing by including an imputed value based upon a market rate of return on the equity in the home. This proved to be quite large, and comprises 10 per cent of the total value of full income and a much higher fraction of the full income of retired people. In addition, we made what might be regarded as a very conservative imputation of the valuation of production and enjoyment that takes place within the home when we placed a value on non-employed time. This has resulted in what we believe to be a realistic picture of far higher levels of material well-being among our aged respondents than their low pension-incomes would suggest.

We would stress the conservative assumptions we have made in computing full income. For instance, we have placed no valuation on what Stretton has referred to as the reciprocity between a richly endowed private sphere and a richly endowed public sphere (Stretton 1976, p. 191). By this Stretton refers to the beneficial effects, both to productivity at work and to the utilisation of the public sphere generally, that come from richly endowed homes of the kind that have been customary in Australia. There is an analogy here with our earlier claim that there is reciprocity between a good social security system and full employment.

As the technical means of production improve, public and private producers are able to give their workers higher pay and shorter hours. They can also produce more and better domestic equipment at lower prices. The rising wages enable households to buy the domestic equipment, the shorter hours leave them time to use it. Human capital from better education improves their capacity to use it: it equips and motivates people to read a wider range of books and papers, acquire higher skills, manage more complicated equipment, enjoy a wider range of arts and more skilful and demanding recreations. In return such households can provide the public and private sectors with adaptable people to meet their increasingly complex human capital needs. (Stretton, unpublished manuscript.)

Note that we are not suggesting that home production can readily serve as a substitute for paid employment. Pahl's sombre findings in Britain were that home production occurred in direct proportion to the level of income. The contrast was between households with money being productive and busy ones and households without money being unproductive and idle ones. Pahl's explanation for this is that home production requires both equipment and reasonably high morale—both of which were lacking among the unemployed he studied (Pahl 1984).

• The Future •

As in the previous section, we outline the direction we believe policy should take rather than attempt a detailed treatise on housing policy. A detailed list of all government intervention in the field of housing in Australia would be very long indeed. It would include regulation of and aid to house-buyers, to tenants, to landlords, and national strategies that attempt to co-ordinate the diverse effects of the actual mix of interventions. It would cover the fields of taxation, finance, building and zoning regulations and public housing. Rather than discuss all these issues, we will focus on what we see to be the overall direction we believe policy should take.

We agree with Stretton that 'common sense suggests that government's best and most popular course may be (i) to see that the nation's poorest housing is at least safe, healthy, and of a standard to allow its occupants to hold their heads up as respected members of society, and (ii) to enable all competent households to have effective choices of the main housing types' and tenures (Stretton, unpublished manuscript). The emphasis here is on making choice possible. Not all people wish to buy a home, but many of those who do are prevented by the special risks in home-buying discussed above, particularly in times of high unemployment. The best answer is to avoid high unemployment. But even in times of low unemployment, as experienced in Australia from 1945 to 1973, policies such as rental-purchase may be necessary. The issue is primarily one of making credit available to people on terms that take realistic account of their circumstances. Two examples are rental-purchase schemes that allow tenants to convert their rental payments to equity, and the provision of level rather than sloped credit—that is, loan repayments that start low and rise over time as the borrower's income rises in step with inflation and real growth.

COMMUNAL PROVISION OF GOODS AND SERVICES

The level of communal provision in Australia of certain goods and services is very high indeed. In 1988–89, government cash benefits were the equivalent of 11 per cent of average gross private income of all households. Yet non-cash benefits in the form of housing, health and education services, and non-cash social welfare were the equivalent of no less than 19 per cent of private income. Putting this another way, these four types of direct non-cash provision alone added 22 per cent to household disposable income (ABS 1992, Table 1). As we saw in Chapter 4, the inclusion of the net value of these goods and services in household income produces a picture of substantially greater equality than does income alone (Table 4.4). Yet it is not 'free-income' like other income in the sense that it is not available to us to be spent at will. Why not simply redistribute cash income, and let people choose for themselves what they will spend it on? Is it not paternalism for the state to decide the goods and services on which, on average, households will spend more than a fifth of their disposable income?

What is at issue here is why it is that a more or less equal distribution of some goods (especially health and education) is sought, but not of others (such as cars or shoes). Why is it that we adopt a policy of what Tobin has called 'specific egalitarianism' —that is, 'the view that certain specific scarce commodities should be distributed less unequally than the ability to pay for them' (Tobin 1970)?

These questions are at the heart of the debate on the relationship of the welfare state and freedom, a debate that has been summarised in masterly form by Goodin (1988, p. 331). The provision of goods and services by the welfare state does indeed reduce the freedom of some people by placing obstacles to their acting in certain ways. But it also enhances the freedom of other people by removing obstacles to *their* acting in certain ways. And to complicate matters, we are not simply talking of limiting the freedom of taxpayers and enhancing that of welfare recipients. We are at times talking about simultaneously limiting *and* enhancing the freedom of each set of people— taxpayers, citizens and welfare recipients. The one person may be a member of all three of these groups.

Citizens as taxpayers have their freedom reduced in that they cannot dispose of their property as they please. Citizens have their freedom reduced by not being able to display diverse tastes for public services; or pursue alternative arrangements once the 'immortal' institutions of the welfare state are in place. Recipients of services lose freedom to pursue their own preferences (as opposed to those of the Ministry of Health or Education); they are also restricted by red tape.

The other side of the coin is that some of these 'restrictions' may be seen as trivial, or may even be freely chosen. The myth of Ulysses and the sirens illustrates one set of circumstances when we are willing to bind ourselves to enhance our freedom (Elster 1979). It is not irrational to accept one's weakness of will, and to bind oneself in such a manner as to prevent weak-willed behaviour (often oriented toward short-term gains at the expense of more distant ones). I may, for instance, be aware of my tendency to consume for trivial purposes resources that are crucial to the health of others, and *choose* to support a health service that *limits* my irresponsible tendency. Or I may be aware of a difficulty in saving and choose to be forced to contribute regularly, perhaps to a superannuation scheme or to payment of a mortgage.

In addition, other freedoms may be enhanced. We have discussed earlier in this book Walzer's argument about separation of spheres in the sense that we may not wish to live in a society where money can buy everything. Another way of putting this is to say that we take some things so seriously (blood transfusion, sex, human life, voting, community membership) that we fear their very meaning would be destroyed or contaminated by the market.

A second argument for governments altering the allocation of specific goods rather than just money income is that specific goods are, at least in part, fungible. That is, to provide a family with free access to health care and education will free up income, which they would otherwise have spent on these things, for expenditure on other things. Provision of particular goods may thus be an economical way of achieving horizontal equity—for example, recognising the greater needs of people with school-age children or chronic ill-health.

A further argument for specific egalitarianism is that there are some resources which have a special role in facilitating equality of opportunity, in enabling individuals to function satisfactorily or in marking them out as citizens in a shared community. What constitutes such a resource, to which people are often said to have a 'right', is contested ground. But there is likely to be widespread agreement that they should include basic education, health services, access to the law and the protection of the state. If such things were left to be purchased from the market, and there continued to be the view that access to similar levels of basic service for all was necessary, then inequality in the distribution of income would have to be greatly reduced. Put another way, inequality in the distribution of income is more acceptable if it does not result in similar inequality in access to the basic resources of citizenship (however these may be defined). Compression of the distribution of income is costly and difficult and may entail more restrictions on freedom than does the redistribution of particular commodities in kind. Thus, inequalities in the vital material resources may be more efficiently reduced, and overall freedom maintained, by strategies of specific egalitarianism than by the alternative of levelling of incomes.

There is a fourth set of reasons, well known to economists, for government provision of particular goods or services. This set comprises public goods (a technical term) and goods which generate large externalities. Examples are the provision of street signs, control against infectious disease, light houses and much environmental protection. The market will not provide efficient quantities of such goods unless induced to do so by the judicious use of taxes, charges and other price signals by government. The arguments presented above for not simply relying upon individual choices are intended to apply even if there are no public goods or externalities arguments for doing so.

Market failures arise not only from public goods and externalities, but also, as we noted above, from moral hazard and asymmetric information. A well-informed government is able to use its coercive powers to overcome some of these sources of market failure, to provide a more efficient insurance system than would emerge from the market. This provides a rationale for some government involvement in health, unemployment and old-age insurance.

There is a further sense in which the idea of externalities can be drawn on here. It is that taxpayers (the ones to be coerced in order to finance the provision of specific commodities) may be willing to pay for the provision of particular goods and services (such as education for their children or health services) to those who are unable to buy these themselves, but not to pay for a range of other things which the recipient person may choose to buy if given the money instead. That is, the taxpayer may have a sense of specific egalitarianism which says he or she is prepared to finance some forms of consumption but not others. They may be prepared to pay for food for hungry children, but not to pay for a night on the town for their parents. If cash rather than goods in kind were given to low-income people on the grounds of respecting their preferences and maximising their freedom to choose, this would be at the expense of diminishing the respect for the preferences of the taxpayer. We note this in order to draw attention to the fact that even a decision to maximise individual freedom of choice does not resolve the issue of whether support for low income people should be paid in the form of cash or in the form of more equal access to particular goods and services.

It is no accident that many of the institutions of the welfare state had their origins in war. This is in part because wartime scarcity means that the usual objections in terms of efficiency to non-market distribution are less urgent. In addition, a quite different issue arises, namely, the desire for the purposes of prosecution of war for specific social arrangements. For instance, British social policy was heavily influenced by the alarming findings of the *Report of the Inter-Departmental Committee on Physical Deterioration* (1904, cmd. 2175) documenting the physical and intellectual standards of recruits during the Boer War (Titmuss 1963, p. 80). Titmuss points out that war has also influenced social policy when the standards of nutrition, education, and health that had been achieved for the armed services were extended to the population at large, often in explicit recognition of their part in bearing the burdens of war (ibid.). However, it is one thing to note that the institutions of the welfare state were strongly influenced by war or the immediate aftermath of war; it is quite another to conclude that this justifies their continuation. We believe the public provision of goods and services can be justified, but the components of such schemes do need frequent re-examination.

The market has unparalleled efficiency properties. In recognition of this, it should be replaced as the allocating mechanism for specific commodities only where a clear and strong case can be made. In addition, some of the efficiency properties of the market can be mimicked even where the basis for establishing a claim on resources is something other than income. It is this line of reasoning which lies behind, for example, the idea of using education vouchers to ensure that access to education is not dependent upon one's income.

Where a market or market-like allocation is not used, it is necessary to pay particular attention to the incentive structures which face the people who determine the costs of the system (the suppliers and/or the customers); to regulate; and to impose tight budget constraints. In his survey of OECD social welfare systems, Barr (1992) concludes that 'successful strategies embrace two key elements: social insurance and a regulatory regime which includes stringent financial control' (p. 793).

We summarise these views on criteria for design of a social welfare system as follows:

- identify any *efficiency* grounds for government provision of (or mandating for) specific aspects of social welfare and the form of that involvement which would give the most efficient outcomes
- identify the redistributive and social cohesion goals of the welfare system
- identify any specific commodities which are to be kept in a separate sphere, such that access to them is determined by criteria other than one's income
- identify any separate argument for using the service in question as a vehicle for redistributing income (such as enhancement of freedom or the achievement of horizontal equity).

• The Future •

Our proposals for public provision of goods and services can be summarised as follows.

As a general rule, we would wish to see incomes high enough for
people to be able to exercise the widest possible choice. But there
are many occasions when we would support the provision of services or of tied cash grants.[11] Our reasons are:

- The redistribution of income that would be required to enable
all to purchase what we would regard as reasonable levels in such
areas as health and education would be so massive as to be unrealistic and inefficient.

- There are some services whose meaning would be so changed
if delivered by the market that we would not welcome such a
move. The classic instance is a blood transfusion service (Titmuss
1971).

- Paternalism is not always undesirable. The compulsory education of children, perhaps against the wishes of parents, is one
example. We may go further and say that whereas we generally
respect people's preferences, we may not respect their preferences
for risk. The basis of the argument is that people are notoriously
bad at assessing 'low probability, high risk' ventures, and when a
government insists on, say, the installation of automobile air bags
that inflate on impact it is assuming citizens do not have a considered preference for death over life (Goodin 1988, p. 319).

- The taxpayers who finance the provision of services may have
a preference for specific egalitarianism.

- There are public goods that all must enjoy if anyone does (law
and order, public health). If we rely on voluntary provision, the
problem of 'free riders' who wait for someone else to pay is such
that gross underprovision results.

- There are goods whose production or consumption imposes
effects on others who are not party to their production or consumption (external effects).

- We would repeat our argument made above in relation to
housing. Even where we favour market provision of services in
general (as in the case of housing), some aspects (such as the conditions under which finance is made available to some would-be
purchasers) may merit public intervention.

222

- A more contentious argument may be based on the analogy with community commitments made in time of war. Most liberals baulk at talk of 'community commitments', except perhaps in emergencies such as occur during wartime. Outside such emergencies, they would argue that 'the community' should not commit citizens to anything so strong as national goals. However, we believe such talk can be justified in the context of the discussions in this chapter on the decisive impact of high levels of unemployment. The consequences are so serious for the whole of society (and not just for the unemployed) that a strong case can be made for low rates of unemployment to be a national goal. Such a commitment could bring in its train a commitment to the provision of certain public services.

For instance, Esping-Andersen has pointed out that the simultaneous quest for full employment, the protection of living standards, the avoidance of insider–outsider divisions, and fiscal responsibility imply a set of 'terrible trade-offs'. In such a context, he suggests—or at least raises as an open question—the option of 'accepting wage flexibility and low-paid service jobs on the condition that the welfare state commits itself to offering educational guarantees as a basic right of citizenship throughout a person's entire life cycle' (Esping-Andersen, 1991). In other words, a welfare state can assist towards a goal of full employment in more ways than one. We have already discussed that role in terms of income maintenance during periods of transition. We also discussed how good housing can promote the desired flexibility. Here, we are saying that the guarantee of solid and continuing education can be used for the same purpose. Esping-Andersen's proposal also answers the question of why this cannot be left to the market. The people he has in mind as being most affected by the need for this 'flexibility' will be above all low-paid workers in marginal service jobs. They are precisely the people who would *not* be likely to be in a position to cover their educational needs from their own savings.

CONCLUSION

We see this book in three ways: 1) as a 'how to' book on the measurement of material well-being; 2) as a description, using these methods, of Australia at one point in time; and 3) as proposals for the future.

In the 'how to' sections, we argue that in the balancing-act between measures that are simple enough to make the story intelligible and complex enough to be credible, the scale has swung too far in the direction of simplicity. We have sought to redress this imbalance, and provided rather more complex measures than the usual ones—of current income and poverty lines.

When we use these more complex measures, our account of material well-being in Australia at one point in time is a generally positive one. The broad picture is not one of stark contrasts in terms of inequality or of poverty. In addition, we find only a weak tendency for misery to accumulate in the same groups. That is, those who are on the bottom of one measure of well-being are rarely on the bottom of all measures.

There are no guarantees that our positive findings will continue in the future. In particular, we attribute much of what we have found to a long period of full employment, to sensible housing policies, and to a 'good enough' social welfare system. All of these elements are now at risk. Our proposals for the future are centred on reasserting a goal of low levels of unemployment. If that goal were abandoned, or proved to be unrealisable, we know of no set of policy proposals that could enable our account of Australia at the end of the 1980s to hold good in the future.

NOTES

1 '[T]wo nations: between whom there is no intercourse and no sympathy; who are as ignorant of each other's habits, thoughts, feelings, as if they were dwellers in different zones, or inhabitants of different planets; who are formed by different breeding, are fed by different food, are ordered by different manners, and are not governed by the same laws ... the RICH and the POOR'. (*Sybil*, II, V [1845] Oxford University Press, 1950, p. 67).

2 The countries involved are: Britain, US, Sweden, Austria, Canada and Australia.

3 A strong, but by no means atypical sample: 'Let's get a few facts straight. Australia is one of the most unequal societies in the world' (Phil Raskall, 'The Widening Gap', *Modern Times*, March 1992, p. 9).

4 There are indeed theoretical models of what would be required. The assumption that full employment is an unrealistic goal underlies most proposals for a Basic Income—that is, an untaxed, unconditional payment to all citizens (Walter 1989; Parker 1991; Van Parijs 1990, 1991, 1992).

5 The 'insurance' in question has no actuarial mechanism, and it involves compulsion. However, it mimics private insurance far more closely than does the Australian version of social insurance, which is insurance only in the sense that it offers protection against certain risks (Barr 1992).

6 In 1980 there were about 75000 people who had been unemployed for more than one year and they comprised about 18 per cent of total unemployment. Chapman, Junankar and Kapuscinski (1992) project this figure to rise to over 400000 people by 1993. By early 1992, the long-term unemployment and the percentage was rising.

7 Knight (1921).

8 For an excellent discussion of the efficiency case for the social welfare system (among other things) see Barr (1992). Much of our discussion of this point draws on this source.

9 The wartime reports of the Joint Committee on Social Security were an exception (1940–46).

10 We have been greatly assisted in this section by discussions with Hugh Stretton, who has, in addition, generously permitted us to draw on an unpublished manuscript of his. He is not responsible for our actual interpretation.

11 We leave aside the question of whether tied cash grants (such as scholarships that can be used only for educational purposes) are preferable to free services. We see that as essentially a technical issue.

Appendices

Appendices

APPENDIX 1:

THE AUSTRALIAN STANDARD OF LIVING STUDY (ASL)

• Study Design •

The study draws heavily on the Swedish level of living studies (Erikson and Åberg 1987), though its chief focus is on material well-being. A self-completion questionnaire was used, though interviewers were used to explain the questionnaire to respondents, and, if necessary, to assist those with language or literacy difficulties.

• The Sample •

The sample frame was taken from a sub-sample of that of the Australian Family Project, a major survey conducted by the Australian National University, a full description of which may be found in AFP Working Paper No.1 (Bracher 1988). In brief, the sample was based on the 1981 Census and covers all metropolitan and other urban areas in the country as well as the more densely populated rural areas. For reasons of economy, remote rural areas covering about 1.4 per cent of the total population were excluded. Also excluded were non-private and temporary dwellings such as hospitals, institutions and caravan parks, covering a further 4.4 per cent of the population. In total, the sample covers over 94 per cent of the national population.

The sample used in the survey was based on a four-stage design stratified by area in which the probability of selection at each stage was proportional to the number of private dwellings in the area. The full AFP sample of 5130 dwellings was located in 216 Census Collectors' Districts selected from four strata—namely major urban centres of 100 000 people or more, large towns of 14 000 or more, small towns of 1000 or more, and the rural balance. The ASL subsample of one-third of the AFP sample was restricted to 128 Collectors' Districts. Two of the eight AFP sample towns were omitted, and also two of the six AFP sample rural areas. Interviewers were given a list of all dwellings in their area with the dwellings selected for interview marked in advance. No replacements were made in cases of non-contact or refusal.

• Fieldwork Outcome •

Fieldwork was conducted by AGB:McNair, and financed by a grant from the Australian Research Grants Council. Two pilot studies were conducted, while the main field phase in all states was from 9 November to 7 December, 1987.

A total of 1578 dwellings was approached. Of these, 151 were excluded either because they were non-residential, non-existent, obviously vacant or contained no person within the scope of the survey (men and women who are usual residents, aged 20–74, or married to an eligible person). Of the remaining 1427 dwellings, complete listings of residents were obtained for 1206. The balance of 221 dwellings represent refusals or non-contacts. The 1206 listings showed 1.8 persons per household to be eligible, a total of 2224 persons. The survey produced 1696 usable questionnaires, a response rate of 76 per cent of identified eligible persons. However, assuming there were also 1.8 eligible persons per household among the 221 dwellings for which we have no information, the estimated total eligible is 2622. The response rate for this estimated total is 65 per cent.

• Comparability with Census Data •

One obvious check on the outcome of a survey is to compare the results with known data from the most recent census. When the ASL is compared with the 1986 Census, the results are reassuring.

Table 1: *Age by sex*

	CENSUS 1986		ASL	
Age	Male	Female	Male	Female
20–24	13.0	12.6	11.6	12.0
25–29	13.0	12.9	15.3	14.8
30–34	12.3	12.3	11.1	13.5
35–39	12.4	12.2	12.2	12.1
40–44	10.9	9.6	10.9	11.4
45–49	8.4	7.9	8.1	6.7
50–54	7.3	7.0	8.2	6.9
55–59	7.5	7.2	7.5	7.2
60–64	6.8	7.1	6.6	6.2
65–69	5.2	5.9	5.0	5.2
70–74	4.1	5.2	3.7	3.9
20–74	49.9	50.1	48.2	51.8

The smaller proportion of the oldest age-groups found in the survey than in the Census can be explained in part by the fact that 200 000 people aged over 65 live in non-private dwellings, and are not included in the sampling frame of the survey.

Table 2: *Labour force status (age 20 to 64)*

	CENSUS	ASL
In labour force	65.3	65.9
Not in labour force	44.7	44.1

Table 3: *Housing tenure*

	CENSUS	ASL
	(25–)	(20–74)
Owned	37	31
Mortgage	30	35
Renting	19	22
Other	14	14

Table 4: *Country of birth*

	CENSUS	ASL
	(age 20–)	*(age 20–74)*
Australia	71.7	74.7
Other	27.8	23.7
Missing	0.5	1.6

APPENDIX 2:

TWO-STAGE LEAST SQUARES REGRESSION ESTIMATION OF THE LINK BETWEEN INDIVIDUAL ATTRIBUTES AND LEVEL OF INCOME

The personal attributes which cause high or low levels of income include some that are exogenous (such as family background) and some that are likely to be endogenous (such as education and labour force status). To obtain unbiased estimates of the effect of the endogenous variables it is necessary to use a technique such as two-stage least squares in which instrumental variables replace the original variables in the final equation.

Each of the endogenous variables has been estimated using the set of exogenous variables as the explanators. The explanatory power of these equations is mostly small. A consequence of this is that the predicted values of the endogenous variables will not be efficient instruments in the second stage of the two stage least squares regression.

There is an intermediate group where endogeneity is possible but probably not strong. These are marital status, health and proportion

Table 5: *Ordinary least squares regression explaining the sources of different versions of income*

VARIABLE	FULL INCOME COEFFICIENT		T STATISTIC		FULL INCOME NET GOVERNMENT COEFFICIENT		T STATISTIC	
	Males	Females	Males	Females	Males	Females	Males	Females
Constant	-7019.843	-12839.000	-1.082	-1.913	210.382	-4856.958	0.034	-0.753
Parents' class	-1232.998	-597.620	-1.297	-0.620	-1086.148	-544.789	-1.182	-0.588
Migrant from Eng.-speaking country	-2950.166	-2715.611	-1.673	-1.369	-2898.267	-2614.468	-1.700	-1.370
Migrant from non-Eng.-speaking country	-2717.891	-2266.928	-1.598	-1.319	-2709.679	-2304.001	-1.647	-1.394
Loss on end of marriage	-24.375	-1387.2602*	-0.050	-3.253	-18.563	-1345.684*	-0.039	-3.281
Health	3435.862*	4136.856*	2.950	3.432	3241.651*	3735.883	2.879	3.222
Married	707.535	5387.700*	0.407	2.620	-1688.188	2687.184 -1005	1.359	
Age	330.590	642.714*	1.247	2.466	228.373	491.882	0.891	1.962
Age squared	1.555	-1.765	0.529	-0.606	2.767	0.180	0.974	0.064
Years of education	966.173*	1184.483*	4.056	4.577	879.359*	1121.103*	3.818	4.504
After-tax hourly earnings	1374.337*	629.840*	9.770	6.328	1321.340*	620.163*	9.714	6.479
Currently unemployed	-2327.333	-12560.000*	-0.713	-2.628	-1949.099	-11154.000	-0.618	-2.426
Not in labour force	2200.116	-4427.031*	0.886	-2.873	3372.930	-3576.056*	1.405	-2.413
R2 (adjusted)	0.363	0.349			0.352	0.342		
Deg. of freedom	498.000	489.000			498.000	489.000		

Table 6: *Ordinary least squares regression explaining the sources of different versions of income*

VARIABLE	EQUIVALENT INCOME COEFFICIENT		T STATISTIC		FAMILY INCOME COEFFICIENT		T STATISTIC	
	Males	Females	Males	Females	Males	Females	Males	Females
Constant	5162.936	-2622.290	1.201	-0.552	-11325.000*	-17685.000*	-2.386	-3.450
Parents' class	-934.890	-396.071	-1.485	-0.581	-1627.907*	-777.221	-2.342	-1.056
Migrant from Eng.-speaking country	627.794	-192.980	0.538	-0.138	602.062	-662.613	0.467	-0.437
Migrant from non-Eng.-speaking country	-1478.098	-627.422	-1.312	-0.516	-833.594	-587.660	-0.670	-0.448
Loss on end of marriage	268.090	-400.063	0.825	-1.326	159.976	-574.762	0.446	-1.764
Health	1443.664	2235.966*	1.872	2.622	2390.149*	3350.725*	2.807	3.638
Married	-61.510	2749.622	-0.053	1.891	10678.000*	13329.000	8.404	8.487
Age	4.077	278.466	0.023	1.511	450.615*	761.223*	2.324	3.824
Age squared	1.639	-1.241	0.843	-0.602	-4.111	-7.812*	-1.914	-3.512
Years of education	601.684*	867.807	3.814	4.741	777.244*	1007.377*	4.463	5.095
After-tax hourly earnings	677.118*	181.767*	7.268	2.582	860.782*	287.186*	8.369	3.777
Currently unemployed	-3314.022	-6895.049*	-1.534	-2.040	-1910.740	-8800.285*	-0.801	-2.410
Not in labour force	-2339.623	-4972.542*	-1.423	-4.563	-3779.955*	-7639.148*	-2.082	-6.490
	R2 (adjusted)		0.256	0.210	R2 (adjusted)		0.450	0.412
	Deg. of freedom		498.000	489.000	Deg. of freedom		498.000	489.000

of property lost on divorce. Because the instruments available are not ideal, this intermediate group has been included directly, without the use of instruments.

The drawback of the OLS procedure is that there is likely to be some endogeneity among the variables. This makes it difficult to identify with precision which variables have a significant effect. The difficulty with the two-stage least squares procedure is that the available instruments are not very precise. This means that a good deal of information is being wasted by using the instrument rather than the original variable. Because the choice as to which is the preferred approach is not clear cut, we present the results of the OLS estimations in Tables 5 and 6 on pp. 230 and 231. These may be compared with the results of the two-stage least squares procedure which are to be found in the text.

• BIBLIOGRAPHY •

ABS 1992, *1988–89 Household Expenditure Survey, Australia. The Effects of Government Benefits and Taxes on Household Income,* (cat. 6537.0) (Canberra: ABS).

— — 1991a, *Australian Demographic Statistics,* June Quarterly 1991 (cat. 3101.0) (Canberra: ABS).

— — 1991b, *Year Book Australia,1991* (Canberra: ABS).

— — 1990a, *Socio-Economic Indexes for Areas,* (cat. 1356.0) (Canberra: ABS).

— — 1990b, *1988–89 Household Expenditure Survey: Household Characteristics* (cat. 6531.0), (Canberra: ABS).

— — 1989, *1986 Income Distribution Survey,* (cat. 6523), (Canberra: ABS).

Andre, J. 1992, 'Blocked Exchanges: A Taxonomy', *Ethics* 103, pp. 29–47.

Aquinas, T. 1974, *Summa Theologiae,* vol. 38 *Injustice,* Latin text and English Translation, Blackfriars (London: Eyre and Spottiswoode).

Arneson, R. J. 1989, 'Introduction. Symposium on Rawlsian Theory of Justice', *Ethics,* 99, pp. 695–710.

Ash, T. G. 1989, *The Uses of Adversity* (London: Granta Books).

Atkinson, A. B. 1989, *Poverty and Social Security* (London: Harvester Wheatsheaf).

Australian Institute of Health 1987, *Health Differentials for Working Age Australians* (Canberra: Australian Institute of Health).

Australian Labor Party 1987, 'The Third Hawke Government', An Address by the Prime Minister, 23 June 1987.

Baldwin, P. 1990, *The Politics of Solidarity: Class Bases of the European Welfare State 1875–1975* (Cambridge: Cambridge University Press).

Barr, N. 1992, 'Economic Theory and the Welfare State: A Survey and Interpretation', *Journal of Economic Literature*, 30, pp. 741–803.

Barry, B. 1990, 'The Welfare State Versus the Relief of Poverty', *Ethics*, 100, pp. 502–29.

Becker, G. 1965, 'A Theory of the Allocation of Time' *Economic Journal*, 75, pp. 493–517.

Berlin, I. 1955–56, 'Equality'. *Proceedings of the Aristotelian Society*, pp. 310–11.

—— [1969] 1979, *Four Essays on Liberty* (Oxford: Oxford University Press).

Besley, T. 1990, 'Means Testing versus Universal Provision in Poverty Alleviation Programmes' *Economica*, 57, pp. 119–29.

Beveridge, W. 1942, *Social Insurance and Allied Services* (London: HMSO, cmd. 6404).

Blinder, A. 1980, 'The level and distribution of economic well-being', in M. Feldstein, ed., *The American Economy in Transition* (Washington: NBER).

Booth, C. 1903, *Life and Labour of the People In London,* Second series, 'Industry', vol. 3 (London: Macmillan).

—— [1889] 1902, *Life and Labour of the People in London,* vol. 1 (London: Macmillan).

Boxill, B. R. 1991, 'Wilson on the Truly Disadvantaged', *Ethics*, 101, pp. 579–92.

Bracher, M. D. 1988, 'The Australian Family Project', Working Paper no. 1, Australian Family Project, Australian National University (Canberra).

Bittman, M. 1991, *Juggling Time: How Australian Families Use Time* (Canberra: Office of the Status of Women).

Bradbury, B., Doyle, J. and Whiteford, P. 1990, 'Trends in the disposable incomes of Australian families, 1982–83 to 1989–90', Social Policy Research Centre, University of New South Wales, *Discussion Paper* no. 16.

Bradbury, B. and Saunders, P. 1990, 'How Reliable are Estimates of Poverty in Australia? Some Sensitivity Tests for the Period 1981–82 to 1985–86', Social Policy Research Centre, University of New South Wales, *Discussion Paper* no. 18.

Brecht, B. 1966, *Galileo* (New York: Grove).

Briggs, A. 1961, *A Study of the Work of Seebohm Rowntree, 1871–1954* (London: Longmans).

Brownlee, H. 1990, *Measuring Living Standards* (Melbourne: Australian Institute of Family Studies).

Buhmann, B., Rainwater, L., Schmaus, G. and Smeeding, T. M. 1988, 'Equivalence Scales, Well-Being, Inequality, and Poverty: Sensitivity Estimates Across Ten Countries Using the Luxembourg Income Study (LIS) Database', *Review of Income and Wealth*, 34, pp. 115–42.

Caldwell, J. C. 1986, 'Routes to Low Mortality in Poor Countries', *Population and Development Review*, 12, pp. 171–220.

Cannadine, D. 1985, Review of G. Himmelfarb, *The Idea of Poverty,* in *London Review of Books*, 24 January, pp. 15–16.

Cass, B. 1986, 'The Case for the Review of Aspects of the Australian Social Security System', *The Social Security Review* (Canberra: DSS).

Castles, I. 1992, 'Living Standards in Sydney and Japanese Cities: A Comparison', in K. Sheridan, ed., *The Australian Economy in the Japanese Mirror* (St Lucia: Queensland University Press).

Chapman, B., Junankar, P. and Kapuscinski, C. 1992, 'Projections of Long Term Unemployment', *Australian Bulletin of Labour*, 18, pp. 195–207.

Clark, C. M. H. 1955, 1966, *Selected Documents in Australian History* (Sydney: Angus & Robertson) vol. 2, p. 660

Clark, J. B. 1908, *The Distribution of Wealth* (Boston: Boston, Ginn and Co.).

Coffield, F., Robinson, P. and Sansby, J. 1980, *A Cycle of Deprivation? A Case Study of Four Families* (London: Heinemann).

Commission of Inquiry into Poverty 1975, *First Main Report, Poverty in Australia* (Canberra: AGPS).

Culyer, A. J. 1983, *Health Indicators: An International Study for the European Science Foundation* (Oxford: M. Robertson).

Daly, H. E. and Cobb, J. B. 1989, *For the Common Good* (Boston: Beacon Press).

Deaton, A. 1979, 'The Distance Function in Consumer Behaviour with Application to Index Numbers and Optimal Taxation', *The Review of Economic Studies*, 46, pp. 391–405.

Dendy, H. 1895, 'The Meaning and Methods of True Charity', pp. 167–79 in B. Bosanquet, ed., *Aspects of the Social Problem* (London: Macmillan).

Department of Health and Social Security (Great Britain) 1980, *Inequalities in Health: Report of a Research Working Group Chaired by Sir Douglas Black*.

Department of Social Security 1985, *Pensioner Fringe Benefits* (Canberra: AGPS).

Diener, E., Horowitz, J. and Emmons, R. A. 1985, 'Happiness of the Very Rich', *Social Indicators Research*, 16, pp. 263–74.

Dilnot, A. 1990, 'The Distribution and Composition of Personal Sector Wealth in Australia', *Australian Economic Review*, 89, pp. 33–40.

Disraeli, B. [1845] 1950, *Sybil: or The Two Nations* (Oxford: OUP).

Donnison, D. 1991, *A Radical Agenda* (London: Rivers Oram Press).

Duncan, O. D. 1975, 'Does Money Buy Satisfaction?', *Social Indicators Research*, 2, pp. 267–74.

— — 1969, 'Inheritance of Poverty or Inheritance of Race?', pp. 85–110 in D. P. Moynihan, ed., *On Understanding Poverty* (New York: Basic Books).

Easterlin, R. A. 1980, *Birth and Fortune* (New York: Basic Books).

— — 1974, 'Does Economic Growth Improve the Human Lot? Some Empirical Evidence', pp. 89–125 in P. A. David and M. W. Reder, *Nations and Households in Economic Growth* (New York: Academic Press).

— — 1973, 'Does Money Buy Happiness?', *The Public Interest*, 30, pp. 3–10.

Eatwell, J., Milgate, M. and Newman, P., eds, 1987, *The New Palgrave: a Dictionary of Economics* (London: Macmillan).

Economic Planning and Advisory Council (EPAC) 1988, *Trends in Private Saving*, Council Paper no. 36 (Canberra: AGPS).

Edwards, H., Gates, R. and Layton, R. 1966, *Survey of Consumer Finances*, University of Sydney and Unversity of NSW.

Edwards, M. E. 1981, *Financial Arrangements Within Families* (Canberra: National Women's Council).

Elder, G. 1981, 'History and the Life Course', pp.77–115 in D. Bertaux, ed., *Biography and Society* (Beverly Hills: Sage)

— — 1974, *Children of the Great Depression* (Chicago: University Press).

Elster, J. 1979, *Ulysses and the Sirens*, (Cambridge: Cambridge University Press).

Encel, S. 1970, *Equality and Authority* (Melbourne: Cheshire).

Erikson, R. 1990. 'Politics and Class Mobility—Does Politics Influence Rates of Social Mobility?', pp. 247–65 in I. Persson, ed., *Generating Equality in the Welfare State: The Swedish Experience* (Oslo: Norwegian University Press).

Erikson, R. 1984, 'Social Class of Men, Women and Families', *Sociology*, 18, pp. 500–14.

Erikson, R. and Åberg, R. 1987, *Welfare in Transition. A Survey of Living Conditions in Sweden 1968–1981* (Oxford: The Clarendon Press).

Erikson, R. and Fritzell, J. 1988, 'The Effects of the Social Welfare System in Sweden on the Well-Being of Children and the Elderly', pp. 309–30 in J. L. Palmer, T. Smeeding and B. B. Torrey, eds, *The Vulnerable* (Washington: The Urban Institute Press).

Erikson, R. and Goldthorpe, J. H. 1992, *The Constant Flux: A Study of Class Mobility in Industrial Societies* (Oxford: The Clarendon Press).

— — 1987a, 'Commonality and Variation in Social Fluidity in Industrial Nations. Part 1: A Model for Evaluating the FJH Hypothesis', *European Sociological Review*, 3, pp. 54–77.

Erikson, R. and Goldthorpe, J. H. 1987b, 'Commonality and Variation in Social Fluidity in Industrial Nations. Part II: The Model of Core Social Fluidity Applied', *European Sociological Review*, 3, pp. 145–66.

Erikson, R., E. Hansen, S.Ringen and H.Uusitalo, eds 1987, *The Scandianavian Model: Welfare States and Welfare Research,* (New York: M. E. Sharpe).

Erikson R. and Uusitalo, H. 1987, 'The Scandinavian Approach to Welfare Research', pp.177–93 in Robert Erikson et al., eds, *The Scandinavian Model: Welfare States and Welfare Research* (New York: M. E.Sharpe).

Esping-Andersen, G. 1991, 'The Welfare State in the Reorganisation of Working Life', pp. 1–9 in P. Saunders and D. Encel, eds, *Social Policy in Australia: Options for the 1990s*, Proceedings of National Social Policy Conference, Sydney, 3–5 July 1991, SPRC Reports and Proceedings no. 96.

— — 1990, *The Three Worlds of Welfare Capitalism* (Cambridge: Polity Press).

Eyles, J. 1990, 'Objectifying the Subjective: the Measurement of Environmental Quality', *Social Indicators Research*, 22, pp. 139–53.

Fogelman, K., Fox, A. J. and Power, C. 1989, 'Class and Tenure Mobility: Do They Explain Social Inequalities in Health Among Young Adults in Britain?', pp. 333–52 in Fox, J., ed., *Health Inequalities in European Countries* (Aldershot: Gower).

Foster, C. 1988, *Towards a National Retirement Incomes Policy*, Issues Paper no. 6, Social Security Review (Canberra: AGPS).

Galston, W. 1982, 'Defending Liberalism', *The American Political Science Review*, 76, pp. 621–9.

Garfinkel, I. and Haverman, R. 1977, 'Earnings Capacity, Economic Status and Poverty', *Journal of Human Resources*, 12, pp. 49–70.

Goedart, T., Halberstadt, A., Kapteyn, A. and Van Praag, B. 1977, 'The Poverty Line: Concept and Measurement', *Journal of Human Resources*, 12, pp. 503–20.

Goldthorpe, J. H. 1980, *Social Mobility and Class Structure in Modern Britain* (Oxford: The Clarendon Press).

Goodin, R. E. 1988, *Reasons for Welfare* (Princeton: Princeton University Press).

Gorsuch, R. 1974, *Factor Analysis* (Philadelphia: Saunders).

Gould, S. J. 1988, *The Mismeasure of Man* (Harmondsworth: Penguin).

Gravelle, H. and Rees, R. 1981, *Microeconomics* (London: Longman).

Green, G., Coder, J. and Ryscavage, P. 1992, 'International Comparisons of Earnings Inequality for Men in the 1980s', *Review of Income and Wealth*, 38, pp. 1–15.

Gregory, R. and Daley, A. 1990, 'Can Economic Theory Explain Why Australian Women are So Well Paid Relative to their US Counterparts?', Centre for Economic Policy Research, Discussion Paper no. 226, Australian National University.

Gruen, F. H. 1989, 'Australia's Welfare State—Rearguard or Avant Garde?', Centre for Economic Policy Research, Discussion Paper no. 212, Australian National University.

Grusky, D. B. and Hauser, R. M. 1984, 'Comparative Social Mobility Revisited: Models of Convergence and Divergence in 16 Countries', *American Sociological Review*, 49, pp. 19–38.

Gunton, R. 1971, 'A Distribution of Personal Wealth in Australia: 1967–68', paper presented to 43rd ANZAAS Congress, Brisbane.

Hancock, K. J. 1976, *A National Superannuation Scheme for Australia*, Final Report of the National Superannuation Committee of Inquiry, (Canberra: AGPS).

Hancock, W. K. 1930, *Australia* (London: Ernest Benn).

Hanushek, E. 1986, 'The Economics of Schooling: Production and Efficiency in the Public Schools', *Journal of Economic Literature*, 24, pp. 1141–77.

Harding, A. and Mitchell, D. 1992, 'The Efficiency and the Effectiveness of the Tax-Transfer System in the 1980s', *Australian Tax Forum*, 9, pp. 277–303.

Hartwell, R. M. 1961, 'The Rising Standard of Living in England, 1800–1850', *Economic History Review*, 13, pp. 397–416.

Headey, B., review of Frank M. Andrews ed., *Research on the Quality of Life*, *Social Indicators Research*, 21, pp. 445–50.

Headey, B. and Wearing, A. 1988, 'The Sense of Relative Superiority—Central to Well-being', *Social Indicators Research*, 20, pp. 497–516.

Henderson, R. F., Harcourt, A. and Harper, R. J. A. 1970, *People in Poverty: A Melbourne Survey* (Melbourne: Cheshire).

Hesse, M. 1978, 'Theory and Value in the Social Sciences', pp. 1–16 in C. Hookway and P. Petit, eds, *Action and Interpretation: Studies in the Philosophy of Social Interpretation* (Cambridge: Cambridge University Press).

Hetzel, B. 1980, *Health and Australian Society* (Ringwood: Penguin).

Hetzel, B. and McMichael, T. 1987, *The LS Factor: Lifestyle and Health* (Ringwood: Penguin).

Hewson, J. and Fischer, T. 1991, *Fightback! The Liberal and National Parties' Plan to Rebuild and Reward Australia* (Canberra: Parliament House).

Higgins, Justice H. 1907, *The Harvester Judgment (Ex parte H. V. McKay)*, *Commonwealth Arbitration Reports*, 2, pp. 2–18.

Himmelfarb, G. 1984, *The Idea of Poverty* (London: Faber and Faber).

Hinrichs, K. 1991, 'Irregular Employment Patterns and the Loose Net of Social Security: Some Findings on the West German Development', pp. 110–27 in M. Adler et al., eds, *The Sociology of Social Security* (Edinburgh: Edinburgh University Press).

Hirsch, F. 1977, *Social Limits to Growth* (London: Routledge).

Hobsbawm, E. J. 1957, 'The British Standard of Living, 1790–1850', *Economic History Review*, 10, pp. 46–68.

Hobsbawm, E. J. and Hartwell, R. M. 1963, 'The Standard of Living During the Industrial Revolution: A Discussion', *Economic History Review*, 16, pp. 119–146.

Hochschild, J. L. 1991, 'The Politics of the Estranged Poor', *Ethics*, 101, pp. 560–78;

Illsley, R. 1990, 'Comparative Review of Sources, Methodology', *Social Science and Medicine*, 31, pp. 229–36.

Ishida, H., Goldthorpe, J. H. and Erikson, R. 1991, 'Intergenerational Class Mobility in Postwar Japan', *American Journal of Sociology*, 96, pp. 954–92.

Jencks, C. 1989, 'What is the Underclass—and is it Growing?', *Focus*, 12, pp. 14–26.

Johansson, S. 1976, 'Towards a Theory of Social Reporting', Swedish Institute for Social Research, September.

Joint Committee on Social Security 1940–43, *Reports*, nos. 1–9, CPP, (vol. II).

— — 1944–45, *Reports*, nos. 1–9, CPP, (vol. II).

— — 1945–46, *Reports*, nos. 1–9, CPP (vol. III).

Jones, M. A. 1990, *The Australian Welfare State* 3rd edn (Sydney: Allen and Unwin).

Joseph, K. and Sumption, J. 1979, *Equality* (London: John Murray).

Kaelble, H. and Thomas, M. 1991, pp. 1–56 in Y. S. Brenner, H. Kaelble and M. Thomas, *Income Distribution in Historical Perspective* (Cambridge: Cambridge University Press).

Kakwani, N. 1991a, 'Aggregate Welfare and Growth Rates in OECD Countries: 1960 to 1988', Centre for Applied Economic Research working paper 1991/1, University of NSW.

— — 1991b, 'Performance in Living Standards: an International Comparison', (University of New South Wales Press).

— — 1986, *Analyzing Redistribution Policies: A Study Using Australian Data* (Cambridge: Cambridge University Press).

Katzenstein, P. J. 1985, *Small States in World Markets: Industrial Policy in Europe* (Ithaca: Cornell).

Knight, F. H. 1923, 'The Ethics of Competition', *The Quarterly Journal of Economics*, 37, pp. 579–624.

— — 1921, *Risk, Uncertainty and Profit*, (Boston: Houghton Mifflin).

Kotlokoff, L. and Summers, L. 1981, 'The Role of Intergenerational Transfers in Aggregate Capital Accumulation', *Journal of Political Economy*, 89, pp. 706–32.

Lancaster-Jones, F. 1975, 'The Changing Shape of the Australian Income Distribution, 1914–15 and 1968–69', *Australian Economic History Review*, 15, pp. 21–34.

Lane, R. E. 1978, 'Markets and the Satisfaction of Human Wants', *Journal of Economic Issues*, 13, pp. 799–827.

Lerman, R. and Yitzhaki, S. 1985, 'Income Inequality by Income Source: A New Approach and Applications to the United States', *Review of Economics and Statistics*, 67, pp. 151–6.

Lewis, O. 1969, 'The Culture of Poverty', pp.187–200 in D. P. Moynihan ed., *On Understanding Poverty* (New York: Basic Books).

Loch, C. S. 1910, *Charity and Social Life* (London: Macmillan).

Lovell, K., Richardson, S., Travers, P. and Wood, L. (1993), 'Resources and Functionings: a New View of Inequality in Australia', in W. Eichhorn, ed., *Models and Measurement of Welfare and Inequality* (Berlin:Springer Verlag).

Lydall, H. 1968, *The Structure of Earnings* (Oxford: Oxford University Press).

Mack, J. and Lansley, S. 1985, *Poor Britain* (London, George Allen and Unwin).

Malthus, T. R. [1798] 1960, *Essay on Population*, ed. G. Himmelfarb, (New York, Modern Library).

Marcuse, H. 1969, *An Essay on Liberation* (London: Allen Lane).

Marshall, T. H. 1981, *The Right to Welfare* (London: Heinemann).

McCallum, J. and Beggs, J. 1991, 'Determinants of Household Wealth: Assets of Divorcing Couples in Australia', *Australian Economic Review*, 96, pp. 57–66.

McConnell, C. and Brue, S. 1992, *Contemporary Labor Economics* 3rd edn (New York: McGraw-Hill Inc.).

McDonald, P. 1986, *Settling up: Property and Income Distribution on Divorce in Australia* (Sydney: Prentice Hall).

McLean, I. and Richardson, S. 1986, 'More or Less Equal? Australian Income Distribution Since 1933', *Economic Record*, 62, pp. 67–81.

McLean, I. and Pincus, J. 1983, 'Did Australian Living Standards Stagnate between 1890 and 1940?', *Journal of Economic History*, 43, pp. 193–202.

McMichael, A. J. 1985, 'Social Class (As Estimated by Occupational Prestige) and Mortality in Australian Males in the 1970s', *Community Health Studies*, 9, pp. 220–30.

McNabb, R. and Richardson, S. 1989, 'Earnings, Education and Experience: is Australia Different?', *Australian Economic Papers*, 28, pp. 57–75.

McRae, S. 1986, *Cross Class Families:A Study of Wives' Occupational Superiority* (Oxford: The Clarendon Press).

Mishra, R. 1990, *The Welfare State in Capitalist Society* (London: Harvester Wheatsheaf).

Mitchell, D. 1991, *Income Transfers in Ten Welfare States* (London: Gower).

Nussbaum, M. 1990, 'Aristotelian Social Democracy', in R. B. Douglass, M. Mara and H. S. Richardson, eds, *Liberalism and the Good* (New York: Routledge).

— — 1986, *The Fragility of Goodness* (Cambridge: Cambridge University Press).

O'Farrell, P. 1986, *The Irish in Australia* (The University of New South Wales Press).

Orosz, E. 1990, 'The Hungarian Country Profile: Inequalities in Health and Health Care in Hungary', *Social Science and Medicine* 31, pp. 847–57.

Paglin, M. 1975, 'The Measurement and Trend of Inequality: a Basic Revision', *American Economic Review*, 65, pp. 598–609.

Pahl, J. M. 1989, *Money and Marriage* (Basingstoke: Macmillan Education).

Pahl, R. 1984, *Divisions of Labour* (London: Blackwell).

Parker, H., ed. 1991, 'Basic Income and the Labour Market', *BIRG Discussion Paper no. 1* (London: Basic Income Research Group).

Phelps Brown, H. 1988,*Egalitarianism and the Generation of Inequality*, (Oxford: The Clarendon Press).

Phlips, L. 1983, *Applied Consumption Analysis* (Oxford:North Holland).

Piachaud, D. 1987, 'Problems in the Definition and Measurement of Poverty', *Journal of Social Policy*, 16, pp. 147–64.

Piggott, J. 1988, 'The distribution of Wealth: What is It, What does It Mean, and Is It Important?', *Australian Economic Review*, 83, pp. 35–41.

— — 1984, 'The Distribution of Wealth in Australia—A Survey', *Economic Record* , 60, pp. 252–65

Podder, N. and Kakwani, N. 1976, 'Distribution of Wealth in Australia', *Review of Income and Wealth*, 22, pp. 75–92.

Portocarero, L 1987, *Social Mobility in Industrial Societies: Women in France and Sweden* (Stockholm: Swedish Institute for Social Research, Doctoral Dissertation series 3).

Prosser, W. R. 1991, 'The Underclass: Assessing What We Have Learned', *Focus*, 13, 2, pp. 1–18.

Raskall, P. 1992, 'The Widening Income Gap', *Modern Times,* March, p. 9.

— — 1977, 'Who's got what in Australia: The Distribution of Wealth', *Journal of Australian Political Economy*, 2, pp. 3–6.

Rawls, J. 1971, *A Theory Of Justice* (Cambridge, Mass.: Harvard University Press).

Reid, J. and Lupton, D. 1991, pp. xi–xxii in J. Reid and P. Trompf, eds, *The Health of Aboriginal Australians* (Sydney: Harcourt Brace Jovanovich).

Reser, J. P. 1991, 'Aboriginal Mental Health: Conflicting Cultural Perspectives', pp. 218–91 in J. Reid and P. Trompf, eds, *The Health of Aboriginal Australians* (Sydney: Harcourt Brace Jovanovich).

Richardson, S. 1979, 'Income Distribution, Poverty and Redistributive Policies', pp. 11–62 in F. H. Gruen, ed., *Surveys of Australian Economics* vol. 11 (Sydney: George Allen and Unwin).

— — 1981, 'A Comparison of Public and Private Sector Employee Compensation', in N. Fisher, ed., *Prospects for Public Sector Industrial Relations* (Canberra: Canberra College of Advanced Education).

Richardson, S. and Travers, P. 1992, 'Cash Income and Full Income: Does the Difference Matter?', *Working Paper 92–* , Department of Economics, University of Adelaide.

— — 1989, 'The Conceptual Flaws in Poverty Lines', *Working Paper 89-6*, Department of Economics, University of Adelaide.

Ringen, S. 1985, 'Towards a Third Stage in the Measurement of Poverty', *Acta Sociologica*, 28, pp. 99–113.

Rivlin, A. 1975, 'Income Distribution: Can Economists Help?, *American Economic Review,* 65, pp. 1–15.

Ross, R. 1990, 'A Probit Analysis of the Factors Influencing Labour Market Success of Aborigines in New South Wales', Social Policy Research Centre, University of New South Wales, *Working Paper* no. 27.

Ross, R. and Whiteford, P. 1990, 'Income Poverty among Aboriginal Families with Children: Estimates from the 1986 Census', Social Policy Research Centre, University of New South Wales, *Working Paper* no. 20.

Rowntree, B. S. 1941, *Poverty and Progress* (London: Longmans).

— — [1901] 1902, *Poverty. A Study of Town Life* (London: Macmillan).

Rowntree, B. S. and Lavers, G. R. 1951, *Poverty and the Welfare State* (London: Longmans).

Saggers, S. and Gray, D. 1991, 'Policy and Practice in Aboriginal Health', pp. 381–420 in J. Reid and P. Trompf, eds, *The Health of Aboriginal Australians* (Sydney: Harcourt Brace Jovanovich).

Saunders, P. 1990, 'Employment Growth and Poverty: An Analysis of Australian Experience, 1983–1990', *Discussion Paper* no. 25, Social Policy Research Centre, University of New South Wales.

Saunders, P., Hobbes, G. and Stott, H. 1989, 'Income Inequality in Australia and New Zealand: International Comparisons and Recent Trends', *Discussion Paper* no. 15, Social Policy Research Centre, University of New South Wales.

Saunders, P. and Matheson, G. 1991, 'An Ever-Rising Tide? Poverty in Australia in the Eighties', *Discussion Paper* no. 30, Social Policy Research Centre, University of New South Wales.

Saunders, P. and Whiteford, P. 1989, *Measuring Poverty: A Review of the Issues*, Economic Planning Advisory Council, *Discussion Paper* 89/11, (Canberra: AGPS).

— — 1987, *Ending Child Poverty: An Assessment of the Government's Family Package*, Social Policy Research Centre, University of New South Wales, *Reports and Proceedings* no. 69.

Sawyer, M. 1976, 'Income Distribution in OECD Countries', *OECD Economic Outlook: Occasional Studies*, July.

Scharpf, F. W. 1991, *Crisis and Choice in European Social Democracy*, (Ithaca: Cornell).

Sen, A. 1990, 'Individual Freedom as a Social Commitment', *New York Review of Books*, 37 (14 June), pp. 49–54.

— — 1987, *The Standard of Living* (Cambridge: Cambridge University Press).

— — 1985, *Commodities and Capabilities* (Amsterdam: North Holland).

— — [1981] 1982, *Poverty and Famines* (Oxford: The Clarendon Press).

— — 1983, 'Poor, Relatively Speaking', *Oxford Economic Papers*, 35, pp. 153–69.

— — 1982, *Choice, Welfare and Measurement* (Oxford: Blackwell).

— — 1973, *On Economic Inequality* (Oxford: The Clarendon Press).

Shanahan, M. 1991. *The Distribution of Personal Wealth in South Australia, 1905 to 1915*, Ph.D thesis, Flinders University of South Australia.

Simey, T. S. and Simey, M. B. 1960, *Charles Booth: Social Scientist* (Oxford, Oxford University Press).

Smith, Adam [1776] 1976, An Enquiry into the Nature and Causes of the Wealth of Nations, R. Campbell, A. Skinner and W. Todd, eds, (Oxford: The Clarendon Press).

Social Welfare Policy Secretariat 1981, *Report on Poverty Measurement* (Canberra: AGPS).

Stanton, D. 1980, 'The Henderson Poverty Line—a Critique', *Social Security Journal*, pp. 14–24.

Stern, J. 1983, 'Social Mobility and the Interpretation of Social Class Mortality Differentials', *Journal of Social Policy*, 12, pp. 27–49.

Stretton, H. 1976, *Capitalism, Socialism and the Environment* (Cambridge: Cambridge University Press).

Taylor, C. 1989, *Sources of the Self: The Making of the Modern Identity* (Cambridge, Mass.: Harvard University Press).

Taylor, C. 1979, 'What's Wrong with Negative Liberty', pp. 175–93 in A. Ryan, ed., *The Idea of Freedom. Essays in Honour of Isaiah Berlin* (Oxford: Oxford University Press).

Thomson, N. 1991, 'A Review of Aboriginal Health Status', pp. 37–79 in J. Reid and P. Trompf, eds, *The Health of Aboriginal Australians* (Sydney: Harcourt Brace Jovanovich).

Thomson, N. 1985, 'Review of Available Aboriginal Mortality Data, 1980–82', *The Medical Journal of Australia. Supplement*, 143, S46–S49.

—— 1984, 'Australian Aboriginal Health and Health-Care', *Social Science and Medicine*, 18, pp. 939–48).

Titmuss, R. M. [1950] 1976, *History of the Second World War. Problems of Social Policy*, (London: HMSO).

—— 1971, *The Gift Relationship* (London: Allen and Unwin).

—— 1963, 'War and Social Policy', pp. 75–87 in *Essays on the Welfare State* 2nd edn (London: Unwin University Books).

—— 1962, *Income Distribution and Social Change* (London: Unwin University Books).

Tobin, J. 1970, 'On Limiting the Domain of Inequality', *The Journal of Law and Economics*, 13, pp. 263–77.

Townsend, P. 1979, *Poverty in the United Kingdom*, (Harmondsworth: Penguin).

Townsend, P. and Davidson, N. 1982, *Inequalities in Health: the Black Report*, (Harmondsworth: Penguin; 1988 republished together with M. Whitehead, *The Health Divide*).

Townsend, P. and Gordon, D. 1991, 'What Is Enough? New Evidence on Poverty Allowing for the Definition of Minimum Benefit', pp. 35–69 in M. Adler et al., eds, *The Sociology of Social Security* (Edinburgh: Edinburgh University Press).

Travers, P. 1991, 'Salami Tactics and the Australian Welfare State', pp. 95–109 in M. Adler et al., eds, *The Sociology of Social Security* (Edinburgh: Edinburgh University Press).

—— 1986, 'Contingent and Noncontingent Effects of Unemployment', *Sociology*, 20, pp. 192–206.

United Nations Development Programme 1990, 1991, 1992, *Human Development Report 1990; 1991, 1992* (Oxford: Oxford University Press).

Usher, D. 1987, 'Income' in *The New Palgrave: A Dictionary of Economic Thought*, J. Eatwell, M. Milgate and P. Newman, eds, (London: Macmillan Press).

Van Haitsma, M. 1989, 'A Contextual Definition of the Underclass', *Focus*, 12, pp. 27–31.

Van Parijs, P. 1992, 'Basic Income Capitalism', *Ethics*, 102, pp. 465–84.

—— 1991, 'Why Surfers Should Be Fed: The Liberal Case for an Unconditional Basic Income', *Philosophy and Public Affairs*, 20, pp. 101–31.

—— 1990, 'The Second Marriage of Justice and Efficiency', *Journal of Social Policy*, 19, pp. 1–26.

Van Praag, B., Hagenaars, A. and Van Weeren, H. 1982, 'Poverty in Europe', *Review of Income and Wealth*, 28, pp. 345–59.

Vickery, C. 1977, 'The Time-Poor: A New Look at Poverty', *Journal of Human Resources*, 12, pp. 27–48.

Vogel, J. 1991, *Social Report for the Nordic Countries* (Copenhagen: Nordic Statistical Secretariat).

Wachtel, P. L. 1983, *The Poverty of Affluence: A Psychological Portrait of the American Way of Life* (New York: Free Press).

Walker, A. 1984, *Social Planning. A Strategy for Socialist Welfare* (Oxford: Blackwell).

Walker, R. 1986, 'Consensual Approaches in the Definition of Poverty: Towards and Alternative Methodology', *Journal of Social Policy*, 9, pp. 18–23.

Walter, T. 1989, *Basic Income* (London: Marion Boyars).

Walzer, M. 1986, 'Justice Here and Now', pp.135–50 in F. S. Lucash, ed., *Justice and Equality Here and Now* (Ithaca: Cornell University Press).

— — [1983] 1985, *Spheres of Justice*, (Oxford, Basil Blackwell).

Waring, M. J. 1991, *Juggling Time: How Australians Use TIme* (Canberra: Office of Status of Women).

Watts, R. 1987, *The Foundations of the National Welfare State* (Sydney: Allen and Unwin).

Whitehead, A. N. [1929] 1978, *Process and Reality* (New York: The Free Press).

Williams, R. 1985, *Ethics and the Limits of Philosophy*, (Cambridge Mass.: Harvard University Press).

— — 1969, 'Foreword' in *Charles Booth's London*, eds, A. Fried and R. M. Elman (London: Hutchinson).

Williams, R. A. 1983, 'Ownership of Dwellings and Personal Wealth in Australia', *Australian Economic Review*, 62 , pp. 55–62.

Wilson, W. J. 1991, '*The Truly Disadvantaged* Revisited: A Reply to Hochschild and Boxill', *Ethics*, 101, pp. 593–609.

Wnuk-Lipinski, E. and Illsley, R. 1990, 'International Comparative Analysis: Main Findings and Conclusions', *Social Science and Medicine* 31, pp. 879–89.

Yates, J. 1991, 'Australia's Owner-Occupied Housing Wealth and its Impact on Income Distribution', Social Policy Research Centre, University of New South Wales, *Reports and Proceedings* no. 92.

• INDEX •